KEY TO THE LOCKED GARDEN
Learning to Enhance the Shabbat Experience

MENORAH

Simcha H. Benyosef

KEY *to the* LOCKED GARDEN

Learning to Enhance the Shabbat Experience

Menorah Books

KEY TO THE LOCKED GARDEN
Learning to Enhance the Shabbat Experience

First Edition, 2018

Menorah Books
An imprint of Koren Publishers Jerusalem Ltd.

POB 8531, New Milford, CT 06776-8531, USA
& POB 4044, Jerusalem 9104001, Israel
www.menorah-books.com

© Simcha H. Benyosef, 2018

Cover Painting © Rachel Lewinson

The publication of this book was made possible through the generous support of *Torah Education in Israel*.

All rights reserved. No part of this publication may be reproduced, stored in a retrieval system or transmitted in any form or by any means, electronic, mechanical, photocopying, or otherwise, without the prior permission of the publisher, except in the case of brief quotations embedded in critical articles or reviews.

ISBN 978-1-940516-79-0, *hardcover*

A CIP catalogue record for this title is available from the British Library

Printed and bound in the United States

בס"ד

לעלוי נשמת
יוסף (חי) ג'ורג'
בן אליהו ואסטרייא ע"ה
תהא נשמתו צרורה בצרור החיים

In eternal memory
A man of refinement and nobility of spirit
Who left a life of business to dedicate himself to learning
Torah with sincere devotion
Whose dedication to the Leshem[1] over decades inspired students
and scholars alike
Who was able to bring people back to Hashem by
explaining hidden truths
Who felt and participated in the suffering of others,
experiencing it as his own
Who accepted the challenge of pain silently and never complained
Who saw his suffering as a rectification *(tikkun)* for the *Shekhina* and
for the People of Israel, to hasten the *Geula*.

לוּלֵי תוֹרָתְךָ שַׁעֲשֻׁעָי אָז אָבַדְתִּי בְעָנְיִי

Had Your Torah not been my delight, then I would have perished in my affliction.

---

1. Rabbi Shlomo Eliyashiv, known as the Leshem, was the grandfather of Rabbi Yosef Shalom Eliyashiv. The Leshem revealed the mystery behind the suffering of the world and of the individual. This teaching helps man to accept his suffering with love by understanding how it serves as a *tikkun*, a rectification or purification, for everyone and everything to bring them to the World to Come *(Olam Haba)*, and receive the ultimate good and happiness, which is unification with Hashem.

בס"ד

לעילוי נשמת
מאיר בן בן ציון ופייגע הוכמן

בס"ד

Rabbi Moses Schatz	משה שץ
17a Givat Shaul St.	רחוב גבעת שאול 17 א
Jerusalem, 95477 Israel	ירושלים עיה"ק ישראל
Tel. 972 2 6512649	תיקון ליל שבועות הרש"ש זיע"א עטרת
Fax 972 2 6535438	תפארת
Author: *Sparks of the Hidden Light*	כתר מלכות על ספירת העומר
	תרשיש שהם וישפה

Jan. 10, 2017 י"ב טבת תשע"ז

I immensely enjoyed Simcha Benyosef's *Key to the Locked Garden: Learning to Enhance the Shabbat Experience,* based on the teachings of Rabbi Moses Luria (1931-2009) z"l. It brings inspiration to experience the true joy of Shabbat in its spiritual essence, beautifully weaving the Arizal's inner theme of Shabbat (taken from the *Shaar Hakavanot*) in the course of the book.

Included in the book are all the pieces of advice from our Sages enabling us to receive the delight of Shabbat, and in particular, encouraging us to accept Shabbat earlier in order to fulfill the mitzvah of *Tosefet* (addition to) *Shabbat,* which is a great mitzvah.

In short, I will say that after reading *Key to the Locked Garden,* my Shabbat experience deepened and is not the same anymore. Benyosef so brilliantly brought the Kabbalistic concepts to life, particularly for the layperson, that even a Kabbalist who is familiar with them will find much that is new to him in reading this book.

I conclude with a blessing that all who read this book may experience a new level of Sabbath delight.

I sign in honor of the Torah,
Rabbi Moses Schatz

בס"ד

I want to recommend this extremely important and advanced sefer. The author should be lauded for the tremendous effort it took to compile the primary sources. May the publication of this sefer bring the Final Redemption and the Great Shabbat ever closer.

Rabbi Abraham Sutton
Author and Mentor
Kiryat Ye'arim, Israel
Zot Chanukah, 2nd of Tevet 5778, December 20, 2017

PLEASE PROTECT THE SANCTITY OF THIS BOOK.
This book contains Sacred Names of God. Please treat it with respect and do not take this book into places that are impure, such as a bathroom.

Note on Hebrew Transliterations
Unless a Hebrew word has found its way into common usage, or is presented as a title or other exception, all transliterated Hebrew words that appear in the text have been *italicized* and, in most cases, are defined on their first usage. A glossary of Hebrew words and idioms is also provided at the back of the book.

Contents

Foreword xv
Acknowledgments xix
To Each Reader xxiii
Prefatory Note: Foundations xxvii

CHAPTER 1
CREATOR OF DARKNESS 1

CHAPTER 2
FIERY COALS OF LOVE 11

CHAPTER 3
A TASTE OF THE WORLD TO COME 19

CHAPTER 4
SPIRITUAL KISSES 27

CHAPTER 5
DEEPER MEANING OF *MENUCHA* – INNER HARMONY 39

CHAPTER 6
***KABBALAT SHABBAT* AND THE EVENING PRAYER** 53

CHAPTER 7
WHEAVENLY DEW 73

CHAPTER 8
SECOND *SEUDA* – ABOVE TIME 81

CHAPTER 9
SOUL COMPANIONS 93

CHAPTER 10
WE ARE THE *KALLA* 101

CHAPTER 11
A TUNNEL UNDER THE THRONE OF GLORY 109

CHAPTER 12
ASCENDING WITH THE *TOSEFET SHABBAT* 129

CHAPTER 13
GROWING WITH THE ADDITIONAL SOUL 145

CHAPTER 14
YOU WILL CALL ME *ISHI* 151

CHAPTER 15
ON THE SIXTH DAY *161*

CHAPTER 16
I CAME INTO MY GARDEN *177*

APPENDIX I
SOUL LEVELS *189*

APPENDIX II
BIRKAT HALEVANA *191*

APPENDIX III
MYSTICAL READINGS FOR THE SHABBAT TABLE *201*

Bibliography 263
Glossary 267

Foreword

This work is based on the teachings of Rabbi Moses Luria zt"l,[2] a descendant of Rabbi Isaac Luria, the holy Ari z"l, and a Chasidic master of our times who brought divine service to an experiential level. Rabbi Luria once confided to Rabbi Yoel Benharrouche, one of his close *talmidim* (disciples), that he came to the world to transmit through his writings the teachings of the Inner Torah that the holy Ari z"l was unable to complete due to his untimely death.

The teachings of the Ari z"l have their origin in the holy Zohar, the book of Inner Torah which was revealed to Rabbi Shimon bar Yochai ("Rashbi"). Rashbi received his revelation not long after the destruction of the Temple. However, for centuries the Zohar was like a precious vessel placed in a spot so high that no one could reach it, until Rabbi Isaac Luria, the foremost sixteenth-century Kabbalist, who is referred to as *HaAri haKadosh* (the holy Ari z"l), spread the light of the Zohar. Unfortunately the holy Ari z"l passed away at the age of thirty-eight, two years before the time he had been granted in potential.

---

2. This was his name throughout most of his life. The name Rafael was added during his last years on account of his illness, so that his works are catalogued under the name Rafael Moses Luria.

Rabbi Moses Luria's explanations shed further light upon the complex teachings of the holy Zohar and of the Ari z"l, adding allegorical explanations based on human relationships that enable us to relate to these lofty concepts.

Rabbi Luria's teachings explain Judaism as a relationship of intense love which only actualizes if both sides focus exclusively upon the Other. There are no words in which I can express my gratitude to our lost Torah master. His Torah will live on, an eternal heritage for generations to come.

My own intention has been to amplify further these beautiful teachings in order to make them available not only to Torah scholars able to grasp the original writings, but to all the Community of Israel.

Upon coming to this world, our soul, previously filled with divine consciousness, now has to deal with total amnesia. We forget who we are, why we are here, and what we came to do. We are placed in a world of darkness whose nature is such that we are not even able to identify it.

Upon starting to write this book my intention was to share with the reader that spiritual darkness is an optical illusion and that all we need to do to dissolve it is to draw to ourselves the Shabbat consciousness. When the Shabbat Queen takes leave of us at the end of Shabbat, most of the Shabbat consciousness leaves as well. *Key to the Locked Garden* transmits the teachings of the Torah's Inner dimension as revealed by the holy Zohar, teaching us how to unlock our inner garden, draw the Shabbat consciousness to ourselves, and retain it during the weekdays. My hope and prayer is that each one of us will retain a love relationship that will be on the verge of our consciousness at every hour of the day:[3] *when you sit in your home, while you walk on the way, when you retire and when you arise.*

This book is addressed to one who is familiar with the Shabbat ritual, but is open to learning about a type of Shabbat in which one attains a meaningful spiritual experience that one could draw upon in the coming weekdays. Chapters Two to Eleven will thus be devoted to the description of such a Shabbat. Then, in Chapters Twelve to Fifteen, we will examine how one who yearns for such a Shabbat experience

---

3. Paraphrasing the *Shema*-declaration of faith; Exodus 6:8.

should prepare throughout the weekdays, and in particular, on Fridays. The last chapter, *I Came into My Garden,* explores the depth of our bond with the Holy One, to seal in our minds what we are striving for.

For this book's cover I selected a painting of *Rachel Imeinu* (the matriarch Rachel), who is often associated with the *Shekhina. Rachel Imeinu's* tears glisten on the leaves at a distance from the tomb, and the tomb is surrounded by a soft glow, suggesting that it is up to each one of us to transform Rachel's tears into an outpouring of joy at the coming of Shabbat, thus paving the way to our desired redemption.

Acknowledgments

I would like to express my gratitude to Rabbi Isaac Abadi for his support throughout this project and for helping me clarify the relevance of personal requests in our divine service.

To Rabbi Moses Schatz, my gratitude for taking time from his magnum opus introducing the teaching of Kabbala, *Mayan Moshe*, to read *Key to the Locked Garden: Learning to Enhance the Shabbat Experience* and write his approbation.

To Arie David, there are no words. May Hashem grant him *kol tuv* (all good things), all the blessings from *Beit Genazai*, the House of Hidden Treasures.

To Ashirah Yosefah, editor-in-chief of Menorah Books, for her guidance and support throughout the years of this book's odyssey.

To Reb Rahmiel Hayyim Drizin, author of author of *Shabbat Meal Meditations,* for going over the mystical readings for the Shabbat Table.

To my son Gabriel Pinchas, for going through the manuscript and helping me realize that the verses I cite in the book have little meaning in translation unless I include the original Hebrew text. May *Hakadosh Barukh Hu* soon bring Gabriel Pinchas and his family to *Eretz Yisrael*

Key to the Locked Garden

on "eagles' wings," with an easy means of sustenance that will enable him to study Torah.

To fourteen-year-old Tova Helfenbaum for reading this book in manuscript form and offering excellent suggestions that I was grateful to adopt. May the Holy One grace Tova with His help to build a *bayit neeman beYisrael* (a true house in Israel) with her true soul companion at the right time, and may she continue using her talents to pave the way for the *geula*.

To Nechama Tehilla Kendle, for editing an earlier version of this book.

A heartfelt thanks to Sarah Kremansky for her generous and expert editing. May the Holy One grant Sarah and her husband Vidali the ability to integrate and implement the deep mysteries underlying the Shabbat experience, as well as to transmit it to their children.

To my student Revaya, for suggesting that I include the "Mystical Readings for the Shabbat Table" as an appendix to this book. May it be divine will that Revaya soon build a true house of Israel, a *binyan adei ad* (an everlasting building) with her rightful soul companion.

To E. Ofier, thanks for an invaluable addition to this book. To M. O. Ghiladi and A. Kletzel, thanks for valid suggestions, which will make the reading of this book easier for others.

To Esther Cameron, for sensitive and knowledgeable editing, which helped bring out the best in this book.

May Hashem bless the work of Rachel bat Chana, the young artist who painted the cover of this book, and help her devote her talents to illuminate this world with the light of His Presence. I am grateful to her husband, Yosef Shmuel, for insisting that I quote fully all the verses alluded to in the poem *"A'ufa Eshkonah* (I will fly away and find rest)" so that the poem may have its full impact on the reader. May Yosef Shmuel be successful in his Torah study. May Rachel and her husband Yosef Shmuel continue to build a true house of Israel, a *binyan adei ad* worthy of becoming a *mikdash me'at* (a small sanctuary) for the Divine Presence.

Acknowledgments

Last but not least, to our beloved Creator, for giving me the strength to hold on to this book during all the years that it took to complete it, until it was ready to transmit its teachings to *Knesset Yisrael* (the Congregation of Israel) with the yearning to speed our awaited *geula* (redemption).

Simcha H. Benyosef
Jerusalem
First light of Chanukah, 25th of Kislev, 5777 (2017)

To Each Reader

As much as I have tried to address the modern reader, still, what I am transmitting is not just a complex study – it is a consciousness which flows down from on High according to the vessel that we prepare within us to receive it. How to refine this vessel is what this book is about. Each person may take on what s/he feels is appropriate at this time.

The Talmud teaches us about Choni who made a circle around himself and told his Maker that he would not leave until rain came down. When studying the Torah's inner dimension, we all have to learn from Choni. We must persist in the pursuit of this divine wisdom, willing ourselves to continue even if all the concepts presented to us are not yet clear in our mind. It often happens that concepts which are at first difficult to grasp will later be perceived at an experiential level, defying translation into words.

Upon finishing this book, I sent it to my research assistant. A month later, I experienced a technical difficulty in my computer because of which I lost all my files – my work of many years. We all receive blows of this kind; what makes the difference is our reaction. What is expected from us is to continue forward undaunted, with the firm faith that the new product will be more refined than the last. I thus revised the book one more time, attempting to clarify it further, and upon checking a source in one of Rabbi Luria's volumes, I found a paper in which years ago I had copied a fragment of his writings. It is my prayer that these beautiful words will speak to all those who find challenging the teachings behind the awesome gift that is Shabbat:

> He who studies Torah and perceives its meaning through effort only discerns the Torah's inner light which became enclosed within his human intellect. In contrast, one who receives the Torah as a gift is also receiving its surrounding light, which is perceived by the eyes of the intellect, above and beyond what may be perceived by the brain. Then even what could not be contained by his brain's vessel, he receives as a gift. However, all this is because he initially struggled with his Torah study: only then did he find it as a gift.
>
> הלומד תורה ומשיג מתוך יגיעה אינו משיג אלה האור פנימי שבתורה שהוא מתלבש בשכל האדם אבל מי שמקבל התורה במתנה מקבל האור מקיף שהוא אור הנראה לעיני השכל לעילא מבחינת ההשגה במוח וגם מה שאינו נכלל בכלי המוח הוא מקבל במתנה. אמנם כל זה משום שבתחילה הדברים יגע בתורה ואחר כך מצאת בבחינת מתנה.

God does not interfere with man's mind processes unless man initiates the process by showing with his Torah observance and diligent study that he desires an expanded consciousness more than anything else in the world. As Rabbi Luria says above, only then does man find this expanded consciousness within himself as a gift, albeit a gift s/he had to work for.

Upon taking the Children of Israel out of Egypt, God caused the people to make a detour rather than leading them by a direct route, lest the sight of war should frighten the people and make them want to return to bondage. God did not miraculously enhance their consciousness so that they would understand that it was better to go forward. Why not? This was the time of open miracles! However, in the new relationship that was being forged, we had to find inner strength to deal with the unknown, based on our total trust of divine providence.

The brain becomes a vessel when we use it to study divine mysteries. Then, when we receive the *neshama yetera* (the additional soul) on Shabbat, our brain is infused with this higher soul. It is up to us to persist in the struggle of Torah study in the faith that our effort will be crowned with the gift of perception and understanding. Moreover, this is particularly true in the case of the study relating to Shabbat on High, since as Rabbi Luria teaches, by observing the Shabbat laws and abstaining on Shabbat from the type of work identified as *melacha* we are rejoicing with *Hakadosh Barukh Hu* (the Holy One, blessed be He) on His day of joy *(anu shovtim vesmechim imo beyom simchato)*.

If I had to lose all my work in order to reach the understanding that it is up to us to persevere in order to receive the wisdom – and transmit it – it would have been worthwhile.

Prefatory Note: Foundations

The aim of this book is to teach Shabbat observance according to the mystical teachings that are revealed in the Zohar and other Kabbalistic works, especially the teachings of the Ari z"l.

We say in the Song of Songs as Shabbat begins: *"ki tovim dodeikha miyayin* (Your [spiritual] love is far more precious to me than wine [the pleasures of this world])." The Sages have interpreted: The innermost secrets of the Torah that were transmitted to us through the oral teachings of the prophets and sages are sweeter to us than the wine of the Written Torah.

All we know from the Written Torah is the prohibition of doing *melacha* on Shabbat. In the oral Torah it is spelled out that the *melachot* that are forbidden on Shabbat are thirty-nine categories of activities – writing, sewing, building, plowing, lighting fire, etc.

These activities are specified because they are the activities that were necessary to build the *Mishkan,* the portable Sanctuary that the People of Israel built in the desert.[4] The *Mishkan* is referred to as *olam katan* (small world); it is seen as a microcosm of the world. Hence the

---

4. Rabbi Imanuel Bar Urian, "HaMishkan ve Haolam," *Matana Tova Yesh Li Beveit Genazai* (Jerusalem: private publication, 5773), 85-86.

Key to the Locked Garden

the thirty-nine *melachot* are spiritually equivalent to Hashem's work in creating the world.

KABBALISTIC TEACHINGS ABOUT CREATION

To understand the meaning of Shabbat according to Kabbalistic teachings, we must understand some of the Kabbalistic teachings about Creation itself, though we can explain these here only in general, simplified terms.

Hashem's divine flow, which creates and sustains the world, comes down to us like a heavenly ladder made up of the different levels of divine revelation. These levels are described in terms of four worlds or spiritual dimensions. The lowest of them is called *Asiya* (Action), and it is the spiritual interface with our physical world. Above *Asiya* is a dimension called *Yetzira* (Formation); then comes *Beriya* (Creation), and only then the dimension of *Atzilut* (Closeness), which is closest to Hashem.

In each of these worlds operates the system of the *sefirot*, emanations of the divine light. The highest of these is *Keter* (Crown, or divine will). Next comes *Chokhma* (Wisdom), then *Bina* (Understanding), then *Daat* (Knowledge—in a sense which will be explained later). These are known as the "intellectual" *sefirot*. Below these are six *sefirot* that are known as *midot* (measures or qualities) which characterize both divine and human action: *Chesed* (Lovingkindness), *Gevura* (Restriction), *Tiferet* (Harmony), *Netzach* (Dominance), *Hod* (empathy), and *Yesod* (foundation). Finally comes the *sefira* known as *Malkhut* (Kingship).

Below the spiritual dimensions lies our world. Despite its lowliness, it is in this world that the purpose of Creation was fulfilled, for the Creation was motivated by Hashem's desire for a *dira batachtonim* (a dwelling-place below).

In addition to the worlds of divine revelation above us, there are also lower worlds, known as the worlds of the *klippot* (shells or husks). These are the result of a stage of Creation when the divine light was poured into vessels that were too weak to hold it and they broke, so that the light fell down and became encased in husks. The worlds of the husks are considered to be the realm of evil, or the *sitra achra* (other side).

Prefatory Note: Foundations

THE SHEKHINA

The word *"Malkhut"* has many nuances of meaning. In general, it refers to the "body" of all the king's subjects relating to the king as sovereign ruler and accepting his decrees willingly, not as they do towards a *memshala* (government). The aspect of *Malkhut* whose goal is to supervise man below, with the intention that divine kingship in the world will be clear to all, is known as the *Shekhina*. The word *"Shekhina"* stems from the Hebrew root ש-כ-ן SHKHN (to dwell) and refers to the level of divine revelation closest to us.[5]

This last level of divine revelation appears to us as having a feminine character. She is conceived of as distanced from *Hakadosh Barukh Hu* and longing for reunion with Him. Shabbat is the time when the *Shekhina* and *Hakadosh Barukh Hu* come together in *yichud* (unification) helped by our Sabbath observance.

Furthermore, the *Shekhina* is identified with *Knesset Yisrael* (the Community of Israel). *Knesset Yisrael* is a code expression for something else much bigger than its literal translation seems to imply. The higher aspect of each of the souls of the People of Israel is attached to the Holy One on High together with all the other souls of Israel in a collective entity called *Knesset Yisrael*.

The inner dimension of the Torah distinguishes between *Knesset Yisrael Above* (our collective soul roots attached to Hashem on High), and *Knesset Yisrael Below* (namely, our collective souls in the world below in a state of spiritual togetherness under our physical forms). *Knesset Yisrael Below* thus refers to the collectivity of our souls, even though each one of these seems to be an independent entity that gives life to its body.

These are complex teachings forming part of a consciousness that is acquired gradually. For the sake of simplicity, however, we will refer to the Divine Presence as "the *Shekhina*" and will use the expressions

---

5. There are several references in the Torah to the revelation of the *Shekhina*. One of them comes in Genesis 18:25, when the patriarch Abraham tries to convince his Maker not to destroy the city of Sodom for the sake of fifty righteous men who could be dwelling among the evil inhabitants of the town. Abraham exclaims: *"Chalila lakh* (It would be sacrilege to ascribe this to You)!" When reading the verse in English we do not notice anything unusual, but if we read it in Hebrew we realize that "You" is expressed by the feminine form of the second person pronoun.

Knesset Yisrael Above and *Knesset Yisrael Below* interchangeably with the *Shekhina Above* and the *Shekhina Below* (*Shekhina Elyona* and *Shekhina Tataa*, in the language of the Zohar), because the technical differences between these terms are beyond the scope of this book.

The concept of the *Shekhina* is bound up with that of the souls of Israel. Our soul is an entire spiritual structure made up of many levels, each one of which is the counterpart of a specific state of consciousness. The highest of these levels of our soul structure cleaves to Hashem in the heavenly world, and we call it our soul root. In the *Aleinu* prayer that comes at the end of our three daily prayer services, we say *"uShekhinat uzo begovhei meromim* (and the might of His *Shekhina* is on the loftiest heights)." This alludes to the point in which all our heavenly souls cleave to Hashem on High.

When the highest point of all our heavenly souls – namely, *Knesset Yisrael Above* – is cleaving to Hashem on High, then the People of Israel below become a spiritual entity whose inner souls, in a state of togetherness, are attached to Hashem. This spiritual entity under our physical forms is referred to as *Knesset Yisrael Below*.

To help us understand the relationship between the *Shekhina* – that is, *Knesset Yisrael* – and the souls of Israel, the *Tikunei Zohar* suggests an image:

> Our sages have established the relationship between the *Shekhina* and the souls of Israel; the light of the *Shekhina* may be likened to that of a torch whereas the light of the souls may be compared to that of candles)."[6]
>
> דְהָכִי אוּקְמוּהוּ רַבָּנָן, דְנִשְׁמָתִין דוֹמִין קֳדָם שְׁכִינְתָּא כְּנֵרוֹת לִפְנֵי הָאֲבוּקָה

A great sage of the early twentieth century, Rabbi Yehuda Fedaya, made an analogy which helps us understand divine revelation at the level of the *Shekhina*. Imagine that all the Jewish people in the world were standing in a valley, trying to warm themselves in the sunlight after a harsh

---

6. *Tikunei Zohar* (Jerusalem: Yeshivat Nahar Shalom, n.d.), 7a.

winter. But there is a cloud overhead, and the light that seeps through is not the sun's radiance but a meager light. The cloud represents the barrier formed by our transgressions, which desensitize us and prevent us from experiencing our closeness to Hashem. The poor light under the cloud represents our impaired ability to receive the *shefa* (divine bounty) from Above. And on a different level the poor light also stands for the *Shekhina*'s pain at not being able to give us the bounty stemming from the higher levels of divine revelation.

Another *mashal* (parable) about the *Shekhina* is found in the Zohar: A king's children acted badly, so he sent his children into exile. He also sent his wife, the queen, so that she could protect them. However, the king soon felt that without his loved ones, there was no point in having a palace, so he destroyed it.[7] When the king's desire for the queen and their children intensifies, says the Zohar, as the verse says,[8] לִים הִנֵּה זֶה עוֹמֵד אַחַר כָּתְלֵנוּ מַשְׁגִּיחַ מִן הַחֲלֹנוֹת מֵצִיץ מִן הַחֲרַכִּים – *He was standing behind our wall, supervising from the windows, peering through the lattices.* In a similar way, explains the Zohar, the People of Israel, even though that at the time of the Temple destruction, they left the King's palace and went into exile, they took with them His dwelling place, that is, they took the Shekhina with them. And, since the King's desire was to bring them back soon, He allowed them to take the Shekhina with them. When the holy King's desire intensifies to be with the Queen, as on the Shabbat and festival days, He comes,[9] מְדַלֵּג עַל הֶהָרִים מְקַפֵּץ עַל הַגְּבָעוֹת – *leaping over mountains, skipping over hills.*

The king is Hashem, the palace represents our Holy Temple, and the queen is the *Shekhina on High*, who encloses all of our collective souls at the point in which our souls are attached to Hashem. The queen's children are *Knesset Yisrael Themselves*, namely, the collective entity of our inner souls dwelling in this world under physical garments, empowered by our Torah observance to contribute to the divine plan.

Painful as is the distancing of the *Shekhina Below* from the higher levels of divine revelation, this separation serves the purpose

---

7. Ibid., 115a.
8. Paraphrasing the Song of Songs 2:9.
9. Paraphrasing the Song of Songs 2:8.

of preventing the other side – the forces of impurity – from deriving sustenance from the divine radiance on High. (Again, the expression *Shekhina Below* refers to the aspect of the *Shekhina* who is attached to *Knesset Yisrael Below*.) In the Ultimate Future the *Shekhina* will recover all the light that was once her own.

Chapter 1

Creator of Darkness

The inner dimension of the Torah understands darkness as a state of mind rather than as a physical restriction of light.[1] At the very beginning of the account of Creation, it says, "and the darkness He named 'Night.'" [2] This tells us that the concepts "night" and "darkness" are equivalent. The Hebrew letters of the word "*Layla* (night)" allude to the inner dimension of these terms, for we may rearrange the same letters to form the word "*yelala*" (wailing). Darkness thus designates the emotions threatening to overcome us when we feel distant from *Hashem* (God), such as an anxiety that may lead us to despair.

We may fight darkness by drawing light to ourselves from the highest source – Shabbat. On Shabbat, the night has the same quality of daylight as the day itself. After each of the six days of Creation we read "And there was evening, and there was morning" and the number of the day. However, with respect to the Sabbath the verse says: "By the

---

1. The following analysis of prayer is adapted from Rabbi Luria, "Yaakov Tikken Tefilat Arvit," in *Sefer Beit Genazai al Parshiyot HaTorah, Kolel Biurim Uferushim Laparshiyot: Bereshit ["Sefer Beit Genazai al Parshiyot HaTorah"]* (Jerusalem: R. M. Luria, 5761), vol. 2, 683ff.
2. Gen. 1:5; *The Living Torah*, translated by Rabbi Aryeh Kaplan (New York: Moznaim Publications, 1981).

seventh day, God completed His work … ."[3] The words "and there was evening, and there was morning" do not appear, for the entire Shabbat is considered light.

On Shabbat night there is the same kind of spiritual light as there is during the daytime. Even though there is physical darkness, this is not the same type of darkness as there is throughout the week, which causes the week nights to be called "night." The darkness of Shabbat night is of a different kind.

In our morning prayers, when we bless Hashem for creating darkness *(boreh choshekh)*, we are really referring to the light in the heavenly world of *Beriya* (Creation), which radiates with such intensity that we have no means of perceiving it. That is why we refer to it as darkness. The light that Hashem shines on us throughout Shabbat is of the same type as that of *boreh choskhekh*, so intense that we cannot grasp it. To that end, the Holy One gives us tools to expand our consciousness, thus enabling us to receive the Shabbat light: One of these is the Shabbat additional soul; another is the additional *Amida* (standing prayer) we refer to as *Mussaf*.

The inner purpose of the additional soul is to help us focus our entire mind on the Almighty.[4] As a result, our ability to feel His Presence intensifies, particularly at the time of prayers. Moreover, the additional soul also sharpens our sense preceptions, allowing us to use all our physical senses as a means to lift the veil of concealment separating us from the Beloved. The *Mussaf Amida* prayer was included in the Shabbat ritual, in addition to our three daily prayers, because saying *Mussaf* helps us absorb the divine light stemming from *Keter* (Crown). We shall see in the pages to come that the light of *Keter* is emitted on the seventh day of each week.[5]

---

3. Gen. 2:2. *Tanach: The Stone Edition* (New York, Mesorah Publications, 1996). All the citations from Chumash and Tanakh will be from this edition unless otherwise noted.
4. Adapted from Rabbi Moshe Luria, "Maamar Neshama Yetera BeShabbat," *Sefer Beit Genazai Kolel Maamarim Ubiurim al Derekh Haavoda meyusadim al divrei ha Ari z"l Luria, be'inyanei Shabbat ["Sefer Beit Genazai: Maamarei Shabbat"]*, 1st ed., 85-89.
5. Adapted from Rabbi Moshe Luria, "Selichot Bechodesh Elul Ubimei Hateshuvah, "*Sefer Beit Genazai: Sefer Beit Genazai: Kolel Inyanei Teshuva Bechodesh Elul, Rosh Hashanah, Aseret Yemei Teshuva, Yom Hakippurim, Chag Hasukkot, Ushmini Atzeret*

The darkness of the night comes to the world when the forces of *dinim* (strict justice) overwhelm the heavenly dimensions, causing the state of constriction that we call the darkness of the night. The *dinim* forces are spiritual forces dwelling outside the realm of holiness, in what we would call the realm of evil, or "the other side," which stands in contrast with the realm of holiness, representing Hashem's Presence. The outside forces only exist in virtue of the fragments or sparks of holiness that they snatch from the souls of those who transgress divine will as expressed in the Torah. Without these sparks, they would not have any existence. The outside forces are actually part of the plan of Creation. By allowing both good and evil to exist, Hashem established a system in which man has free will to choose between the deeds bringing light and those causing darkness.

In order to understand the inner darkness caused by these forces of impurity on High and below, and how to distance ourselves from them, we must reflect on the special nature of the bond between the Creator and the People of Israel. As described in the Introduction, the higher aspect – the root – of each of the souls of the People of Israel is attached to the Holy One on High, together with all the other souls of Israel, in a collective entity called *Knesset Yisrael Above*. When the highest point of all our heavenly souls – namely, *Knesset Yisrael Above* – is cleaving to Hashem on High, then the People of Israel below become a spiritual entity whose inner souls, in a state of togetherness, are attached to Hashem. This spiritual entity under our physical forms is referred to as *Knesset Yisrael Below*.

Rabbi Moshe Luria zt"l writes:

> As it is taught in the holy Zohar, the inner purpose of all the *mitzvot* (commandments) is to [help us reach] passionate attachment to Hashem; the message is that by means of this [effort we supply as we engage in the performance of *mitzvot*] we may attain [what the Prophet Ezekiel refers to as] the "time for love." And, if it can be said, this is His main will and delight. [6]

Veavodat Yom Kippur Bamikdash Ubiurim BaRambam Hilkhot Teshuva ["Sefer Beit Genazai – Massekhet Teshuva –Hilkhot Teshuva"] (Jerusalem: R.M. Luria, 5767), 36-38.
6. "Chiko Mamtakim," *Sefer Beit Genazai: Shir Hashirim*, 169a.

Elsewhere, in a similar vein, Rabbi Luria explains:

> The soul comes down to this world so that by fulfilling *mitzvot* and engaging in good deeds she will acquire garments and ornaments of a spiritual nature by means of which she may become pleasing to the King of the world and able to stand before Him and serve Him on High.
>
> One of the ways in which our soul can serve Hashem on High while we are in this world is by means of prayer. At the time of our three daily prayers, there is a spiritual energy interconnecting all the souls of Israel to form the spiritual entity of *Knesset Yisrael* in the state of togetherness of *yichud* (unification) with Hashem.[7]

The word "*yichud*" alludes to the total togetherness only possible at the soul level. Rabbi Luria explains that when there is a *yichud* on High between *Hakadosh Barukh Hu* and our collective soul-roots, the People of Israel below are included as well. And then the People of Israel below are in a state of happiness, perceiving the closeness to *Hakadosh Barukh Hu*. The higher aspect of their soul is able to ascend on High at the time of the *yichud*, and as a result *shefa* is directed to the world below. The unification brought about by our daily prayers brings well-being to all the People of Israel, but those of us who are actually involved in the prayer may feel a special closeness to Hashem at that time.

In an essay on the Song of Songs, Rabbi Luria explains that there are two types of mystical unification of the Holy One with *Knesset Yisrael*.[8] The first is likened to the union of two separate entities. The second may be likened to a bond of total unity in which two entities become one. This is similar to our marriage ceremony, in which we first have to go through the *kiddushin* (betrothal) and only then comes the *nissuin* (completion of the marital bond). The second type of union underlies

---

7. "Ani velo Malach," in *Sefer Seder Leil Shimurim: Kolel Maamarim Ubiurim al Derekh Haavodah: Meyusadim a"d haArizal Luria Beinyanei Seder Leil Pesach Vehaggada shel Pesach* (Jerusalem: unknown, 5750), 240b.
8. "Asher LiShlomo," *Sefer Beit Genazai: Shir Hashirim*, 18ff.

the very purpose of Creation, and each soul of Israel tasted this union at the giving of the Torah, in which the collective souls as well as each individual soul became a dwelling space for the Holy One. The divine intention was that they should achieve this spiritual union through their own efforts.

Rabbi Luria concludes this essay with the verse:

| His mouth is sweet; He is altogether desirable; this is my Beloved, this is my Friend, O daughters of Yerushalayim[9] | חִכּוֹ מַמְתַקִּים וְכֻלּוֹ מַחֲמַדִּים זֶה דוֹדִי וְזֶה רֵעִי בְּנוֹת יְרוּשָׁלָם |

On this verse Rabbi Luria comments:

> [This verse] includes two main elements. One of these is [alluded to by] "His mouth is sweet" in the situation [in which we may relate to Hashem] as "This is my Beloved," evoking Ezekiel's expression the "time for love," which is the time of the heavenly unification taking place every day during our *Amida* prayer and on Shabbat as well as Yom Tov (festive days). At these times we may [attain an experiential perception of the words] "His mouth is sweet," alluding to the delight of divine closeness [while we are engaged in prayer].
>
> [The second element is alluded to by the words] "He is altogether desirable," referring to the time before and after the unification occurring in the *Amida* prayer. [This second aspect before and after prayer] has the quality of *machamadim* (desirable), for it expresses yearning and desire. [At these times we may relate to Hashem] as "This is my Friend" in the sense that this not the time of unification.

---

9. Song 5:16. Translated by Rabbi Avraham Sutton. This translation will be part of the second volume of the Breslov Siddur edited by Rabbi Sutton, forthcoming. Rabbi Sutton may be contacted at <avraham.sutton@me.com>. All quotations from Shir Hashirim will come from this translation unless otherwise noted.

We retain from these teachings that the expression "the time for love" alludes to the moment of *yichud*, not only in our *Amida* on Shabbat and Yom Tov, but also every single day, three times a day. While saying the *Amida* we enter a special state of consciousness in which we may attain a perception of Hashem's love at these times. In contrast, before and after the *Amida* we may also perceive Hashem's closeness, but not in the same way.

Although in our generation we have no conscious perception of the heavenly unification at the time of *Amida* prayer, we are nevertheless infused by the immediacy of an unknown Presence whose vibrant energy fills us with a total sense of fulfillment. The *Amida* enables our soul to replenish its former luminous energy as it rises to the Source. The purpose of the prayers that follow the *Amida* is then to bring this energy down with us to elevate our normal consciousness, helping to enhance our awareness of the Divine until the next time we pray the *Amida*.

Rabbi Luria tells us the secret of how to attain the type of bond we have mentioned:

> In order to initiate the heavenly unification [that is to take place on Shabbat] we must adopt the way of a bride – namely the longing of *Knesset Yisrael* – [to be close to] the Holy One, for the word *"kalla"* (bride) is related to [the expression] *kalot hanefesh* (longing of the soul). [Our soul's longing helps to] give rise to the unification which will take place when the Holy King goes to the field to bring the Queen from the field into the Home. By going to the field [on Friday afternoon] and saying "Come O Bride," we actively arouse divine action on High. *Hakadosh Barukh Hu* then draws *Knesset Yisrael* [close] to Him. As explained in the teachings of the holy Ari z"l, on Shabbat all the worlds ascend on High to the world of *Atzilut* (Closeness).[10]
>
> And this is [the way in which we must understand it] when the Torah asks us to sanctify the Shabbat even though the Shabbat holiness is [a gift which] will keep coming from Above [without requiring our intervention]. Even though [on Shabbat]

---

10. See Chapter 12, "Ascending with the *Tosefet Shabbat*."

special divine lights, as well as the additional Shabbat soul, are directed onto us, still, in order to initiate the unification on High, the People of Israel below have to show the eager attitude of a bride. As a result there is an injunction [which we will explain further] called *Tosefet Shabbat* [addition to Shabbat] to show *Knesset Yisrael*'s yearning for *Hakadosh Barukh Hu*.[11]

In the chapter on *Tosefet Shabbat*, we will examine what we may do on Erev Shabbat (which starts on Thursday night after the evening prayer, and lasts until the Shabbat begins) in order to enable us to receive the Shabbat light at a higher level.

Darkness means exile; it means being in a situation in which we do not feel Hashem's closeness. In contrast, Shabbat is the day in which we gather enough faith to hold on to it for the rest of the week. The mystery of *emuna* (faith) is the consciousness of our contact with Hashem. In other words, it is not just that we believe it but rather that we know it. We can relate to the world around us with an expanded consciousness or with constricted consciousness. The faith that is there for us to absorb on Shabbat is an expanded consciousness in which we are able to push away the constriction of fear and anxiety that beset us the rest of the week. Hashem always keeps an eye on us, but the intensity of His loving look varies according to the way in which we ourselves relate to Him.

The ultimate desire of the Divine is that we should all relate to Him as soul companions.[12] Rabbi Moshe Luria points out that Hashem reveals His love for the People of Israel as He tells them in the Torah: "You shall be My special treasure among all nations,"[13] and, "God your Lord loves you"[14] – and in the Prophets, "I have loved you, says God."[15]

The main feature of the love of soul companions is that it has to be reciprocal, in contrast with the love of *banim* (children) in which the reciprocity is not indispensable. Parental love may be one sided – the

---

11. *Sefer Beit Genazai: Shir Hashirim*, 140-141.
12. The teachings that follow on Shir Hashirim 5:16 are adapted from Rabbi Moshe Luria, "Chiko mamtakim," *Sefer Beit Genazai: Shir Hashirim*," 168ff.
13. Ex. 19:5; trans. Rabbi Aryeh Kaplan, *The Living Torah*.
14. Deut. 23:6; *The Living Torah*.
15. Mal. 1:2.

parent loves the child even when the child is unable to express love in return, nor even realizes s/he has any – but the love of *dodim* (soul companions), expressed in the plural form, has to be actively shared. Consequently, this love was portrayed in Shir Hashirim from both perspectives:[16] One is "My Beloved is mine and I am His," and the other one is "I am my Beloved's and my Beloved is mine," thus indicating that – to the extent that we can express it[17] – the love is equal on both sides. Or rather, as Rabbi Luria writes: "*kesheyesh giluy ahava mishnei tzedadim ze laze* (both sides are aware of this love)." It is thus expressed in the plural form, for it is a double love which stems from both sides: each side feels the love of the other directed toward him, and this is what produces the love of *dodim*.[18]

There is no specific element of *avodat Hashem* (divine service) that one aiming for the bond of soul companion can take on. It is more of an inner expression of one's desire to have such a level of closeness, and that is a very individual thing.

Ahavat Hashem (loving Hashem) and *devekut* (attachment) form an essential part of the *mitzvot* that we have to do. Rabbi Luria teaches:[19]

> The [preceding discussion about soul companions] teaches us a principle regarding the *mitzvot* of loving Hashem and cleaving to Hashem: in addition to the essential issue that these are *mitzvot* like all the others, most importantly, they also [express] the object of divine will directed to completing the relationship of *Knesset Yisrael*, His soul companion.

As will be explained, on Shabbat our closeness to Hashem is like that of soul companions, and we receive a level of emuna which is like the experiential perception of this closeness through the Shabbat *seudot*

---

16. As explained in "BeShaar Hasefer," in Rabbi Moshe Luria, *Sefer Beit Genazai: Kolel Maamarim Uviurim Bemitzvot Tefilla… Uferushim Bedivrei HaAri z"l Beshaar Hakavanot ("Sefer Pitchei Tefilla")* (Jerusalem: R.M. Luria, 5762-5764), vol. 3, 1ff.
17. I am grateful to my teacher, Rabbi Aryeh Kaplan zt"l, for this translation of *kiveyachol*, which is usually rendered as 'as it were' or 'if it can be said.'
18. *Sefer Beit Genazai: Shir Hashirim*, 169.
19. "Chiko Mamtakim," *Sefer Beit Genazai: Shir Hashirim*, 169a.

(meals), which the holy Zohar calls the *seudot* of perfect faith, or the *seudot* of focused consciousness.

The three *seudot* we have on Shabbat are linked to Exodus 16:25, in which the Israelites are given the rules about the manna and Shabbat, because this verse repeats the word *"hayom"* (today) three times.[20] We have these meals in the evening, morning and afternoon, thus indicating that all these times are called *yom* (day), and that on Shabbat the concept of "night" in the weekday sense does not exist.

Whereas on weekdays the *Amida* prayer is the same in the morning, afternoon and evening, on Shabbat each of the *Amida* prayers has a paragraph of its own identifying the unique quality of its time. Rabbi Luria writes:

> The differences in the Shabbat prayers indicate three levels of closeness and *devekut* (attachment) between *Hakadosh Barukh Hu* and *Knesset Yisrael*. [...]
>
> All three levels are [linked with the divine lights of] *daat* (intimate knowledge), evoking the bond of passionate attachment between *Hakadosh Barukh Hu* and Israel.[21]

There is a different level of love called *daat* (knowledge). It is the higher state of *consciousness* in which one achieves a passionate attachment to Hashem. In this higher form of awareness, each spirit merges with the other, so to speak, until they become one.

Daat is the biblical term for the marital union ("And Adam *knew* Eve"). It is the metaphor used in the Song of Songs to describe Hashem's love for Israel. To reach the oneness and passionate attachment of the marital bond, both husband and wife must feel the love with equal intensity, and the love must be exclusive. To cleave to Hashem on the level of *daat*, the love must be mutual and exclusive; we must focus upon

---

20. Ex. 16:25.
21. "Shalosh Seudot beShabbat," in *Sefer Beit Genazai al Parshiyot haTorah: Shemot*, vol. 1 (Jerusalem: R. M. Luria, 5761), 142.

Him all our emotions. Anything short of this cannot be called binding to Hashem with passionate attachment.

Hence by means of the three Shabbat prayers we draw down these three types of light – lights of *daat* (knowledge) imbued with *devekut*. We internalize these lights by participating in the *seuda* following each prayer. When we do this, the consciousness of this closeness can be with us for the entire week.

Chapter 2

Fiery Coals of Love

We recall that the Hebrew letters of the expression *Shabbat l'Hashem* may be regrouped to form the word *"Shalhevet"* (flame), as at the end of Shir Hashirim:[1]

Love's sparks are fiery coals, a flame of the Divine.	רְשָׁפֶיהָ רִשְׁפֵּי אֵשׁ שַׁלְהֶבֶתְ יָ-הּ:

Shabbat is a day in which Hashem's love manifests with the strength of a *shalhevet*. The Zohar points out that concealed within the word *"Bereshit"* (in the beginning) are the Aramaic word *tre* (two) and the Hebrew word *"esh"* (fire).[2] Our Sages thus instituted that when Shabbat comes to a close we should light a candle with multiple wicks and say the blessing to *boreh meorei haesh* (He who creates the illuminations of the fire).[3] If we pay attention to the word *"meorei"* (illuminations) in this blessing, we notice that it is worded in the plural form, for we are

---

1. Song 8:6.
2. *Tikunei Zohar*, Tikun 27, 143b.
3. *The Complete ArtScroll Siddur, Nusach Sefard*, 655.

Key to the Locked Garden

now asking that some of the illumination of our additional Shabbat soul should cast light onto our coming week.

We draw upon ourselves the Shabbat experience with the light of candles, and we leave it with the light of a torch.[4] The candle only lights its immediate surroundings, whereas the torch lights the way before us. The meaning is that we must leave the Shabbat day with the lasting impression of its fire of holiness, and thirst for a quality of closeness to Hashem the intensity of which evokes the flaming torch of the *havdala* (closing service). We want this torch to illuminate the coming week with a spiritual energy that will last until the following Shabbat.

And the Zohar reveals to us that at the time of Havdala, the *Shekhina* is saying:

| Sustain me with *ashishot* (the two illuminations of the fire), [...] for I am lovesick.[5] | סַמְּכוּנִי בָּאֲשִׁישׁוֹת [...] כִּי חוֹלַת אַהֲבָה אָנִי |

Rabbi Luria directs our attention to the word *"ashishot"*, pointing out that this word has it in the word *"esh"* (fire) twice.

The *Shekhina* seems to be asking us to sustain her, and we are left to wonder how we may do that.

Our prayers – in particular the *Amida* – act as vehicle in which the *Shekhina* ascends every day and attains a type of unification with the Beloved at the three times in which we pray during the day: in the evening, in the morning, and then in the afternoon.

---

4. "Beshaarei Shabbat: Ner Biknisat HaShabbat Veavukah Bitziato," *Sefer Beit Genazai: Maamarei Shabbat*, 2nd edition (Jerusalem: private publisher, 5751), n.p. (at the end of the introduction to the volume).
5. Song 2:5.

The *Tikunei Zohar* explains the value of prayer in Hashem's eyes:

> There is no gift [referring to the *Amida*] that is more precious to *Hakadosh Barukh Hu* than a prayer where the person praying has in mind that it should elevate the *Shekhina* for the sake of the heavenly unification.[6]
>
> דְּלֵית דּוֹרוֹנָא חֲבִיבָא קֳדָם קוּדְשָׁא בְּרִיךְ הוּא כְּדוֹרוֹנָא דִשְׁכִינְתָּא

Moreover, on Shabbat it is through our contribution – the contribution of *Knesset Yisrael Themselves* – that the *Shekhina* ascends to the higher aspect of divine revelation, which is why Shabbat is "Shabbat for Hashem" – that is, Hashem's day of joy.

Hence the main way that we, *Knesset Yisrael Themselves*, can help is by saying the formal prayers every day because somehow, the words of the *Amida* have a special property to bring about this union between the *Shekhina* and *Hakadosh Barukh Hu* that other prayers do not have.

Rabbi Luria explains that according to the Ari z"l,[7] the words *"Ata kiddashta"* (You have sanctified), which we say in the Shabbat evening *Amida*, allude to the stage of *kiddushin* (consecration) in our marriage ceremony.[8] After undergoing the *kiddushin* a bride is consecrated to her groom and forbidden to everyone else, but she is not yet permitted to her groom. She will be permitted to him after they go through the next level of union, called *nissuin*.

The idea of *kiddushin* as Shabbat begins is that in order to come together with Hashem you have to separate yourself from everything else. You have in mind: I am giving myself over to Him because He wants me to be with Him on Shabbat, and in doing so, I am leaving my past behind.

---

6. *Tikunei Zohar*, 37b.
7. *Pri Etz Chaim, Shaar HaShabbat*, chapter 13; cited by Rabbi Luria in "Beshaarei Shabbat: Ner Biknisat HaShabbat Veavukah Bitziato" (see note 3 above).
8. The teachings on kiddushin are adapted from Rabbi Moshe Luria, "Ata Kidashta [א] and [ב], *Sefer Beit Genazai: Pitchei Tefilla*, vol. 3, 226ff.

"*Ata kiddashta*" refers to the *kiddushin* between *Hakadosh Barukh Hu* and *Knesset Yisrael*. The legal state of *kiddushin* entails that the outside forces have no longer any right to attach themselves to *Knesset Yisrael* and derive nourishment from her as they do on the weekdays.

On Shabbat the *Amida* prayer has only seven blessings instead of the weekly eighteen. The *Rishonim* (Early Sages) said that this is because Shabbat is the day in which we become Hashem's soul companion, and the Shabbat *Amida* prayer may be likened to the seven blessings of the marital ceremony.[9]

The Bride of the Shabbat *kiddushin* is thus the spiritual entity of *Knesset Yisrael*. As we say the seven blessings of the evening *Amida*, she becomes forbidden to the outside forces.

Three times on Shabbat – once within the *Amida*, then right after we finish the *Amida*, and the third time within the Kiddush at the *seuda* – we say the verse "*vaychulu hashamayim vehaaretz* (the heaven and earth were finished)."[10] This is because we are testifying that *Hakadosh Barukh Hu* created the world in six days, and for testimony to be legally valid you need two or three witnesses. We say it standing up because testimony has to be given standing. In this way we are also acting as witnesses to the *kiddushin*. We want everything we do below to be a mirror replica of what happens on High in order to help the process come to fulfillment.

There is a *piyyut* (liturgical poem) for the Shabbat day authored by Rabbi Masud Abuchatsira, father of the famed kabbalist and miracle worker Rabbi Israel Abuchatsira, known as Baba Sali.[11] This song contains all the elements of the preparation for Shabbat as taught in the

---

9. As mentioned by Rabbi Luria, the names of these early Sages include the Ramban (Nachmanides), the Abudarham, and the Shibolei haLeket.
10. Gen. 2:1.
11. The word made up of the first letter of every stanza forms the acrostic of Rabbi Masud's name.

Shaar haKavanot on Shabbat of the Ari z"l, some of which I discuss in this book.[12] Concerning the *kiddushin*, Rabbi Masud says:

Then must be said the testimony of *kiddushin*, established in the three times [we say] *Vaychulu*,[13] at the time *Chakal Tapuchin Kaddishin* (Field of Holy Apples).[14]	אָז תֹּאמַר עֵדוּת קִדּוּשִׁין. בְּשָׁלֹשׁ וַיְכֻלּוּ נוֹסָדָה. רִאשׁוֹנָה חֲקַל נֶגֶד שי"ן חֲקַל תַּפּוּחִין אַחַר עֲמִידָה. חֲקַל תַּפּוּחִין קַדִּישִׁין. נִקְרֵאת בְּקִדּוּשׁ סְעֻדָּה.

While the six days of Creation are considered a time of building the *dira* (dwelling place) worthy of His Name, Shabbat is the day of *nissuin* between *Hakadosh Barukh Hu* and *Knesset Yisrael*. We derive that the inner purpose of Creation was to attain the bond of *nissuin* between *Hakadosh Barukh Hu* and *Knesset Yisrael*, which is the deeper reason behind our stopping creative activity on Shabbat, for on the day of the marriage ceremony neither bride nor groom work. This bond is also the inner reason behind the Shabbat morning *seuda*. Just as after a wedding there is a reception and there is great joy, so we say in the Shabbat morning *Amida*, "Yismechu beMalkhutkha (They will rejoice in Your Kingship)."

According to the *Rishonim*, there are three different stages to the *nissuin* of *Hakadosh Barukh Hu* and *Knesset Yisrael* on Shabbat. *Kiddushin* occurs in the evening when we say, "*Ata kiddashta*." On Shabbat morning, the phrase "*yismach Moshe* (Moses will rejoice)" in the morning *Amida* anticipates the joy of *nissuin*, which takes place in the *Mussaf* (additional *Amida*). At the peak of the Shabbat experience, on Shabbat afternoon, we say "You are One and Your Name is One and who is like Your people Israel, one nation on earth," for at this time the unification occurs. It is for this reason, according to the Early Sages, that

---

12. My deepest gratitude to Ruth Shira for "discovering" this *piyyut*, and for not only sending it, but for persisting until I took the time to study it and realized that it encapsulates all the elements of Shabbat. At Ruth Shira's suggestion, the *piyyut* is included in its entirety in the Mystical Readings for the Shabbat Table, at the end of the readings for the first *seuda*.
13. See chapter 12, "Ascending with the *Tosefet Shabbat*."
14. See chapter 4, "Spiritual Kisses."

Key to the Locked Garden

the Shabbat afternoon *Amida*, unlike the others, does not include the paragraph *Yismechu beMalkhutcha*, for this is the moment of union, so intense that it goes beyond joy.

And yet according to the Ari z"l, there is no unification at the time of Mincha. The teachings of the *Rishonim* and the Ari z"l do not contradict each other, however, for they are referring to two different aspects of divine revelation. In a nutshell, the Ari z"l is referring to the *Shekhina on High* – our collective soul roots on High attached to *Hakadosh Barukh Hu* – whereas the early Sages are referring to *Knesset Yisrael Themselves* in the world below, under their physical garb.

As mentioned,[15] there are two types of mystical unification of the Holy One with *Knesset Yisrael*.[16] The first is likened to the union of two separate entities, while the second is likened to a bond of total unity in which two entities become one. This is similar to our marriage ceremony, in which we first have to go through the *kiddushin* and only then comes the *nissuin*.

In the light of the preceding, we can only say that it is no wonder that it is the *Shekhina on High*, who is *etzem meatzamav* (part of the essence of the Divine), who attains the first type of unification at the Shabbat *Mussaf*, a bond of total unity in which two entities are attached as one – the bond of One.

Kiddushin and *nissuin* are only required when there are two separate entities, who want to become one single being. Consequently, we – *Knesset Yisrael Themselves* under our physical bodies – are the ones who need *kiddushin* and *nissuin*!

According to the Ari z"l,[17] *Ata kiddashta* in the evening prayer alludes to the higher level of holiness and divine revelation drawn onto the *Shekhina on High* at the beginning of Shabbat, whereas the *yichud* of the *Shekhina on High* occurs at the time of *Mussaf*. This *yichud* is not comparable to the unification at the Giving of the Torah, for

---

15. See chapter 1, "Creator of Darkness."
16. The teachings on the Song of Songs are adapted from Rabbi Moshe Luria, "Asher LiShlomo," *Sefer Beit Genazai: Shir Hashirim*, 18ff.
17. See *Shaar Hakavanot: Shabbat*, cited in Rabbi Moshe Luria, "Asher LiShlomo," *Sefer Beit Genazai: Shir Hashirim*, 18ff.

only once a year on Yom Kippur can the *Shekhina* ascend that high, though this will happen permanently in the Ultimate Future. In our time, however, the *Shekhina* is unable to go that high on Shabbat. As a result, in the afternoon at the time of Mincha in which the unification is even loftier than that at *Mussaf* in the morning, the *Shekhina* is not in a state of joy, and out of empathy with the *Shekhina* we do not say *Yismechu beMalkhutcha*.

As will be discussed in the pages to come, according the *Rishonim*, *Knesset Yisrael Themselves* take over and become the Shabbat soul companion during Mincha and the third meal.

Rabbi Luria here poses a question: We have learnt that we want everything we do below to be a mirror replica of what happens on High in order to help the process come to fulfillment. How, then, can there be a unification involving us below if it is not occurring simultaneously on High?

The answer is that it is our participation below which helps the *Shekhina on High* attain a higher level of fulfillment at the time of the Shabbat *Mussaf* and earns us divine favor as result at the time of Mincha.

Shabbat afternoon is when we have a chance to taste Hashem's love for *Knesset Yisrael* that is like *rishpei esh* (fiery coals).

Furthermore, our divine service also supports the *Shekhina on High*; for from the time in which she returns Home at the beginning of Shabbat, we play an essential role, enhancing her return with the eagerness of our Shabbat preparations; and while she receives levels of holiness on High, we act as the soul companion below. That is the reason why, in each of the Shabbat prayers, we ask *Hakadosh Barukh Hu* to want us as His soul companion. The Sages state that the wife only reaches the inner harmony of rest in her husband's home. Consequently, every time we pray "*Retze na bimenuchatenu* (May You look with favor upon our *menucha*)" in the Shabbat *Amida*, we are saying: "May it be Your will that we will be Your soul companion and find *menucha* in You."

As we will see, our participation in the different steps of the *Shekhina*'s return Home continues all the way through till the end of Shabbat.

Chapter 3
A Taste of the World to Come

The prophet Isaiah promises:

> If you restrain your foot because it is the Sabbath; refrain from accomplishing your own needs on My holy day; if you proclaim the Sabbath "a delight," and the holy [day] of Hashem "honored," and you honor it by not engaging in your own affairs, from seeking your own needs or discussing the forbidden – then you will delight in [al] Hashem.[1]

> אִם תָּשִׁיב מִשַּׁבָּת רַגְלֶךָ עֲשׂוֹת חֲפָצֶיךָ בְּיוֹם קָדְשִׁי וְקָרָאתָ לַשַּׁבָּת עֹנֶג לִקְדוֹשׁ ה׳ מְכֻבָּד וְכִבַּדְתּוֹ מֵעֲשׂוֹת דְּרָכֶיךָ מִמְּצוֹא חֶפְצְךָ וְדַבֵּר דָּבָר: אָז תִּתְעַנַּג עַל ה׳

The words *"az titanag al Hashem"* are translated "then you will delight in Hashem," but *al* means literally "over." The Sages explain that the word *"al"* alludes to a lofty level of divine revelation that is beyond the ability of human translators to render.

---

1. Is. 58:13.

Key to the Locked Garden

Since none of us can truly conceive of or imagine Hashem Himself, we have to think in terms of how He revealed Himself to us. There are different levels of divine revelation and a revelation means that the Holy *Ein Sof* (Infinite Being) condenses His light at different levels of constriction and allows us to call Him by His Names.

For instance, the words in the Haggada *"ubemora gadol zu gilui Shekhina"* (and with great 'awe' means the revelation of the *Shekhina*) tell us that at the moment of the Exodus the Jews experienced a revelation of the *Shekhina*. However, they could not have registered it as an actual vision, because at that time they were still in Egypt, and the *Shekhina* cannot reveal herself where there is impurity. At that point they could only have experienced an inner feeling of awe. In contrast, at the moment when they crossed the sea, they were able to have an actual vision.

In our times Hashem reveals Himself to us through His Names. For example, we may examine Psalm 55, in which King David tells us how hurt he is because his best friend has betrayed him. If we pay attention to the simple meaning of the words, we see that he does not use divine names indiscriminately. On the contrary, different names are applied to different levels of divine revelation, that is, to specific ways in which Hashem interacts with the world.[2] King David calls upon a certain name when he desires to draw downward the type of divine revelation or interaction associated with that name. At the end of the psalm, in verse 23, David's final advice is:

Cast *al* (literally over) Hashem [what you conceive as] your destiny, and He will sustain you.	הַשְׁלֵךְ עַל ה׳ יְהָבְךָ וְהוּא יְכַלְכְּלֶךָ

---

2. For instance, in verse 2 ("Give ear, *Elokim*, to my prayer") he first addresses his prayer to the Divine as *Elokim*. Speaking of his former friend who has slandered him, he says in verse 10: "*Adonai*, (spelled with the Hebrew letters *alef, dalet, nun, yud*), consume and confuse their tongue." The divine name spelled in this way is associated with the execution of strict justice. Then in verse 17 he says, "As for me, upon *Elokim* shall I call." The divine name *Elokim* is associated with the divine attribute of strict justice. He ends verse 17 "and Hashem will save me." To ask for compassion, David addresses the name of *Havaya*, associated with the attribute of mercy. In verse 20, he expresses his deep wish for divine compassion, saying, "May *Kel* (God) hear and answer."

Another example is Hannah, mother of the Prophet Samuel; somehow, she realized that, according to the normal channels of Providence, it might have been decreed on High that she could not have a child, "and Hannah prayed *al Hashem*." [3] Although most of this verse's translations read "and Hannah prayed to Hashem," the Zohar stresses that we have to pay attention to the Hebrew word *al*, for there is no word, indeed no letter in the Torah that does not allude to divine mysteries.[4] The holy commentator Shelah explained that there are different levels in divine revelation: The name *Ad-nai* is a lower form of revelation, the name of *Havaya* an intermediary one, and the name *Ekieh* a higher form.[5] When Hannah – somehow – ascended to the highest level in her prayer, at that level of unconditional lovingkindness in which the concept of merit becomes irrelevant, her wish was fulfilled.

We derive from the preceding that we can relate to Hashem at different levels, and Hashem's Names are directly related to the way we may experience divine revelation. The expression *al Hashem* seems to take us higher than all the other divine revelations. We could liken this level of divine revelation to a crown, just as the crown stands over the head of the king, and not inside his head. This expression may thus be telling us that *al Hashem* is a level of revelation above human perception.

We cannot access this level of revelation directly.[6] Hashem's divine flow comes down to us like a heavenly ladder made up of the different levels of divine revelation, and the Zohar gives names to the different levels to help us integrate the meaning of each level. In general terms (somewhat simplified for our purpose), the higher level of divine revelation is referred to by the Aramaic name *Atika Kadisha* (the Ancient Holy One), is also called *Arikh Anpin* (long countenance), and is part of the infinite light of *Ein Sof*. The word *"anpin"* (countenance) alludes to the Creator's will and desire to create man and reveal His light to His

---

3. I Samuel 1:10.
4. Zohar, Acharei Mot 300 *(Matok Midvash* edition).
5. HaShelah Hakadosh, Hagahot on Masechet Pesachim.
6. The explanation that follows on the different levels of divine revelation is adapted from the work of Rabbi Yaakov Hillel, *Binyan Ariel: Kitzur Vetamtzit Sefer Etz Chayim* (Jerusalem: Machon Ahavat Shalom, 5766), 110-111.

creatures. The word *"arikh"* (long) implies an unconditional compassion which would interfere with our ability to exercise free will.

In contrast with the infinite compassion manifest on the level of *Arikh Anpin*, we have a condensed aspect of Hashem's revelation referred to in the Zohar as *Zeir Anpin* (reduced countenance). This refers to an interaction with the world based on judgment. *Zeir* (reduced) indicates the condensed nature of the light this manifestation of Hashem is imbued with. Still, this manifestation too is called *anpin* (countenance) because this constitutes the main source of our illumination from the Creator. *Zeir Anpin* is referred to in the Zohar as *Kudsha Brich Hu*, in Hebrew *Hakadosh Barukh Hu* (the Holy One, blessed is He), for it is at this level that God relates to man.

The Zohar explains the process of divine flow directed from Above to below:

At the time that the Creator supervises the world and sees that men's deeds are meritorious, He reveals His light to *Atika Kadisha* who is *Arikh Anpin*, who in turn directs his light onto *Zeir Anpin*. All the different aspects of divine providence are then imbued with light, receiving light from the level above and directing it onto the level below. The *shefa* is transmitted directly from above to below, infusing all the levels in turn till this flow reaches the *Shekhina*. All the spiritual dimensions are then filled with light and join together like one single entity, as alluded to in the verse:[7] "Hashem is One and His Name is One."[8]

In contrast, when sin is rampant in the lower world, then *Atika Kadisha* conceals his extended countenance. Consequently, divine flow may not be transmitted directly from one level of revelation to the other, and *dinim* (forces of strict justice) are directed onto the world, because *Atika Kadisha* conceals his light and does not direct it onto the levels below. In the words of Daniel:

I watched till thrones were set up, and the Ancient of Days sat (*ve-atik yomin yativ*), His garment white as snow, and the hair

---

7. Zech. 14:9.
8. Zohar, *Vayikra* 15 a-b.

of His head like clean wool; His throne fiery flames, its wheels blazing fire. [9]

The expression "the Ancient of Days sat," says Rashi, implies that *Hakadosh Barukh Hu* is sitting in judgment on *Malkhut* (i.e. the *Shekhina*). The *dinim* stemming from Above then multiply, reaching the *Shekhina*, and then outside forces are given permission to overcome the forces of lovingkindness and cause suffering in the world below, as alluded to in the verse "the assembly that was gathering against *(al)* Hashem." [10]

As a result, says the Zohar, the aspect of Hashem that is above all others – *Atika Kadisha* – sits alone[11] in judgment, as alluded to in Daniel, and the word "alone" implies that the divine flow remains on High, concealed from the lower levels of revelation or interaction. The latter are then unable to direct divine flow to the world below, and then lovingkindness turns into strict judgment. The *Shekhina* suffers from this situation, for instead of directing divine flow to her children, our holy *Shekhina* has to let loose executioners of strict justice against them!

Such expressions of divine revelation as *Atika Kadisha* appear in many *siddurim* (prayer books) before the Shabbat *seudot* (meals), in the *piyyutim* (hymns) beginning with the Aramaic word *atkinu* (prepare), which we are to read before each of the three *seudot*. Three levels of revelation appear in these *piyyutim*: *Atika Kadisha*, alluding to the level of revelation linked with *Keter* (Crown); *Zeir Anpin*, alluding to *Hakadosh Barukh Hu* (the level of revelation on which Hashem interacts with the world) and *Chakal Tapuchin Kadishin,* which we will discuss further on, alluding to the *Shekhina*. These three levels appear in a different order in the *Atkinu piyyutim* because each of the three *seudot* is dedicated to one of these levels. It is thus important to read these *piyyutim* before each of the three *seudot*.

Reading the *piyyut* from the siddur before each *seuda* is a like a declaration that we would like to be aware of the process alluded to in these concepts, and to contribute to divine joy in any way that is pleasing on High, even if it seems to be challenging to us.

---

9. Dan. 7:9.
10. Num. 27:3.
11. Zohar, ibid.

Key to the Locked Garden

What Hashem wants of us on Shabbat is that we should strive to ascend on High through our preparation for Shabbat as well as through the special *mitzvot* of the day, and thus contribute to the heavenly union occurring on this day. The union is going to happen in and of its own, initiated from Above, for that is the nature of the Shabbat day.[12] However, we are able to contribute before Shabbat through all the preparations included in the *Tosefet Shabbat* supplement, beginning Thursday night and ending when Shabbat comes in,[13] and then on Shabbat by participating in the prayers and the *seudot* following them.

The celebration called *shalom zachar*, held on the eve of Shabbat in honor of a newborn baby boy before his *brit mila* (circumcision), sheds light on the role of the *Shekhina* at the first Shabbat *seuda*.[14] Rabbi Luria gives us the inner meaning of this ceremony. He begins by citing the instruction: "When a bull, a sheep or goat is born, it must remain with its mother for seven days. Then, after the eighth day, it shall be acceptable as a sacrifice for a fire-offering to God."[15] He then cites a Midrash explaining why the animal may only presented on the eighth day. The Midrash says that this is like a king who entered a city and pronounced a decree, saying, "All the people present here will not see me until they first see the queen."[16] In a similar way, *Hakadosh Barukh Hu* says, "Do not bring me a *korban* (offering) until after the Shabbat day." The "queen" is Shabbat. The inner reason why the *brit mila* has to be held on the eighth day is that there should be a Shabbat before the *brit*, so that the newborn may be exposed to the light of Shabbat, which is extended to us at this time.

At the onset of Shabbat, we are to go to the field to welcome our holy *Shekhina* returning from the lower world. The first Shabbat *seuda* is thus that of the *Shekhina* – we are her guests and, if it can be said, she

---

12. See "Maamar Shamor VeZachor," *Sefer Beit Genazai: Maamarei Shabbat*, 2nd ed., 115ff.
13. See Chapter 12.
14. The following teachings are adapted from Rabbi Luria's essay "Shalom zachar," *Sefer Beit Genazai: Kolel Biurim Bearba Mitzvot shel Simcha Shehaav Chayav Laben:* Simcha shel Brit; Simcha shel Pidion; Simcha shel Mitzvot; Simcha shel Nisuim (Jerusalem: Private Publication, 5763), 57-59.
15. Lev. 22:27 *(The Living Torah)*.
16. Midrash Rabbah.

A Taste of the World to Come

becomes like a heavenly hostess taking care of her guests. We thus say to Hashem, "Come O Beloved! Let us go toward the Bride!"

As Rabbi Masud sings:

| Going out to the field, to receive the Shabbat Queen. Sparks of Cain and Abel we must elevate from the depths, causing them to find the hereditary portion [in the Holy Land].[17] My soul yearns, even pines.[18] She will then declare: Here I am. | יְצִיאַת שָׂדֶה לְהַקְבִּיל. אֶת פְּנֵי שַׁבָּת מַלְכְּתָא. נִיצוֹצוֹת קַיִן וְהֶבֶל לַעֲלוֹת מִנֵּי עֲמִיקְתָא. יִמְצְאוּ נַחֲלַת חֶבֶל. נַפְשִׁי נִכְסְפָה גַּם כָּלְתָה. תְּשׁוּעַ תֹּאמַר הִנֵּנִי: |

The eve of Shabbat is the time of the *Shekhina*. This is evidenced by one small variation in the wording of the *Amida* prayer we read on Shabbat. The Shabbat *Amida* contains a special paragraph for each of the three times of Shabbat (in contrast with the *Amida* of the festivals, which is the same for all festivals except for minor changes). However, there is a paragraph in the Shabbat *Amida* which is *almost* the same in all the *Amida* prayers we say on Shabbat. In the evening *Amida* the paragraph reads:

| May You look with favor on our rest. Sanctify us with Your commandments and grant our share in Your Torah; satiate us from Your goodness and gladden our souls with Your salvation, and purify our heart to serve You sincerely. And grant us, O Hashem our God, with love and favor, please grant us Your holy Shabbat as a heritage, and may all of Israel who sanctify Your Name, rest on it. | רְצֵה נָא בִמְנוּחָתֵנוּ. קַדְּשֵׁנוּ בְּמִצְוֹתֶיךָ שִׂים חֶלְקֵנוּ בְּתוֹרָתֶךָ שַׂבְּעֵנוּ מִטּוּבָךְ. שַׂמֵּחַ נַפְשֵׁנוּ בִּישׁוּעָתֶךָ וְטַהֵר לִבֵּנוּ לְעָבְדְּךָ בֶּאֱמֶת. וְהַנְחִילֵנוּ ה' א' בְּאַהֲבָה וּבְרָצוֹן שַׁבַּת קָדְשֶׁךָ וְיָנוּחוּ בָהּ כָּל יִשְׂרָאֵל מְקַדְּשֵׁי שְׁמֶךָ: |

---

17. Paraphrasing Zech. 2:16.
18. Paraphrasing Ps. 84:3.

Here, in the expression *veyanuchu bah* (they shall rest on it), *bah*, referring to Shabbat, is a feminine particle. But in the Shabbat morning *Amida* the same paragraph substitutes the word *"bo"* (on it) which is the masculine form. And in the *Amida* of Shabbat afternoon Mincha it is written *Veyanuchu bam*, using a plural form, which refers to *Knesset Yisrael Themselves*.

As Rabbi Luria continues, when a couple invites people over, it is usually the woman who will care for the guests, making sure that each one is comfortable and has what s/he needs. The same is true, if it can be said, of the *Shekhina* at the time of her *seuda*. Consequently, if a person comes into Shabbat having rectified his behavior of the past week, at the time of this *seuda* a holy *shefa* will come onto him, as it will be directed onto the male baby, to help him enter the covenant of Abraham.

The commentators explain that the idea of *shalom zachar* is to comfort the newborn who is mourning for all the Torah that he learned while in his mother's womb and then forgot on coming into the world. The Sages teach that while an infant is in the womb there is an angel teaching him the entire Torah, and there is a light ignited in its head by the power of which it is able to see from one end of the world to the other. As the infant enters the world, the angel taps its mouth and it forgets all the Torah it learned.

Rabbi Luria objects: Why is the baby being comforted at this special time? Shabbat is not a time appropriate to comfort mourners!

On Shabbat, however, we receive a taste of the World to Come. On Shabbat eve, many family members and dear friends come to join us at the Shabbat table. This is the time that the *Shekhina* rejoins her beloved Soul Companion; and as she does so, every one of us shares in this union and closeness and receives a higher level of soul to rise to the occasion. Moreover, on a Shabbat that is preceded by a *shalom zachar*, this spiritual ascent may be regarded as a "redemption" occurring in the merit of the newborn, which adds holiness to his soul.

The inner meaning of Shabbat is that the *Shekhina* – *Knesset Yisrael* – is coming back home; and every one of us, her children, has to do our share to integrate the consciousness of her coming home more and more.

Chapter 4

Spiritual Kisses

Rabbi Masud sings:

> It is our duty to ignite regularly two lights. The light we are commanded to ignite will reveal two radiant lights: the *shem* (name) *Adnut* in its simple form and the *shem El*, each letter spelled out in full. Three unifications cast their light.[1] The joint numerical value of all their letters adds up to that of the word *"ner"* (light): there will encamp the inner letters of the *shem Shakai* [when spelled in full].
>
> חוֹבָה שְׁתֵּי נֵרוֹת תַּדְרִים. נֵר מִצְוָה יִגְלֶה שְׁנֵי מְאוֹרוֹת מַזְהִירִים. אדנו"ת פָּשׁוּט וא"ל מָלֵא. שָׁלוֹשׁ יִחוּדִים מְאִירִים. מִסְפָּרָם לְנֵר יַעֲלֶה. מִלּוּי שד"י שָׁם יַחֲנֶה:

The Ari z"l tells us to contemplate the light of the Shabbat candles after the blessing has been recited over them.[2] The Zohar reveals to us that at the time of candlelighting, the *Shekhina* is "in the two arms of the King,

---

1. Alluding to the unifications involving the holy names *Havaya-Ekieh; Havaya-Elokim; Havaya-Adnut.*
2. "Hadlakat Nerot Shabbat [alef]," *Sefer Bet Genazai: Pitchei Tefilla*, vol. 3, 103-106.

27

face to face with Him." It is important to realize that the words "embrace" and "unification" allude to different types of bonds on High. For instance, during the ten days from Rosh HaShana to Yom Kippur, the heavenly bond is alluded to in the words *"smolo tachat leroshi"* (He placed His left hand under my head).[3] Then, during the entire Sukkot festival, the bond is alluded to in the words *"vimino techabkeni"* (His right hand embraces me still). Finally, on Shemini Atzeret comes the unification alluded to in the words *"bou venismach ani ve-atem"* (Come and let us rejoice, I and you).

There is a poetic composition included in the prayers we say on the day before Shemini Atzeret, Hoshana Rabba, which alludes to the heavenly embrace at the onset of Shabbat. This hymn speaks of the Community of Israel, who is scattered in exile and still *chavuka udevuka bakh* (she hugs and cleaves to You, Hashem).[4]

The inner meaning of this hymn is that when the *Shekhina* ascends, impelled by all our Shabbat work – by our observance of all the laws at the basic level, and then by our willingness to be open to the inner teachings of the Torah, particularly in what concerns our Shabbat experience – she is finally together with *Hakadosh Barukh Hu*.

As mentioned, there are two main aspects of divine revelation. In the higher aspect of divine revelation, there is a bond of total unity in which the essence of one is attached to that of the other. In a lower aspect of revelation, there is a bond of two separate entities, that of *Hakadosh Barukh Hu* and *Knesset Yisrael*, whose voices we hear intertwined throughout Shir Hashirim, longing for each other, longing for the love of One as at the Giving of the Torah.

The female voice in Shir Hashirim is thus the voice of the *Shekhina* – the Queen in exile. When the Children of Israel within her receive their additional soul, the *Shekhina* ascends to meet her beloved, *Hakadosh Barukh Hu*. But when Shabbat ends she asks the Children of Israel, *"samchuni baashishot* (support me with the [two] illuminations of fire)." These two illuminations represent the Written and Oral Torah, both hewn with fire.

---

3. Song of Songs 2:6.
4. See the *Machzor Beit Yosef: The Complete ArtScroll Machzor – Succos* (New York: ArtScroll Studios, 1987), 779 on the service for Hoshana Rabba.

One of the main ways in which we may support the *Shekhina* is through our involvement in prayer; for every time the People of Israel say the *Amida* prayer, they draw the light from on High toward the *Shekhina*. In the morning and afternoon prayers, the *Shekhina* goes up three full levels by means of the silent *Amida* and another three by means of the repetition, which one can only say with a *minyan* in synagogue. Now at the very beginning of Shabbat, the *Shekhina* goes up three full levels as we say the *Kabbalat Shabbat* prayers, welcoming her as she distances herself from the outside forces, and another three levels while we are saying the Shabbat evening *Amida*. In the beautiful verse in Shir Hashirim "*Kamti ani liftoach ledodi* (I arose to open for my beloved),"[5] the *Shekhina* is alluding to the special unification which occurs while we are saying the Shabbat evening *Amida*.

And on Motzaei Shabbat, the *Shekhina* says:

| My Beloved had turned and gone… I sought Him, but did not find Him; I called to Him, but He did not answer.[6] | [...] פָּתַחְתִּי אֲנִי לְדוֹדִי וְדוֹדִי חָמַק עָבָר בִּקַּשְׁתִּיהוּ וְלֹא מְצָאתִיהוּ קְרָאתִיו וְלֹא עָנָנִי: |

The *Shekhina* is left yearning for our desired Redemption, the time in which the heavenly unification will be permanent as hinted in the verse: "On that day Hashem will be One and His Name will be One."[7] The female voice thus says in the Song, alluding to this desired time:[8]

---

5. Song 5:5.
6. Song 5:6.
7. Zech. 14:9.
8. Song 3:4.

Key to the Locked Garden

I found the One my soul loves. I held Him, determined not to let Him go until I brought Him into my Mother's House and to the chamber of She who conceived me.	עַד שֶׁמְּצָאתִי אֵת שֶׁאָהֲבָה נַפְשִׁי אֲחַזְתִּיו וְלֹא אַרְפֶּנּוּ עַד שֶׁהֲבֵיאתִיו אֶל בֵּית אִמִּי וְאֶל חֶדֶר הוֹרָתִי:

The Zohar clarifies that the expression "my Mother's House" alludes to the *Beit haMikdash shel Maala* (the Temple on High), that is, to the higher aspect of divine revelation – the bond of total unity in which two entities are attached *kechad* (as one). In contrast, "the chamber of her who conceived me" alludes to the *Beit haMikdash* below, may it be promptly rebuilt, and to the *Shekhina*.

At the time of exile, the *Shekhina* longs for her Beloved as hinted in the Song:

At night, on my bed, I sought the One my soul loves. I sought Him but I did not find Him.[9]	עַל מִשְׁכָּבִי בַּלֵּילוֹת בִּקַּשְׁתִּי אֵת שֶׁאָהֲבָה נַפְשִׁי בִּקַּשְׁתִּיו וְלֹא מְצָאתִיו

Night stands for spiritual darkness. And Hashem says: "*Shuvi, shuvi, haShulamit, shuvi, shuvi* (Return, return, O Shulamit, return, return)."[10] *Hakadosh Barukh Hu* calls upon *Knesset Yisrael* to return to Him. The word *"shuvi"* has two of the letters of "Shabbat." Let go of your past, we are being told. Return to the Shabbat realm of holiness where you may receive the lofty light dwelling on High!

It is important to read Shir Hashirim before the onset of Shabbat or immediately after candle lighting.[11] The Zohar reveals that the Song of Songs has to do with the inner meaning of Shabbat. Most

---

9. Song 3:1.
10. Song 7:1.
11. The following teachings stem from Rabbi Luria's essay "Amirat Shir Hashirim Beknisat Shabbat" in *Sefer Beit Genazai: Maamarei Shabbat*, 2nd ed., 303ff.

Spiritual Kisses

of Shir Hashirim tells us about the times of exile after Israel sinned and the First and Second Temples were destroyed. In Temple times the unification between *Hakadosh Barukh Hu* and *Knesset Yisrael* was constant; but after the destruction of the Temple and ensuing exile this was no longer the case, and the distance gave rise to a profound yearning for reunion. Rabbi Luria calls attention[12] to the phrase *melekh asur barehatim* (the Supreme King is bound to you in the merit of your hastening [to serve Him])[13]: Hashem's love for *Knesset Yisrael* as it manifests on Shabbat is likened to that of a king who, when he looks at his beloved, feels his heart bound in his love for her to the point that he cannot not focus his mind on any other matter.

It was Rabbi Akiva who revealed to us how Shabbat manifests the immense love between *Hakadosh Barukh Hu* and *Knesset Yisrael*, and that is precisely why it is important to say the Song of Songs at the appointed time in honor of the heavenly Bride, for it arouses this love on High as below.[14]

In the verse *"samchuni beashishot rapduni betapuchim ki cholat ahava ani* (sustain me with raisins [or: flagons], spread out apples around me, for I am lovesick),"[15] the word *"ashishot"* may be literally translated either "apples" or "flagons," but commentators have pointed out that it contains the word *"esh"* (fire). Thus, the verse conveys the love and pain of separation felt by the *Shekhina*.

The *Shekhina* is asking us to sustain her by opening ourselves to the passionate love that the Sages call *ahava raba*, which the Zohar links with the awe of divine greatness, as, for instance, when we are in fear of doing something that may ruin the quality of love in our relationship with Hashem.

---

12. "Divrei Hakdama" in *Sefer Bet Genazai: Shir Hashirim*, 1-6. Rabbi Luria cites this teaching in the name of an early Sage, Rabbi Abraham Tamakh.
13. Song 7:6.
14. The teaching that follows is adapted from Zohar, Midrash haneelam, Vayera, 98b. Quoted from the introduction to *Sefer Beit Genazai al Parshiyot HaTorah*, 5.
15. Song of Song 2:5; my literal translation based on Ibn Ezra; see the note to this verse in the ArtScroll edition of the Song of Songs.

Key to the Locked Garden

Rabbi Luria teaches in the name of the Maggid of Mezrich that burning love is associated with the awe of divine greatness.[16] The Maggid bases this idea on a Talmudic teaching: *"darko shel ish lechazer al isha* (it is the way of man to search for a woman)."[17] As the Maggid explains,[18] the idea of woman here alludes to the image of one whose lack translates into a deep awe of divine greatness, as in the verse *"isha yirat Hashem hi tithallal* (a God-fearing woman – she should be praised)." [19] As in the verse of the Song of the Sea in which Hashem is likened to *ish milchama* (a man of war), here too the word *"ish"* (man) alludes to *Hakadosh Barukh Hu*, searching for what is described as an *isha* (woman), as alluded to in Proverbs:[20]

| He who finds *isha* (a woman) has found good and has won God's favor. | מָצָא אִשָּׁה מָצָא טוֹב וַיָּפֶק רָצוֹן מה׳ |

As Rabbi Luria explains, if a man finds the "woman" within himself by regarding his deficiency as a reflection of that of the *Shekhina* and realizing that he has nothing other than what the Holy One grants him, he wins Hashem's love in the way that a man loves a woman.

Sometimes Hashem puts us in a position in which all we can do is to realize our powerlessness, and to what extent we owe all we have and are to Hashem. That is our chance to arouse ourselves to feel the *ahava raba* (passionate love) described in Shir Hashirim, which is preceded by a deep awe of divine greatness. We are then ready to become the soul companion who is ready to face *bittul* (nullification) of her will for the sake of the Beloved.

In the first of the two books he published on the inner significance of the Land of Israel, Rabbi Luria expounds the topic of *bittul*.

---

16. *Sefer Beit Genazai: Maamarei Shabbat,* 2 nd. Ed. 304 b.
17. Kiddushin 2b.
18. In Or HaEmet, cited in "Amirat Shir Hashirim beknisat Shabbat," *Sefer Beit Genazai: Maamarei Shabbat,* 2 nd ed., 304b.
19. Prov. 31:30.
20. Prov. 18:22.

He begins by citing two sets of messages in the book of Deuteronomy. The first is:

> For Hashem, your God, is bringing you to a good land: a land with streams of water, of springs and underground water coming forth in valley and mountain; a land of wheat, barley, grape, fig and pomegranate; a land of oil-olives and honey; a land where you will eat bread without poverty; you will lack nothing there; a land whose stones are iron and from whose mountains you will mine copper. You will eat and you will be satisfied and you will bless Hashem, your God, for the good land that He gave you.[21]
>
> כִּי ה' אלֹקֶ'יךָ מְבִיאֲךָ אֶל אֶרֶץ טוֹבָה אֶרֶץ נַחֲלֵי מָיִם עֲיָנֹת וּתְהֹמֹת יֹצְאִים בַּבִּקְעָה וּבָהָר: אֶרֶץ חִטָּה וּשְׂעֹרָה וְגֶפֶן וּתְאֵנָה וְרִמּוֹן אֶרֶץ זֵית שֶׁמֶן וּדְבָשׁ: אֶרֶץ אֲשֶׁר לֹא בְמִסְכֵּנֻת תֹּאכַל בָּהּ לֶחֶם לֹא תֶחְסַר כֹּל בָּהּ אֶרֶץ אֲשֶׁר אֲבָנֶיהָ בַרְזֶל וּמֵהֲרָרֶיהָ תַּחְצֹב נְחֹשֶׁת: וְאָכַלְתָּ וְשָׂבָעְתָּ וּבֵרַכְתָּ אֶת ה' אלֹקֶ'יךָ עַל הָאָרֶץ הַטֹּבָה אֲשֶׁר נָתַן לָךְ:

The second message is:

> A land that Hashem, your God, seeks out: the eyes of Hashem, your God, are always upon it, from the beginning of the year to year's end.[22]
>
> אֶרֶץ אֲשֶׁר ה' אלֹקֶ'יךָ דֹּרֵשׁ אֹתָהּ תָּמִיד עֵינֵי ה' אלֹקֶ'יךָ בָּהּ מֵרֵשִׁית הַשָּׁנָה וְעַד אַחֲרִית שָׁנָה:

The commentators have wondered about the first message: after enumerating all the good properties of the Land of Israel, why does the verse

---

21. Deut. 8:7-10.
22. Deut. 11:12.

say "you will lack nothing there?" This being said, why are all the other details that precede it about Israel necessary?

A closer examination reveals to us that the verses complete each other. Namely, we first have the itemization of all the unique qualities featured in the Land of Israel. Afterward, the verse adds *you will lack nothing there,* stressing that these qualities are beyond any praise one could give.

Rabbi Luria answers that the two sets of messages complete one another. We are first told all the special properties that are in this good Land, and after that we are told that we will lack nothing there: this is an additional property which is above all the others, revealed to us in the Psalms:[23] אִוָּהּ לְמוֹשָׁב לוֹ - *[For Hashem chose Zion] and desired her as His habitation.*

And what is this additional property? It is the essence of good, answers Rabbi Luria, and he explains with an allegory: This may be likened to a woman married to a king, and she is always with him in his palace. The *taanug*-delight of closeness to the Holy One is unparalleled – nothing seems to be delight in comparison to the closeness to Hashem in the way of allegory cited.

The Aramaic expression דלית לה מגרמא כלום - *she has nothing in and of herself* is a key phrase in Kabbala relating to the Shechina, who gave all she had to her beloved counterpart. The point that Rabbi Luria is stressing, however, is not that she *has* nothing but rather that she *wants* nothing other than being with Him. It is as if there is nothing in the world other than the delight of being close to the Holy One – and this is the meaning of the expression "the essence of good." The passage ends "the eyes of Hashem, your God are always upon it, from the beginning of the year to year's end," stressing further that there is no greater pleasure than that alluded to here. All the pleasures, whether material or spiritual, are meaningless in comparison to the heavenly delight suggested by the verse "*az titanag al Hashem* (then you will delight in Hashem)."[24]

What about us, *Knesset Yisrael Themselves,* what do we have to give? The Hebrew word Rabbi Luria used here is *bittul.* After looking

---

23. Ps. 132:13.
24. Is. 58:14.

this word up in every dictionary, I realized that *bittul* is more than just giving; it is a giving of yourself.

What are we giving? we may ask.

We are giving our divine service – the lofty divine service that goes hand in hand with this quality of relationship with the Holy One. A divine service that is the ultimate challenge to fulfill because it often occurs that our spouses do not agree, and our children complain, but we plod on, while at the same time striving not to leave them behind!

And the reward is, as Rabbi Luria reiterates: "There is no good, no delight greater than the above mentioned: neither the physical delights of this world nor the spiritual ones have any meaning or significance in comparison to this heavenly delight which is in the category of 'then you will delight in Hashem.'"

Hashem asked us to be holy for His sake – because He is holy.[25] Trying to emulate Hashem is thus the way to get close to Him. The idea of *bittul* may mean, for instance, biting back a sharp answer to someone who deserves it, with the consciousness that one cannot do that in deference to the *Shekhina*'s Presence. In the order of things, first comes the sense of awe and only then can there be the passionate love we are discussing, and this is what the Zohar means when it says that fearing God has to come before loving Him.[26] We are reminded of the account of the Giving of the Torah, in which first of all there was thunder, lightning, and the powerful sound of the shofar and the people shuddered.[27] In order for the "face to face" union between *Hakadosh Barukh Hu* and *Knesset Yisrael Themselves* to take place, they had to go through the phase of intense awe of divine greatness. As an old Chasidic song has it, "Out of fear of You, I flee to You." [28]

---

25. Lev. 19:2.
26. This concept is explained at length in Chapter One of Simcha H. Benyosef, The Beginning of Wisdom: Unabridged Translation of THE GATE OF LOVE from Rabbi Eliyahu de Vidas' *RESHIT CHOCHMAH* (New Jersey: Ktav Publishers, 2001), 3-21.
27. Paraphrasing Ex. 19:16.
28. Rabbi Moshe Luria, "Ashrei Haam Yodei Terua Lehamshikh Or Haganuz Shemeir BeShabbat Umoed Mizivug Ahava Veyira Shalhevet Yud Heh," *Sefer Ori Veyishi: Yamim Noraim, Kolel Maamarim Uviurim al Derekh Haavoda, Meyusadim al Divrei HaArizal Luria* (Jerusalem: Makhon Shaarei Ziv, 5753), 36-41.

Only in the Ultimate Future will we fully attain this bond with Hashem in which the awe of His greatness is like a vessel to contain our love for Him. That is why, according to some traditions, when praying for the rebuilding of the Temple we add, "And there we will serve You with awe as in the times of old." As Rabbi Luria explains, all the members of *Knesset Yisrael* will be enwrapped by the lofty fear of greatness, and they will then be permeated with Hashem's immense love for the Community of Israel, His soul companion.[29]

The awe of divine greatness permeating us at the inception of Shabbat prepares us to be part of the Community of Israel His soul companion, and to merit participating in the lofty unification of Shabbat morning prayers.

The Zohar reveals to us that it is only before the second Shabbat *seuda*, that we hold in the morning, that we say the verse "*az titanag al Hashem* (then you will delight *al* Hashem)," alluding to an aspect of divine revelation loftier than that of the King and Judge of the weekdays. The reason is that on Shabbat eve we are imbued with the awe of divine greatness as a preparation to attain the level of Community of Israel, His soul companion, and the unification on the morning prayer, when we "delight *al* Hashem."

Consequently, there is no contradiction between awe and love, for one completes the other. The verse says:

| Sustain Me with (*ashishot*) the two illuminations of the fire, spread the apples around Me, for I am lovesick.[30] | סַמְּכוּנִי בָּאֲשִׁישׁוֹת רַפְּדוּנִי בַּתַּפּוּחִים כִּי חוֹלַת אַהֲבָה אָנִי |

The Hebrew word *ashishot* evokes the word *"esh"* (fire), be it fire of suffering or fire of love. The words *"rapduni batapuchim"* (spread the apples around me) is what the *Shekhina* is saying to us. The apples refer to us, the souls of Israel likened to the apples in her orchard, and she is asking that the People of Israel may emulate the *bittul* of the *Shekhina*, who, on

---

29. Ibid.
30. Song 2:5. My translation.

going to the lower worlds on the weekdays, accepted her mission to give her beloved counterpart all she had. On Shabbat the *Shekhina* is referred to as *Chakal Tapuchin Kadishin* (Field of Holy Apples). However, this can only happen by means of what it says in the first part of this verse, "sustain me with the two illuminations of fire," with the fusion of love and awe.

Moreover, the word *"ashishot"* contains the words *"ish"* (man) and *"isha"* (woman), alluding to the bond of soul companions we have discussed. The verse thus ends "I am lovesick," for the People of Israel long to feel this passionate love for Hashem, over and beyond their love for Hashem as heavenly Father.[31] We should thus read Shir Hashirim before the onset of Shabbat, with the intention to arouse the *Shekhina* out of the stupor of exile and bring her together with the King.

As mentioned, we want everything we do below to be a mirror replica of what happens on High in order to help the process come to fulfillment. It is thus on Shabbat eve that we have to read the Song, for in the daytime this bond is already happening and our reading would no longer be relevant. Our reading of the Song serves to arouse in us the awe of divine greatness which impregnates the nighttime, as a preparation for the heavenly unification of *Knesset Yisrael* during the Shabbat *Mussaf* prayer.

According to Rashi, in the first verse of the Song of Songs, the words *"neshikot pihu"* (the kisses of His mouth) convey the desire of the Community of Israel to receive the mysteries of the Torah by means of a type of union comparable to that of bride and groom.[32] In order to clarify this teaching of Rashi, Rabbi Luria explains that the spiritual concept of kisses does not tell us about the essence of closeness to the Holy One, but rather about the divine energy flowing through in this unification. As a result of this energy flow, the mysteries of the Torah are transmitted to us in the way that they were communicated at the giving of the Torah and as they will be communicated in the Ultimate Future. In the words of the Ari z"l, the concept of *neshikin* (kisses) conveys a cleaving of spirits to each other. Rashi thus means

---

31. See Zohar, *Vayikra* 7a.
32. The teachings that follow about the additional soul in reference to the Song of Songs are adapted from Rabbi Moshe Luria, "Kabbalat Tosefet Neshama Be'Erev Shabbat," in *Sefer Pitchei Tefilla*, vol. 3, 67ff.

that through the spiritual 'kiss' the spirit will flow from the heavenly Giver to the receiver.

When Shabbat begins, the Community of Israel is at the very beginning of her Shabbat togetherness with *Hakadosh Barukh Hu* in the heavenly world. As we are reading the Song before the onset of Shabbat, she asks Him to transmit to us the spirit of the additional Shabbat soul coming through at this time for all the People of Israel in the form of a kiss.

It is taught that the order of Creation is renewed every week. Just as upon Creation we were re-created at the onset of Shabbat, as we receive an additional level of soul, for all our spiritual *koma* (stature) grows at this time.

When we read Shir Hashirim, we must not interrupt our reading in any way, not even by making a gesture.[33] In the case of a woman who has small children it is different, however. When a woman interrupts her reading of the Song because of her children, her interruption becomes a *mitzva*.

Shir Hashirim brings about the revelation of the inner purpose of Creation – the unification between *Hakadosh Barukh Hu* and the Community of Israel.[34] We can look at King Solomon's masterpiece as the song of *Hakadosh Barukh Hu* to *Knesset Yisrael* and that of *Knesset Yisrael* to *Hakadosh Barukh Hu*. By saying the Song at this time, it is as if we were imbuing the inner purpose of Creation with light.

The *Shekhina* is thus called *Chakal Tapuchin Kadishin* (Field of Holy Apples) at the beginning of Shabbat. As we say "Come O Bride," she is aroused with longing to be with the Beloved and put an end to the weekday separation. Her upward progress from level to level mirrors our steps in observing Shabbat *kehilkhato* –according to the *halakhot* (laws) of Shabbat – for the word *"halakha"* is cognate to *halicha* (walking). Our Shabbat observance is a path on which she walks to rejoin the Beloved.

---

33. As taught in Rabbi Alexander Ziskin, *Yesod Veshoresh Haavoda*, edited by Yehoshua Heshel Zinkober (Jerusalem: private publication, 5747), 384.
34. *Sefer Pitchei Tefilla*, vol. 3, 450.

Chapter 5

Deeper Meaning of *Menucha* – Inner Harmony

Rabbi Luria devotes time and care to transmitting the significance and implication of the expression *hasachat hadaat* (focusing). *Hasachat hadaat* alludes to the ability to use our *daat* (knowledge) to remove everything from our consciousness as it were a blackboard from which we were erasing anything that is not relevant so that we can focus on one issue totally. That is what Shabbat allows us to do – to focus exclusively on our bond with Hashem. In contrast, when we become involved in *melachot* (creative activities), this special focusing stops on High as it does below. If there is no *hasachat hadaat* from us to Hashem, it will not be there either from Hashem to us, and then there cannot be a unification, which is what Shabbat is all about.

There are spiritual dimensions – heavenly worlds – above us preventing us from experiencing divine closeness on the weekdays in the same manner we do on Shabbat or Yom Tov. The lowest of them is called *Asiya* (Action), and it is the spiritual interface with our physical world. Above *Asiya* is a dimension called *Yetzira* (Formation); then comes *Beriya* (Creation), and only then the dimension of *Atzilut* (Closeness), which is closest to Hashem.

The idea of *melacha* is connected with the *Shekhina* when she is below, in the world of *Asiya*. We do *melacha* on the weekdays in order to build up the *Shekhina's* connection with the level of divine revelation in which Hashem acts as King, and on Shabbat we refrain from doing *melacha* in order to finalize the connection.

Doing *melacha* on Shabbat brings the *Shekhina* back down to where she was suffering on weekdays, waiting for the ascent to her rightful place on High.

An aside is in order to develop the concept of *melacha* and its significance on High as explained by a contemporary kabbalist, Rabbi Imanuel Bar Urian.[1]

The word *"melacha"* (plural *melachot)* is from the same root as *malach* (angel), whereas *avoda* (work) stems from the word *"eved"* (servant). Just as an angel is spiritual and miraculous, so is his *shelichut* (the mission he accomplishes) imbued with a spiritual nature. In a similar way, a *melacha* (creative activity) produces a spiritual effect of an ethereal nature. In other words, a *melacha* causes a totally new spiritual creation to come and enclose itself in the object of the *melacha*.

In contrast, a servant is physical and his work is material and revealed, meaning that is clear to the onlooker. In a similar way, the word *"avoda"* conveys a physical undertaking that does not renew any spiritual force in the world. It is thus permitted to do *avoda* work on Shabbat,[2] for it does not bring a new creation to the world. This is not the case with the *melacha*, for it brings about a spiritual renewal. In fact, when we do a *melacha* or a *mitzva*, an angel is created as a result; this angel is intimately connected to our soul, and upon doing this *mitzva* or *melacha* his spiritual force is added to that of our soul and makes it more complete.

The *melachot* that are forbidden on Shabbat are the activities that were necessary to build the *Mishkan*, the portable Sanctuary that

---

1. In the section that follows, we will transmit the teaching of Rabbi Imanuel Bar Urian in his book *Matana Tova Yesh Li Beveit Genazai*, 79ff.
2. E.g. sweeping a room, clearing the table and washing the dishes after the first Shabbat *seuda* because they will be needed for the next day; to be distinguished from the *avoda* (service) specifically connected with the Temple.

the People of Israel built in the desert.[3] The *Mishkan* is referred to as *olam katan* (small world); it is seen as a microcosm of the world. Consequently, the *melachot* required for building the *Mishkan* reflect their spiritual counterpart, the activities which were required for creating the world. Hence the *melachot* that are forbidden on Shabbat are spiritually equivalent to Hashem's work in creating the world.

At Creation the Holy One selected sparks of holiness from a lower world – the name and nature of which are part of a spiritual process that is beyond our scope – and elevated most of them, leaving some of them behind in order to enable us to complete the job. Every time that we perform a good deed, our soul goes down to this lower world and selects holy sparks from there with the intention of elevating them.

Our spiritual task during the six weekdays is to become involved in the thirty-nine *melachot* that produced Creation. As we are doing a *melacha* – even if we are not consciously aware of this process – our soul goes down to the lower world and selects the holy sparks connected with the particular *melacha*, and on Shabbat elevates them to their proper place on High, called the *olam hatikkun* (world of rectification).

The divine *melachot* that led to Creation are considered rectifications, as they required selecting good elements from the bad and elevating them. Alas, when Adam, the first man, sinned, all the rectifications that the Creator had brought about by means of the *melachot* of Creation fell and once again became imbedded in the space of *klippot* (evil husks), among the evil elements of this lower world. As a result, Adam's soul lost the lofty character it had before the sin; and all the souls of Israel, which were the choicest part of Adam's soul, fell into this lower world as well. The souls of Israel then became disjoined, split into six hundred thousand particles. The mission confided to each soul as it is born in this world thus depends on the place to which this soul fell in the mentioned lower world. According to the nature of its fall, so will be the rectifications the soul will be asked to do in the world. Since each soul fell into a different place within this lower world, each soul will come to the world in order to rectify the specific type of evil that permeated the place of its fall.

---

3. Rabbi Bar Urian, op. cit., 85-86.

The task of the People of Israel is to restore the world to the ideal state it had before Adam's sin, by going down into this lower world and selecting the good from the bad. Whenever a person makes a good choice in his life, not only in actual deed but also in his thoughts and speech, it means that his soul went down to this lower world and liberated a holy spark from the evil which surrounded it. When this spark ascends, it will join the aspect of the man's soul that is on High and will become part of it.

To the extent that we can express it, each Jewish soul is thus the Creator's partner in the task of rectifying the world, for man's relationship with Hashem may be likened to the woman's bond with her husband. Without his wife, a man cannot give birth to an infant, for she is the one who gives form to her husband's seed, and from the food she eats will be formed the body of the infant. After the stage in its mother's womb, the infant is born with body and soul. The work performed by the People of Israel accomplishes a purpose similar to that of the newborn in the sense that, if it can be said, *Hakadosh Barukh Hu* may not form the *olam hatikkun* (world of rectification) without the sparks elevated by the descent of each soul into the lower world.

The preceding teaching is the mystery of all the descents and ascents that each soul experiences in this world, for by means of the above process each soul becomes enriched with all the good sparks it selects. Moreover, on a larger scale, the heavenly world becomes rectified as a result of man's action below. This process is also the mystery of the *Shekhina*; for whenever a soul descends to this lower world, the *Shekhina* goes down as well in order to help it accomplish its *melacha* of selection. The *Shekhina* encloses herself within the souls of Israel, to help them succeed in their *melacha* of selection. Together with the *Shekhina* many heavenly powers from the world of *Atzilut* also go down – all the *sefirot* (emanations) from *Atzilut* which enclose themselves in the *Shekhina* and act as helpers to the souls of Israel, and as protectors to defend them against the forces of the other side.

The *Shekhina* thus helps the soul, surrounding it in order to protect it from the *klippot* dwelling in the lower world, to prevent the *klippot* from attaching themselves to the soul and attracting some of the soul's light to themselves. Furthermore, the *Shekhina* ensures that the liberated sparks will ascend to their proper space in Eden, for the *Shekhina* is the one who elevates these sparks.

In the light of the preceding we may understand why a *pegam* (flaw) comes about when a *melacha* is done on Shabbat and not on the weekdays, for on the weekdays the soul receives a great amount of help from the heavenly world to face its descent. Equipped with this powerful protection, the souls thus do not become tainted by the other side when they come down to perform their rectification of the world.

Rabbi Bar Urian adds:

> This is not the case on Shabbat, for on this day all the heavenly powers ascend to their proper place on High, and do not go down to the lower world. Consequently, when a man does a *melacha* on Shabbat – Heaven forbid – he drags down with him to the lower world the forces of holiness to whom his soul on High is attached, but without all the divine help prevalent on the weekdays. Since the heavenly powers do not go down with his soul, the latter is unprotected in its task of selecting the good from the bad. In consequence, the forces of evil and the other side are able to overcome this soul at the time he goes down [from the world of *tikkun* where his soul dwells on Shabbat] to their space below, and the quality of death dwells over it. The person is thus liable to the death penalty. Such is thus the flaw that comes about when one does a *melacha* on Shabbat: understand all this.[4]

These teachings from Rabbi Bar Urian help us understand Rabbi Luria's aforementioned teaching that doing *melacha* on Shabbat brings the *Shekhina* back down to where she was suffering on weekdays, waiting for the ascent to her rightful place on High. And yet there is a difference between the *Shekhina*'s descent on the weekdays and her descent on Shabbat, for on the weekdays she goes down accompanied by many heavenly powers who protect her against the *klippot*, whereas on Shabbat these powers remain on High. Consequently, she must go down without

---

4. Rabbi Bar Urian, op. cit., 117.

any protection, together with the soul of the person who wants to do a *melacha* on Shabbat.

If we play close attention to the Hebrew of the verse (Ex. 31:14) that prescribes the death penalty for Shabbat desecration, we notice that in the expression *mechaleleiha* (those who desecrate her), Shabbat is referred to in the feminine gender. Hence those who know that Shabbat represents the *Shekhina* realize that it is the *Shekhina* herself that is desecrated by Shabbat violations. This is why a Jew who does a *melacha* on Shabbat is liable to the death penalty if Shabbat is desecrated in a willful act.[5] (If it happened accidentally or out of ignorance, the desecrator could regret his wrongdoing, bring an offering to the Temple and attain expiation.) Some insight into the reason for the severity of this penalty can be gained from the Sages' explanation for the decree that a non-Jew who *keeps* Shabbat is liable to the death penalty. They say that it is as if a king was together with his wife the queen and a person came and put his head in between them.[6] And the same parable applies to a Jew who desecrates Shabbat, for he is putting his head, namely the decision he has made to do *melacha*, between the level of divine revelation in which Hashem acts as King and the *Shekhina*, thus interrupting the *yichud* between them.

Although the person who desecrates Shabbat is only liable to the death penalty if he or she did so willfully, still, even if s/he does so accidentally, the consequence remains the same – the *Shekhina* is desecrated. Yet Shabbat itself forgives the one who transgresses unintentionally. After he heard that one who does a *melacha* by mistake is forgiven, King David composed the "Song for the Shabbat Day" that we sing at the beginning of Shabbat.

We cannot help sympathizing with the *Shekhina* who is distant from her Beloved during the weekdays. We have to understand, however, that if we inwardly object to this, we object to Creation itself.[7] Before she

---

5. In Torah law the death penalty is imposed only where the doer was warned explicitly before committing the act and where there were two witnesses to the act.
6. "Mechaleleiha Mot Yumat," *Sefer Pitchei Tefilla*. vol. 3, 214.
7. As noted by Rabbi Daniel Frish in his commentary *Matok Midevash* on Zohar, *Vayeshev* 181a.

Deeper Meaning of Menucha – Inner Harmony

was diminished, the *Shekhina* received her light directly from the higher levels of divine revelation, as does the aspect of Hashem to Whom we relate as King and Judge. Had the *Shekhina* continued to be in a constant state of togetherness with Hashem, the world below would have always been permeated with Hashem's lovingkindness – there would not have been any evil in the world. There would not have been any evil impulse and people would have been like angels. There goes Creation! Man would not have had the freedom to act, to strive against all odds to fulfill the will of his Creator for the sake of a unique love relationship – the love relationship we experience on Shabbat. There would not have been room for reward and consequence of error. Hashem thus asked of the *Shekhina* that, for His sake, she should accept to be affected by the Torah observance of the souls of Israel rooted in her. It is thus our challenge to strive to the utmost in our Torah observance and to rectify our past mistakes, which were the cause of the *Shekhina*'s exile.

In the Ultimate Future the *Shekhina* will recover all the light that was once her own.

The building of the Temple was meant to happen only after the Children of Israel entered the Land. However, in order to help the Children of Israel rectify the sin of the Golden Calf, the Holy One asked them to build the *Mishkan* in the desert.[8] As Rabbi Luria points out, the Torah portion *Vayakhel*, in which the Israelites are asked to donate all the elements needed for the *Mishkan*, begins with the verse:

These are the things that Hashem commanded, to do them.[9]	אֵלֶּה הַדְּבָרִים אֲשֶׁר צִוָּה ה' לַעֲשֹׂת אֹתָם

---

8. The following section is adapted from "Shabbat UMishkan Chibur Shamayim Vaaretz," *Sefer Beit Genazai al Parshiyot HaTorah: Shemot*, vol. 2, 1212ff.
9. Ex. 35:1.

We are ready to hear about these 'things to be done,' but the very next verse tells us about Shabbat observance and, as Rabbi Luria points out, Shabbat is a state of non-doing:[10]

What happens on Shabbat is that the lower world of *Asiya* ascends on High as a result of *shevita* (refraining from creative activities). The reason why in *Parashat Ki Tissa*[11] we are instructed *laasot et haShabbat* (to make the Shabbat) is that what people do in the world below is referred as *asiya*.

At the inception of Shabbat, we must have in mind that all work, whether the physical jobs or the spiritual elements of our divine service having to do with weekday activity, is now completed and we do not think about it. In the verse that follows, after reminding them about Shabbat, Moses tells the Children of Israel to donate the elements for the *Mishkan*. By expressing the things that Hashem commanded in the plural form, Moses was thus including Shabbat observance as well as the building of the *Mishkan* itself. As a result, since Shabbat and the *Mishkan* were both meant to be a solace for the state of severance and concealment of the *Shekhina*, the word *"menucha,"* which literally means "rest," is applied to both. In the *Amida* prayer that we say on Shabbat, Shabbat is described as a day of *menucha*, and as King David sings, Hashem says of the Temple:

| This is My resting place forever. Here I dwell, for I have desired it.[12] | זֹאת מְנוּחָתִי עֲדֵי עַד פֹּה אֵשֵׁב כִּי אִוִּתִיהָ |

Rabbi Luria highlights that the Temple and Shabbat are often mentioned together, for they are both the *dira batachtonim* (dwelling-place below) that is desired on High.[13] The inner significance of the word *"menucha"* is thus that it eases the pain of concealment. On the conclusion of Creation, the verse reports:[14]

---

10. Ibid., 1214a.
11. Ex. 31:15.
12. Ps. 132:14.
13. *Sefer Beit Genazai: Maamarei Shabbat,* 2nd ed. 157.
14. Gen. 2:1-3.

Deeper Meaning of Menucha – Inner Harmony

Thus the heaven and earth were finished, and all their array. By the seventh day God completed His work which He had done and He abstained on the seventh day from all His work which He had done [...]. because on it He *shavat* (abstained) from all His work.

וַיְכֻלּוּ הַשָּׁמַיִם וְהָאָרֶץ וְכָל צְבָאָם: וַיְכַל אלקים בַּיּוֹם הַשְּׁבִיעִי מְלַאכְתּוֹ אֲשֶׁר עָשָׂה וַיִּשְׁבֹּת בַּיּוֹם הַשְּׁבִיעִי מִכָּל מְלַאכְתּוֹ אֲשֶׁר עָשָׂה [...] כִּי בוֹ שָׁבַת מִכָּל מְלַאכְתּוֹ

Noticing that the word *"shavat"* (ceased to work) is spelled with the same letters as Shabbat, the midrashic Sages explain that when Creation was completed at the end of the sixth day, the world was still lacking *menucha*, a word alluding to an inner state of harmony, physical as well as spiritual. *Menucha* only came to be with the Shabbat day.

We may ask: what does it mean that the world was lacking harmony and Shabbat was what brought about this form of harmony? On Shabbat all the elements of Creation that ensure the running of the world continue to function just like they do on the weekdays!

To the extent that we can express it, the *menucha* required was for *Hakadosh Barukh Hu* Himself.[15] The injunction to refrain from *melacha* – as written on the First Tablets – is a consequence of the Divine's cessation of work after Creation. Moreover, on the Second Tablets the prohibition of *melacha* on Shabbat is called a remembrance of the Exodus from Egypt, and we are told observe the Shabbat day: "in order that your slave and your maid servant may rest *(yanuach,* from the same root as *menucha)* like you."[16]

We thus ask in the Shabbat *Amida* prayer: *"Retze na bimenuchatenu* (May You look with favor upon our *menucha*). Based on the teaching of the Sages that a woman only has *menucha* in her husband's house, the commentator Abudarham explains that our request voices that of

---

15. The teaching that follows is adapted from "Lemaan yanuach kamokha," *in Sefer Beit Genazai: Maamarei Shabbat,* 2nd ed.154ff.
16. Deut. 5:14.

the Community of Israel.[17] A woman in the world below knows that her husband is going to sustain her and she does not have to worry about the future. In a similar way, on this day, all of us who make up the Community of Israel are like the wife in a state of *menucha* with the sense of being guarded from Above. We therefore stop all business pursuits, although sometimes that is very hard. Some people have to face the threat that they will lose their jobs or means of sustenance if they do not work on this day, and yet they stop all work activity in a gesture of total *bittul* before Hashem. Then they somehow switch from weekday worry to the Shabbat *menucha* of the Community of Israel, His soul companion.

Rabbi Luria stresses that at the Exodus from Egypt we were chosen to become what the Zohar expresses as *Zivuga veMatronita de Kudsha Brich Hu* (Hashem's soul companion and Queen).

We thus say in the Song of Songs as Shabbat begins: *"ki tovim dodeikha miyayin* (Your [spiritual] love is far more precious to me than wine [the pleasures of this world])." The Sages have interpreted: The innermost secrets of the Torah that were transmitted to us through the oral teachings of the prophets and sages are sweeter to us than the wine of the Written Torah. All we know from the Written Torah is the prohibition of doing *melacha* on Shabbat, but not the explanation of the spiritual implications.

In contrast, the prophets and sages instituted the prohibitions of discussing secular topics *(daber davar)* and of touching anything not relevant to the Shabbat experience, things designated as *muktze*. Instead of becoming frustrated or bored at the forced inactivity, the warning that we must avoid anything that is not related to Shabbat helps us understand that there is a whole other way of relating to the stopping of creative activity.

Finding ourselves in a situation in which we are prohibited not only from doing certain activities but also from touching anything related to them, or even speaking about them, is what helps us attain a momentous experiential perception. The inner purpose of all these requirements is so that we may taste the *menucha* of the Community of Israel, Hashem and the Community of Israel, His soul companion.

---

17. Rabbi David Abudarham, *Perush Haberakhot Vehatefilot Aburdarham Hashalem* (private publication; for information write to Ch. Gittler, R. Bilu 4, Tel Aviv).

Deeper Meaning of Menucha – Inner Harmony

The prohibition of speaking of daily matters on Shabbat is not an easy issue! If a guest or an important family member starts to discuss a topic related to weekday activities that are forbidden on Shabbat, the host and hostess often are at a loss as to how to stop them. And yet that is what they should do! In one case, a Shabbat guest was sharing her experiences with idolatry before she did *teshuva*. The host felt uneasy but did not have the courage to silence this woman, who was twice his age. On the following night, for the first time in over two decades, the host was unable to rise for the Midnight Prayers. Upon asking his rabbi, the latter said that there was no question that he had been prevented from rising at this auspicious time because he had allowed a discussion about idolatrous practices on Shabbat, without trying to prevent it.

We learn from the Zohar that Rabbi Shimon bar Yochai asked his mother herself to refrain from discussing weekday matters on Shabbat, and the commentators explain: "Because speaking of weekday matters on Shabbat gives strength to the [angels] appointed over the weekdays on Shabbat, and that [brings about] a great damage."[18]

That is where a woman's wisdom comes in, for a woman has many ways of diverting the topic of conversation without being abrasive. If she is unable to do that, then she could use tact and care to ask the person to stop speaking of non-Shabbat topics, in such a way as to avoid hurting anyone's feelings.

Avoiding secular speech on Shabbat is indeed one of the biggest challenges of the Shabbat experience, and that is where man has an opportunity to show his Maker to what extent he is attempting to give joy on High. A person may know an important piece of information relating to secular matters that would enable him to 'shine' and draw attention on himself if he discussed it at the Shabbat table. If instead he refrains, his silence is like a body language that will speak for itself.

---

18. *Chok leIsrael Hameforash: Lilmod Bechol Yom Keseder Parshiyot HaTorah, Mikraot min Torah, Neviim UKetuvim*, vol. I (Bereshit) (Jerusalem: Bloom Sefarim, 5760), 174. This edition, which includes in the Zohar selections the glosses of Rabbi Daniel Frish, may be obtained in Judaica bookstores in the U.S. or by writing in Hebrew to Rabbi Bloom at Rechov Yoel 30, Jerusalem, Israel.

Furthermore, every time that we overcome the evil impulse to engage in secular speech on Shabbat, our involvement in the *tikkun* (spiritual repair) that our soul achieves will deepen, and we will be granted the skill to avoid secular discussions on Shabbat in a wise manner.

These teachings derived from the inner dimension of the Torah are very sweet to us. For while we follow the injunctions against doing work on Shabbat because these are "the King's orders," the invitation to rest as Hashem did after the work of Creation shows us the love with which *Hakadosh Barukh Hu* relates to us – a love of soul companions. These teachings "sweeter than the wine of Torah" came to the Children of Israel when they were in the depths of their fall, to give them strength by transmitting the mystery of *shamor* (guarding [Shabbat]). The teachings revealed to them how, if they left all their load behind and became *shomer Shabbat* (guarding the Shabbat laws), they would be guarded from Above and attain the sweetness of His love, of receiving His love and responding in kind.

Rabbi Luria writes:[19]

The People of Israel also need to refrain from creative activity because just like there has to be a state of total focusing in the case of the Giver – that is, *Hakadosh Barukh Hu* – so too there has to be the same quality of focusing in the case of the receiver, *Knesset Yisrael*. Consequently, they also need to refrain from creative activity. This is the message of the two Shabbat lights, for as it is known, the word *"ner"* (candle) alludes to the *yichud* (unification). [...] The idea of *ner* thus conveys that the Giver on High, just like the Receiver below, both have to be in a state of cessation of activity.	גם כלל ישראל צריכים משום שכשם שצריך הסחת דעת בדבר כך צריכים הסחת בנוק׳ כנסת ישראל ולכן הם צריכים לשבות ממלאכה. וזו ההוראה של שני נרות דולקות בשבת להורות כידוע שנר מורה על היחוד [...], היינו נר מצד הדכר ונר מצד הנוק׳ ושניהם צריכים משום כך שביתה.

---

19. The teachings that follow are adapted from "VeShameru Benei Israel et HaShabbat," *Sefer Pitchei Tefilla*, vol. 3, 213-214.

Just as we reach the state of *menucha* here below by leaving everything behind and giving ourselves to the Shabbat experience, so it is true on High. By accepting the mission to go to the lower words on the weekdays, the *Shekhina* gave to her beloved Counterpart all she had, and when He illuminates her with His light on the Shabbat day, she has *menucha*.

This light constitutes the mystery of Shabbat. The time is soon to come for a new light to shine on Zion for the Community of Israel and, in particular, for all those who have strived to become the *dira batachtonim*, thus fulfilling the purpose of Creation. As the verse says: *"veasu li mikdash veshachanti betocham* (They will make Me a Sanctuary and I will dwell within them)."[20]

---

20. Ex. 25:8.

Chapter 6
Kabbalat Shabbat and the Evening Prayer

As we begin to say the *Kabbalat Shabbat* prayers to welcome Shabbat, we should initially close our eyes and remained silent for a few moments, imbued with reverential awe before the Divine Presence.

After saying Psalm 29, we sing *Lekha Dodi*, welcoming Shabbat as heavenly Bride:[1]

Come, my Beloved [God], to greet the Bride!	לְכָה דוֹדִי לִקְרַאת כַּלָּה
Together let us welcome the Shabbat Queen!	פְּנֵי שַׁבָּת נְקַבְּלָה
"Observe" (*shamor*) and "Remember" (*zachor*) –	שָׁמוֹר וְזָכוֹר בְּדִבּוּר אֶחָד. הִשְׁמִיעָנוּ אֵל הַמְיֻחָד
The One God caused us to hear in a single utterance.	ה' אֶחָד וּשְׁמוֹ אֶחָד
Hashem is one and His Name is one.	

---

1. Translation of "Lekha Dodi," Rabbi Avraham Sutton.

The word *"zachor"* appears at the Giving of the Torah, in the First Tablets:[2] *"Zachor et yom haShabbat lekadsho* (remember the Shabbat day to sanctify it)."[3] The word *"shamor"* appears in the Second Tablets that Moses gave the Children of Israel after they repented of making the Golden Calf:[4] *"Shamor et yom haShabbat lekadsho* (Guard the Shabbat day to keep it holy)." In the First Tablets, Hashem Himself gives us the reason behind Shabbat, saying that it is on this day that He ceased Creation and withdrew to the spiritual dimension. The Second Tablets are a remembrance of the Exodus from Egypt, and Moses is the one who gave them to us. The relation of Shabbat to the Creation and the Exodus is mentioned in the first and second paragraphs of the Kiddush prayer recited over wine before the Shabbat evening meal.

Rabbi Luria explains the connection between Shabbat and the Exodus as follows: Even Pharaoh and the Egyptians believed in God's creation of the world, for Yosef had informed Pharaoh about it when interpreting his dreams. Accordingly, they believed in that aspect of God which is associated with the name *Elokim*, whose *gematria* (numeric value) is the same as that of *hateva* (the nature). But Pharaoh did not believe in the miraculous *hanhaga* (divine providence) associated with The Name that is written with four letters. To believe only in *Elokim* is to believe that there is a Higher Power who created the world and then left it to be run by means of constellations; to believe in God as represented by The Name of four letters (one circumlocution for which is *Havaya* [Being]) is to have the consciousness that this Higher Power is the very lifeforce of the world we live in, and that He is involved in all that happens in the world, big and small. That is what the *shem Havaya* teaches – this kind of unique, personalized divine supervision and guidance. And that Pharaoh did not believe –until it was revealed to him through the Ten Plagues and all the miracles that broke the rules of nature.

---

2. Ex. 20:8. Trans. Rabbi Aryeh Kaplan, *The Living Torah*.
3. The teaching that follows on *zachor* and *shamor* are adapted from "Maamar Zachor veShamor," in *Sefer Beit Genazai: Maamarei Shabbat*, 2nd ed., 115ff.
4. Deut. 5:12.

Thus, Shabbat reminds us not only that Hashem created the world, but also that *Hakadosh Barukh Hu* Himself guides the world, and that He did not submit the world's supervision to the constellations.

Moreover, the word *"zachor"* represents *Hakadosh Barukh Hu*, whereas the word *"shamor"* represents the *Shekhina*.[5] At the beginning – that is, before Creation – they were in a state of total togetherness, for the soul roots of Israel were attached to the Holy One on High even before Creation, and our souls are rooted in the *Shekhina*. The *Shekhina* then was severed from her Beloved and given the mission of going down to the dimensions below to gather the holy particles fallen from her children's souls and redeem them. As a result, even though *shamor* and *zachor* were said "in one utterance," still they were inscribed in the Torah in different places. *Zachor* is in the Book of Exodus, whereas *shamor* is in Deuteronomy.

Rabbi Luria analyzes the words of *Lekha Dodi*:

Arise and come forth from the midst of [confusion and] upheaval.	קוּמִי צְאִי מִתּוֹךְ הַהֲפֵכָה

This line tells us why the *Shekhina* has to go down on the weekdays, rather than staying on High all the time where she belongs. We are told about the fallen particles of holiness that she is to redeem.

You have dwelt long enough in the vale of tears.	רַב לָךְ שֶׁבֶת בְּעֵמֶק הַבָּכָא

We tell her, "You can now get up and leave these dark spaces, for the light is shining on you from Above."

Shake the dust [of exile] off yourself – rise up!	הִתְנַעֲרִי מֵעָפָר קוּמִי.

---

5. The following teachings about "Lekha Dodi" stem from Rabbi Luria, "Lekha Dodi Likrat Kalla [Alef]," *Sefer Pitchei Tefilla*, vol. III, 174ff.

Key to the Locked Garden

This portrays the *Shekhina* on weekdays, as she goes down to the world below that of *Atzilut*; this lower world is referred to as dust as an indication of the darkness and impurity of exile.

> Awake, arouse yourself, for Your light has come. [...] Hashem's glory has already been revealed upon you!
>
> הִתְעוֹרְרִי הִתְעוֹרְרִי. כִּי בָא אוֹרֵךְ קוּמִי אוֹרִי עוּרִי עוּרִי שִׁיר דַּבֵּרִי. כְּבוֹד ה' עָלַיִךְ נִגְלָה

We are the ones to arouse her and help her ascend to a space of light in which she will "sing the song [of Redemption]," songs of Hashem's Throne of Glory. And as we go out to the field to greet her, we say to her: "This light will illuminate you as well."

> Be not ashamed or humiliated. Why are you downcast? Why are you agitated? The afflicted of My people will find refuge in you, and the [holy] city will be rebuilt upon Your ruins
>
> לֹא תֵבוֹשִׁי וְלֹא תִכָּלְמִי. מַה תִּשְׁתּוֹחֲחִי וּמַה תֶּהֱמִי. בָּךְ יֶחֱסוּ עֲנִיֵּי עַמִּי. וְנִבְנְתָה עִיר עַל תִּלָּהּ.

When the *Shekhina* is below, she feels that she cannot look at the light of His countenance, the great light which is above her. We now have to strengthen her, reminding her that she can and must go up, and enter the palace of the King where she belongs. When she is on High, it will be as if the Temple were rebuilt, as hinted to in the words "The city will be rebuilt upon Your ruins." We also encourage her by telling her: "The afflicted of My people will find refuge in you." We remind her that the People of Israel – her children – will find comfort in her, and when she goes up, they will ascend as well.

> Those who violated you will be destroyed. Those who devoured you will be removed far away.
>
> וְהָיוּ לִמְשִׁסָּה שֹׁאסָיִךְ וְרָחֲקוּ כָּל. מְבַלְּעָיִךְ

Kabbalat Shabbat and the Evening Prayer

All those who keep the light away from you will be annihilated. The *Shekhina* fears that when she ascends, all those evil forces who cleave to her during the week will be able to go up as well. We therefore tell her that outside forces will not be admitted on High, for they are separated from her as Shabbat starts. That is why the verse ends "Your God will rejoice over you," referring to the joy on High at the Shabbat togetherness, when the forces of evil are powerless.

> But your God will rejoice over you as a groom rejoices over his bride.   יָשִׂישׂ עָלַיִךְ אֱלֹהַקְיִךְ כִּמְשׂוֹשׂ חָתָן עַל כַּלָּה.

When She is below in her aspect of the *Shekhina* below, She is like a bride who is not always together with her groom, but up at the Source she is, as we find in the last stanza, a "crown for her Husband."

> Spring forth to the right and to the left.   יָמִין וּשְׂמֹאל תִּפְרוֹצִי

We are alluding to the *Shekhina*'s awaited encounter with Her beloved and to Their embrace as the women of Israel ignite the Shabbat lights.

> Enter in peace, O crown for her Husband!
> With song, with joy, and with exultation!
> Into the heart of the faithful of the chosen people
> Enter, O Bride! Enter, O Bride!
>
> בּוֹאִי בְשָׁלוֹם עֲטֶרֶת בַּעְלָהּ
> גַּם בְּשִׂמְחָה בְּרִנָּה וּבְצָהֳלָה.
> תּוֹךְ אֱמוּנֵי עַם סְגֻלָּה:
> בֹּאִי כַלָּה. בֹּאִי כַלָּה.

We now say "*Boi Kalla* (Enter, O Bride)," asking for the time to come in which She will be permanently the "crown for her Husband." From Hashem will then glow a light into the heart of the "faithful of the Chosen People." We will then "rejoice and exult," for the *Shekhina* will leave the state of lowliness in which she is at this time of exile and acquire the full splendor of Kingship which is rightfully hers. In the siddur published by Rabbi Mordechai Eliyahu, *Siddur Kol Eliyahu*,[6] we are told after the last line to say in a whisper:

| Enter O Bride, Shabbat Queen[7] | בּוֹאִי כַלָּה שַׁבָּת מַלְכְּתָא |

It is at this point that we receive the *nefesh* level of the Shabbat additional soul.

It is up to us to remember: the more darkness prevails, the greater the light that will follow it. It is not possible to find pearls without the darkness of the ocean to reveal their whiteness.

The Zohar teaches that at the onset of Shabbat the *Shekhina on High* extends a spirit of holiness onto the Children of Israel below as we are receiving the Shabbat Queen, who is our holy guest.[8]

After *Lekha Dodi*, we say two more psalms and then the *Arvit* (evening prayer), consisting of the evening *Shema* and its blessings, followed by the Shabbat evening *Amida*. Just before the *Amida* we say the prayer beginning *"Hashkivenu* (Lay us down to sleep)," which ends:

| Who spreads the *sukkat shalom* (shelter of peace) upon us, upon all of His people Israel and upon Jerusalem[9] | הַפּוֹרֵשׂ סֻכַּת שָׁלוֹם עָלֵינוּ וְעַל כָּל עַמּוֹ יִשְׂרָאֵל וְעַל יְרוּשָׁלָיִם: |

Just before we say the final verse we should have in mind that we are receiving the *neshama yetera* (additional Shabbat soul). For according to the Zohar, it is at this time that the *sukkat shalom*, who is the *Shekhina*,

---

6. *Siddur Kol Eliyahu haShalem. Al pi piskei Maran HaRishon LeTzion HaRav HaGaon Mordechai Eliyahu* (Jerusalem: Hotzaa "Darkhei Horaa LeRabanim," 5762).
7. The words *"Shabbat Malketa"* in the last line (replacing the usual repetition of *Boi Kalla*) are a Kabbalistic practice. When saying this, we have the intention of receiving the *nefesh* level of the Shabbat additional soul.
8. Zohar Bereshit 48a; cited in the Friday Zohar selection of the *Chok LeIsrael* on *Chayei Sarah*.
9. *Complete ArtScroll Siddur: Nusach Sefard*, ed. Rabbi Nosson Scherman (New York: Mesora Publications., 1985), 365.

gives the People of Israel the additional Shabbat soul. Why? asks the Zohar. Because all the souls dwell within her, and as she spreads her wings upon her children, she extends to each soul of Israel new levels from their own souls on High.

The Zohar reveals that this added measure of consciousness allows us to forget our daily matters and our sources of sorrow and frustrations, in a process alluded to in the verse:

| Hashem grants you relief from your distress and your anxiety[10] | הָנִיחַ ה' לְךָ מֵעָצְבְּךָ וּמֵרָגְזְךָ וּמִן הָעֲבֹדָה הַקָּשָׁה |

As Rabbi Masud tells us:

| Pray *Arvit* with awe, with a loud voice and good reasoning.[11] Say the blessings of the Shema with pleasantness, with focused intention, according to the mystery alluded to in the verse, "Contemplate and see that Hashem is good."[12] [As we say *ufros alenu*,] extend [upon us] the additional soul level.[13] Focus your intention in the midst of a congregation of people. Enlighten me by granting me the essence of the name *Shaddai*. | יִתְפַּלֵּל עַרְבִית בְּאֵימָה. בְּקוֹל גָּדוֹל בְּסוֹד טַעַם. בִּרְכוֹת שְׁמַע בִּנְעִימָה. בְּכַוָּנָה וּבְטוּב טַעַם. וּפֵרוּשׁ תּוֹסֶפֶת נְשָׁמָה. תְּכַוֵּן בְּתוֹךְ קָהָל עַם. נִשְׁמַת שַׁדַּ"י תְּבִינֵנִי: |

It is thus not just because of our will power or mental discipline that we are able to forget about all that troubles us on the weekdays! Receiving the additional soul is what enables us to switch to a different reality in which these problems have no existence.

---

10. Is. 14:3.
11. Paraphrasing Ps. 119:66.
12. Alluding to Ps. 34:9, "Test for yourselves and you will see how good Hashem is; happy is the man who takes refuge in him." The mystery of Shabbat as an experiential perception of divine closeness is embedded in this verse.
13. See Chapter 12, "Ascending with the *Tosefet Shabbat*."

Key to the Locked Garden

Between the *Hashkivenu* and the *Amida* we say,[14] right before beginning the *Amida*:

The Israelites shall thus keep (*Veshameru*) the Shabbat, making it a day of rest for all generations, as an eternal covenant. It is a sign between Me and the Israelites that during the six weekdays God made heaven and earth, but on Saturday, He ceased working and withdrew to the spiritual.[15]

וְשָׁמְרוּ בְנֵי יִשְׂרָאֵל אֶת הַשַּׁבָּת לַעֲשׂוֹת אֶת הַשַּׁבָּת לְדֹרֹתָם בְּרִית עוֹלָם: בֵּינִי וּבֵין בְּנֵי יִשְׂרָאֵל אוֹת הִוא לְעֹלָם כִּי שֵׁשֶׁת יָמִים עָשָׂה ה' אֶת הַשָּׁמַיִם וְאֶת הָאָרֶץ וּבַיּוֹם הַשְּׁבִיעִי שָׁבַת וַיִּנָּפַשׁ:

The light directed onto us at this time of Shabbat is of the same kind as the light of Creation.

Veshameru is a form of *shamor*. As above-mentioned, the word *"shamor"* represents the *Shekhina*, whereas the *zachor* represents *Hakadosh Barukh Hu*. By saying a form of the word *"shamor"* at this time, we are reminded that on Shabbat evening the People of Israel become the *nukva* (female companion) of *Hakadosh Barukh Hu*. As taught by a kabbalistic commentator known by the name of his work, *Emek haMelech*, on Shabbat evening we are imbued with reverential awe (in the morning with love). The theme of awe will also be sounded in the *Eshet Chayil* (Woman of Valor) passage that will be read at the table before Kiddush: "*Ishah yirat Hashem hi tithallal* (A God-fearing woman – she should be praised)."

As we saw earlier,[16] the Maggid of Mezrich teaches in *Or Ha'emet* that by experiencing reverential awe of divine greatness, the People of Israel become the *nukva* (female companion, that is, the woman) – and then, as the Talmud teaches, "it is the way of man to search for a woman."

---

14. The teachings that follow are adapted from "VeShameru benei Israel et haShabbat," *Sefer Beit Genazai: Pitchei Tefilla*, vol. 3, 213-214.
15. Ex. 31:16-17. Trans. Rabbi Aryeh Kaplan, *The Living Torah*.
16. See the teachings in Chapter 8, "Spiritual Kisses."

Kabbalat Shabbat and the Evening Prayer

The word "man" here refers to *Hakadosh Barukh Hu*, to the extent that words can express it, searching for what is described as a "woman" as alluded to in Proverbs.[17] It is in the morning that we enter the dimension of *zachor* associated with *Hakadosh Barukh Hu*, and in *Mussaf* the *yichud* takes place.

The preceding helps us understand the meaning of the verse

> Now, Israel, what does Hashem, your God, ask of you, only to fear Hashem your God.[18]
>
> וְעַתָּה יִשְׂרָאֵל מָה ה' אֱלֹהֶיךָ שֹׁאֵל מֵעִמָּךְ כִּי אִם לְיִרְאָה אֶת ה' אֱלֹהֶיךָ

Rabbi Luria comments:

> [The above-mentioned verse] means just this: that it [i.e. becoming imbued with divine greatness] *is the only way* that one can become the *nukva*. Then, love naturally follows when *Hakadosh Barukh Hu* relates to us as the *zachar* (man) in the way suggested in the Talmud: "It is the way of man to search for a woman [with love]." In turn, the People of Israel become imbued with love, as water mirrors a loving look.[19]
>
> כלומר, רק זה שעל ידי כך נעשים בחינת נוק׳, ואהבה ממילא באה על ידי הדבר שדרכו של איש לחזור אחר אשה באהבה ועל ידי זה מתעוררים כלל ישראל באהבה כמים הפנים לפנים

Rabbi Luria is telling us something astounding: experiencing reverential awe, in particular at the inception of Shabbat, *is the only way* that we will be able to take on the image of the *nukva* who finds favor before Hashem.

---

17. Prov. 31:30.
18. Deut. 10:12.
19. Paraphrasing Prov. 27:19.

The only way? Those are strong words; and in our times, we are not even sure of how to identify the feeling that is expected of us. We are not even sure we understand what it means to experience awe of divine greatness.

Elsewhere, Rabbi Luria writes, "It is impossible to attain the level of the Community of Israel, His soul companion, other than by [experiencing] awe of divine greatness, for in so doing, she becomes the *nukva*."[20]

Rabbi Luria illustrates this point with the moment at the inauguration of the *mizbe'ach* (altar) when Moses says to Aaron "Come near to the altar."[21] These words imply that Aaron was hesitating. Rabbi Luria cites the work *Torat Kohanim*, which illustrates Aaron's hesitation with the story of a young girl who gets engaged to a man and upon realizing that her bridegroom is a great king feels paralyzed and is unable to go forward. Rabbi Luria writes:

> The example needs an explanation: why is [Aaron's hesitation] likened specifically to that of a woman getting married to a king? The example could have been about a man who comes to minister before the king and feels embarrassed by the king's greatness, in particular when we are dealing with the King of all kings, Whose Divine Presence dwelt in the Sanctuary. We are led to conclude that an aspect of the *Kohen Gadol* (High Priest) may be likened to a woman getting married to a king, for the soul of the *Kohen Gadol* gathers all the souls of the People of Israel at the roots on High; he is the heart and brain of the People of Israel.[22] He represents *Knesset Yisrael*, about whom it is said, *Knesset Yisrael* Your soul companion.[23]

---

20. *Sefer Beit Genazai: Maamarei Shabbat*, 2nd ed. 305.
21. Lev. 9:7.
22. The topic of the *Kohen Gadol* as heart and brain of the People of Israel is expanded in Simcha H. Benyosef, "Ten Days of Repentance: King Above, King Below," *Living Kabbalah* (New York: Continuum Publishers, 1999), 114-120.
23. "Kerav el Hamizbeach," in *Sefer Beit Genazai al parshiyot HaTorah: Vayikra*, vol. 1, 292-293.

Kabbalat Shabbat and the Evening Prayer

Since on Shabbat, the beloved soul companion is what we yearn to become, Aaron's example may be a model. With the help of this model we may have a perception of what is desired of us when standing to welcome the *Shekhina* in *Kabbalat Shabbat*, as well as later on in the *Amida*.

In his books[24] on the mystical significance of the Land of Israel, Rabbi Luria expounded on this topic. The Shabbat day was imbued with holiness from the time of Creation, as the verse says,[25] "*vaykadesh oto* (and He sanctified it)." And yet we find that we are still commanded to "remember the Shabbat day to sanctify it."[26] Why do we have to sanctify it if Shabbat's sanctity comes from Above and is permanent?

Rabbi Luria answers:

Even though it is clear that Shabbat is a holy day in its essence, still, its holiness is Above, and is not extended within the *midot* (measures); therefore, we may not perceive it.[27]	אמנם נראה שזה ברור שהשבת הוא יום קדוש בעצם מהותו אבל הקדושה היא לעילה מהתפשטות בתוך המדות ולכן אין בה השגה.

Midot is another term for the *Sefirot*. In Rabbi Aryeh Kaplan's brilliant exposition of the principles of Kabbala, *InnerSpace*, we find:

> The *Sefirot* are generally referred to as *Midot*, which means literally "measures" or "dimensions," and by extension, attributes or qualities. It is through the *Sefirot* that God limits His Infinite Essence and manifests specific qualities that His creatures can grasp and

---

24. Two volumes of *Sefer Beit Genazai: Eretz Israel* have been published. Eight thousand pages are stored away in Rabbi Luria's computer, which have never seen the light of day.
25. Gen. 2:3.
26. Ex. 20: 8.
27. *Sefer Beit Genazai Eretz Yisrael, Kolel Biurim Beinyanei Kedushat Eretz Yisrael Umaaloteiha ("Sefer Beit Genazai: Eretz Israel")*, vol 1., 174b.

relate to. As such, the *Sefirot* act variously as filters, garments or vessels for the light of *Ain Sof* that fills them.[28]

We now understand Rabbi Luria's comment: the holiness originally imprinted onto the Shabbat day was not enclosed into vessels and is thus too high for us to receive it unless... as Rabbi Luria continues,

The Torah thus says, "Remember the Shabbat day to sanctify it" – meaning that we must draw down the holiness from the very source of this holiness, so that it may be felt by the entire creation.

וזה מה שאמרה תורה זכור את יום השבת לקדשו, הכונה שאנו נמשיך התפשטות הקדושה משורש הקדושה כך שתהי' מורגשת על כל הבריאה [...].

How do we draw down the Shabbat holiness? Not by means of words, answers Rabbi Luria; not by reading prayers. The Zohar tells us that the beginning of Shabbat is imbued with the quality of *shamor*, which literally means "guarding the Shabbat" and is associated with awe of the Divine. It is thus by experiencing awe of the Divine that we begin to draw downward the Shabbat holiness. In contrast, the Shabbat day is imbued with the quality of *zachor* (remember) and is associated with love of the Divine.

Rabbi Luria thus suggests another way of experiencing awe of divine greatness,[29] as taught by the Ramban (Nachmanides). In commenting on Deuteronomy 5: 12 and 15 ("Observe the Shabbat day to sanctify it, as Hashem your God, has commanded you. [...] And you shall remember that you were a slave in the land of Egypt"),[30] the Ramban teaches:

---

28. Rabbi Aryeh Kaplan, *Inner Space* (Jerusalem: Moznaim Publishers, 1991), 40. (Note: In the corner of his manuscript, Rabbi Kaplan wrote the title *InnerSpace*; but it appears as *Inner Space* in the published work.)
29. *Sefer Bet Genazai: Eretz Israel*, vol. 1, 175.
30. Deut. 5:12 and 5:15.

And in the way of the Truth [the mystic teachings of the Kabbala], we can further add to this [subject, by saying] that this commandment was given with [the expression] "Guard [the Sabbath-day to keep it holy]," in order that we may "fear the Glorious and Fearful Name," and therefore he commands us to remember the "mighty hand and the outstretched arm" that we saw at the Exodus from Egypt, and from it the fear [of G-d] is to come to us, as it is said, "And Israel saw the great work which the Eternal did upon the Egyptians, and the people 'feared' the Eternal." And "therefore the Eternal thy G-d commanded thee to keep the Sabbath day" so that the congregation of Israel be the partner to the Sabbath, as hinted to in the words of our Rabbis. The student [learned in the mysteries of the Cabala] will understand.[31]

ועל דרך האמת נוכל עוד להוסיף בזה כי הדבור הזה בשמור ליראה את השם הנכבד והנורא, ועל כן יצונו שנזכור את היד החזקה והזרוע הנטויה שראינו ביציאת מצרים, וממנו לנו היראה כמו שאמר וירא ישראל את היד הגדולה אשר עשה ה' במצרים וייראו העם את ה' ועל כן צוך ה' אלקיך לעשות את יום השבת שתהא כנסת ישראל בת זוגו לשבת כנרמז בדברי רבותינו והמשכיל יבין.

Hence, according to the Ramban, we may experience reverential awe by having in mind the divine action in the Ten Plagues. As it is clear from the end of the citation, Ramban associates our ability to relate to divine awe to *Knesset Yisrael*'s role as Shabbat's soul companion.

The Baal haTurim points out that the initial letters of the words הַשַּׁבָּת לַעֲשׂוֹת אֶת (*la'asot et haShabbat* [to make the Shabbat]) form the word אהל (*ohel* [tent]), which brings to mind the Portable Sanctuary.

---

31. Ramban (Nachmanides): *Commentary on the Torah,* translated by Rabbi Dr. Charles B. Chavel (New York: Shilo Publishing House, 1976), vol. 5, 66.

This means, according to Rabbi Luria, that *Hakadosh Barukh Hu* would go down to the Temple to dwell with the Children of Israel, and the same happens every single Shabbat.[32]

The words *"veshameru benei Israel"* as we are about to enter the *Amida*, thus evoke the divine awe that we are to experience at this time, and when we aim to do that, Shabbat becomes לְדֹרֹתָם *(ledorotam)*, the next word in the verse, which is translated as "for their generations." A close look at this word, however, reveals that there is a missing letter *vav*. Written as it is, the word could be read as *lediratam*, (for their dwelling place) – as the sages expound, a place appropriate for the dwelling of a man and his wife.

The verse continues: *berit olam beini uvein bnei Israel* (an eternal covenant between Me and the Children of Israel). *Berit Olam* (an eternal covenant) has the same numeric value as *yom haShabbat* (the Shabbat day). And Rabbi Luria points out:

> This is not as if Hashem were telling us, "Today you are My wife, only for the length of Shabbat, but tomorrow in the weekdays you are not My wife." Rather, [the idea of a Shabbat as a dwelling space shared by husband and wife] is an eternal covenant in which we enter a marital contract forever. Each Shabbat, however, is a new creation in which we will re-experience this quality of bond, for it was imprinted in the Shabbat day forever.
>
> שאין זה בחינה של היום את אשתי רק בשבת ולמחר בחול אין את אשתי אלא שזה נעשה ברית עולם וקידושין על לעולם אלא שאחר כל שבת הוא בריאה מחודשת...

We could ask: How could it be forever? Shabbat is only one day!

The verse says, however, that "during the six weekdays God made heaven and earth, but on the seventh day He ceased working and withdrew to

---

32. Adapted from "VeShameru Benei Israel et HaShabbat," *Sefer Pitchei Tefilla*, vol. 3, 213-214.

the spiritual." And Rashi explains that on Shabbat all Creation returns to its Source, and then on Sunday we enter a new Creation. We derive from the preceding that all the ascents that the People of Israel experience on Shabbat are not temporary experiences for that particular day. Rather, this particular aspect of Creation is completed on every Shabbat and ascends on High, to be rebuilt anew on the following Shabbat.

Rabbi Luria continues:

> Among the verses [about Shabbat] it is written: "And the Israelites shall thus keep the Shabbat." [Namely] we are to rest on it and not become involved in [what constitutes] creative activities, "making it a day of rest for all generations," [that is,] in the way of a *dira* (dwelling place) for *Knesset Yisrael* His soul companion, "an eternal covenant. It is a sign forever between Me and the Israelites." The initial letters of *ot hi leolam* (it is a sign forever) form the word *"ohel"* (tent).
>
> ובכללות פסוקים אלו נאמר ושמרו בני ישראל את השבת לשבות בו ולא לעשות מלאכה לעשות את השבת לדרתם כמבואר בחינת דירה כנ״י ב״ז ברית עולם ביני ובין בני ישראל אות היא לעולם ר״ת אהל.[33]

Again,[34] the idea of an *ohel* is associated with the *Mishkan* in the desert in which *Hakadosh Barukh Hu* was able to dwell with *Knesset Yisrael*. The *Mishkan* was a *dira batachtonim* (dwelling place here below), as we ourselves aim to be on Shabbat. The words "to make Shabbat" thus intimate that it is up to us to become a dwelling place for Hashem.

The Hebrew word *dira* (dwelling) implies the togetherness of *ish veishto* (husband and wife).

There are two purposes behind Shabbat:

1. *Hakadosh Barukh Hu* wanted to benefit His children by making Himself known to them.

---

33. Emphasis mine.
34. Note that above the letters of *"ohel"* were also discovered in the phrase *"la'asot et haShabbat."*

2. Hashem wanted each one of us to become a *dira batachtonim* for the Divine Presence.[35]

The first purpose is thus Hashem's will to benefit His children by revealing to them the glory and greatness of His Presence; there is no greater good than this. This first purpose is intertwined with the second purpose in the sense that Hashem wanted to delight in a special bond with the Community of Israel, whether as Father to His children or as Husband and Wife, but the latter is only possible when there is a *dira batachtonim* made available. So long as the People of Israel were in exile, however, this idea of *dira batachtonim* as well as that of *devekut* was not relevant:

| This bond in which, if it can be said, *Hakadosh Barukh Hu* and the People of Israel have an interrelationship, may not come to fruition unless there is a dwelling place below enabling Hashem to be together with Israel. However, as long as He is unable to dwell together with them the idea of *dira* does not apply. Particularly when they are in a state of exile, the state of *devekut* and the ideal of dwelling together while sharing an intimate bond may not come to be.[36] | [...] אלא שבחינה שהיא דבקות קוב״ה וישראל וכביכול מקבלים דין מן דין אין זה יכול להיות אלא כשיש לו דירה בתחתונים ואז הוא בא לשכון יחד עם כלל ישראל אבל כל עוד שאינו יכול לדור עמהם יחד ולא שייך ענין הדירה של תשבו כעין תדורו ובפרט כשהם בבחינת גלות אין שייך דבקות וישיבה יחד. |

The words "particularly when they are in a state of exile" allude to the present situation of the Temple, which is the ultimate *dira batachtonim*.

---

35. "Retzeh Vehachalitzeinu BeShabbat," *Sefer Beit Genazai: Maamarei Shabbat*, 2nd ed. 516ff.
36. "Shabbat haYom l'Hashem veRashbi bechinat Shabbat," *Sefer Beit Genazai: Maamarei Shabbat*, 2nd ed., 43ff.

It is only true on the weekdays, however, that while we are in a state of exile this intimate bond may not come to be. On every single Shabbat we have a new opportunity to experience such a bond, imbuing us with spiritual strength for the coming week.

The Shabbat meal we hold at night is a manifestation of the second purpose of Creation, for at that time each of us is a vehicle for the manifestation of His Presence. On Shabbat evening at the time of the first *seuda* we become His dwelling place below, and in a similar way, the idea of *dira* is a place where a husband and wife live together. This alludes to the highest bond with Hashem, that of soul companion.

SEUDA OF THE FIELD OF HOLY APPLES

The Shabbat evening meal is known as the *seuda* of the Holy Apple Field. The Ari z"l wrote in the *Shaar Hakavanot* about the Kiddush of Shabbat evening: You should stand at your place at the prepared Shabbat table and say aloud: *"Da hi seudata dachakal tapuchin kadishin* (This is the feast of the Field of Holy Apples)." Elsewhere, the Ari z"l stresses that it is important to say the statement *"Atkinu seudata"* after saying Kiddush over the wine and before washing our hands ritually in order to make a blessing over the challa bread.

As noted previously, we say the verse *"Vaychulu hashamayim vekhol tzvaam* (the heaven and earth were finished, and all their array)" three times at the beginning of Shabbat: within the text of the Shabbat evening *Amida*, right after this *Amida*, and in the text of the Kiddush we say on Shabbat evening before the *seuda*. Every time we say *"Vaychulu,"* *Malkhut* receives light from Above in her *mochin* (mentality). When we say it for the third time, in the Kiddush, *Malkhut* becomes referred to as *Chakal Tapuchin Kadishin* (Field of Holy Apples).

The *peshat* (literal understanding) of this verse is that *Hakadosh Barukh Hu* created the world and ceased His involvement with Creation on the seventh day. We thus wonder how is our faith in Hashem's creation related to *Malkhut's* receiving her additional light. As we have in mind the intention to elevate the *Malkhut* and draw divine *mochin* toward her, we ourselves benefit; for Shabbat becomes for us the *yoma denishmata* (soul day) that it was intended to be. Just like *Malkhut*, every time we say *"Vaychulu,"* we also receive an added layer of consciousness from our additional Shabbat soul.

We mentioned earlier that according to the *Rishonim* (early sages), *Hakadosh Barukh Hu*, *Knesset Yisrael* and Shabbat act at different times as *chatan* (groom) and *kalla* (bride). The Bride of the Shabbat *kiddushin* is the spiritual entity of *Knesset Yisrael*. We saw as well that the idea of *kiddushin* as Shabbat begins is that in order to come together with Hashem we have to reach a level of *bittul* (nullification) in which we are willing separate ourselves from everything else. We have in mind: I am giving myself over to Him because He wants me to be with Him on Shabbat, and in doing so, I am leaving my past behind.

The preceding will help us understand the significance of our saying the verse beginning with *vaychulu*, for this verse subsumes the belief that *Hakadosh Barukh Hu* created the world *yesh me ayin* (from nothingness) and He sustains it by Himself, for the world has no independent existence of its own. On the weekdays there is a concealment of the Divine Presence, and it may seem that the Creation has an independent existence; but on Shabbat divine light permeates our consciousness and it becomes clear that there is no other. Only on Shabbat do we reach such a consciousness, and it comes about because of *Malkhut's* ascent on High and receiving from her beloved counterpart light in her *mochin*. The effect in the world below is that at the beginning of the first *seuda* of Shabbat, in particular after we say *"Vaychulu"* for the third time in the Kiddush, we receive the clear faith that *ein od milevado* (there is nothing other than His Presence). In other words, there is no reality other than Hashem. Consequently, by saying *"Vaychulu"* we are stating our *bittul,* expressing our willingness to become Hashem's *Malkhut*.

GREETING THE ANGELS OF PEACE

The Talmud teaches[37] that on Shabbat evening, two angels of peace accompany a man from the synagogue to his home. One is a good angel, and the other is a bad angel. If upon arriving home, they find the table set, the bed freshly made, and the candles lit, the good angel says, "May it be His will that the same occurs next Shabbat," and the bad angel answers "Amen" against his will. And if the opposite occurs, the bad angel says, "May it be His will that the same occurs next Shabbat," and the good angel replies "Amen" against his will.

---

37. Shabbat 119b.

We must try to understand this challenging teaching; for the angels accompany man in order to honor him, and in what way does the company of a bad angel honor man? Furthermore, why are both referred to as "angels of peace" if one of them is a bad angel?

The meaning is that a clean and orderly home is the sign of an effort to welcome the *Shekhina* – *Malkhut* – and shows that the man is striving to elevate his physicality so that body and soul are united in the yearning for closeness. When this is the case, the good angel exclaims, "May this be his situation next Shabbat as well," and the bad angel replies against his will, "Amen."

However, it may be that the preceding is not the scene they find upon coming home, for this particular man is not ready for his *gashmiut* (physicality) to ascend to the level of his *ruchniut* (spiritual being). This man thus remains on the same spiritual level he was on the weekdays, struggling against his impulse for evil which incites him on Shabbat as it does on weekdays. Now, the spiritual mission of the bad angel is precisely to help this man win the struggle. He is referred to as a "bad angel" because the man is trying to drawn down the light by overcoming evil. The angel thus says, "May this be this man's situation on next Shabbat as well," namely, may he continue his involvement in divine service in the same way. And the good angel, who wants the spiritual elevation of one's physical being on the Shabbat, answers "Amen" against his will.

Consequently, both are called "angels of shalom (peace)" for they both want *shlemut* (perfection) in man's service. However, there are two ways of attaining this *shelemut*: the way of the weekdays and the way of the Shabbat. The Zohar thus teaches that when man comes home from synagogue, two angels come with him, one from the right side and the other one from the left side, while the *Shekhina* is over his head. When they enter his home and they find the table set and the candles burning, and also see that the man and his wife have a harmonious relationship and receive the auspicious guest with joy, the *Shekhina* says, "He is mine!" She then says, "Israel, in whom I take glory."[38]

---

38. Rabbi Luria cites this teaching in the name of the Zohar, in "Kiddush Leil Shabbat," *Sefer Pitchei Tefilla*, vol. 3, 262a.

Chapter 7

Heavenly Dew

The second Shabbat *seuda* transports us to the very Source of light, which we refer to as *Atika Kadisha*.[1] Rabbi Luria gives a parable, which, although limited, illustrates the level of divine revelation called *Atika Kadisha*: Let us imagine a small child whose father wants to give him a new garment. At first, the child does not understand that it is a good thing and starts crying when they come and dress him with the garment. When the child is older, he does understand that what he is receiving is good for him but he does not really know in what way. When he is older still, he understands why it is wonderful for him to have this new garment and he rejoices. The completion of his growth is when he rejoices together with his father who gave him the garment. Like the child in the parable, we are unable to identify divine *shefa* when it begins to flow down to us from the source of blessings at the level of revelation of *Atika Kadisha*.

All the good *hashpaot* (flows of blessing) emanating from Above are initially concealed from us. This may be likened to a tree planted in

---

1. Adapted from "Be'atika Talia Milta," *Sefer Beit Genazai al haTorah: Shemot*, vol. 1, 420ff. Rabbi Luria cites the example of the child in the name of the Maggid in *Or Ha'emet*.

the ground: initially, it is only a seed that we plant in the ground and it has to rot, enmeshed between earth and ashes – but that is the root of the tree. Afterward, when the tree itself develops, we know that this is the place where the fruit will grow. Still, at this point we cannot see anything until the fruits themselves begin to grow.

The same is true of the *shefa* that comes to us from Heaven: it has to come down through all the levels of divine revelation until it reaches us. Hence, at the time that the *shefa* is first emitted, we do not see anything – much like the seed that will become a tree first has to rot before it starts to sprout – and it is only after a time that we receive the revelation of lovingkindness. Consequently, before we receive any good that Hashem gives us, we experience a period of *katnut* (restricted consciousness and concealment) because it has to go through all the levels of revelation before it reaches us.

The second Shabbat *seuda* brings to realization the aftermath of the Exodus from Egypt, in which as mentioned, we were chosen to become what the Zohar expresses as *zivuga vematronita de Kudsha Brich Hu* (Hashem's soul companion and Queen). Consequently, at the time of the second *seuda*, we are actually no longer thought of as a *kalla* but much more than that.

As we will see, at the second *seuda* – known as the *seuda* of *Atika Kadisha* –we are at the peak of the mountain, so to speak. Even at that lofty level, however, we may still contribute to the divine joy.[2]

Another event in which the Children of Israel received a light of salvation directly stemming from that high level that we call the peak of the mountain – *Atika Kadisha* – took place when they left Egypt and reached the Sea of Reeds. When they saw all the dangers before them, they started to pray to Hashem to save them. In truth, from the beginning of their prayer, the light of salvation had begun to flow toward them from Heaven – but they did not know this. Now, when they saw that the Egyptians were after them in hot pursuit, their instinct told them to cry out to Hashem. *Hakadosh Barukh Hu* then told Moses: "This is not the time to cry out to Me." This means that prayer was not what they had

---

2. Adapted from "Zecher Nes Keriat Yam Suf," *Sefer Beit Genazai al haTorah: Shemot*, vol. 1, 427ff.

to do at that time. Hashem was hinting to them that their salvation was dependent on the concealed divine *ratzon* (will) that gave rise to Creation, which is referred to as *Atika Kadisha*, and had thus already been emitted on High. However, the salvation was still at the level of Atika, concealed at the root of divine will. Thus they could not see the salvation yet, but they had to focus on the *bitachon* (trust) that they soon would.

Furthermore, the type of salvation they required at this point had to do with a purpose of Creation which is above divine revelation to man. Consequently, it is beyond our ability to communicate with this aspect of Hashem through prayer.

When a *hashpaa* (flow) is emitted from Heaven for us, the Torah gives us specific *mitzvot* so that we can merit receiving this flow and actually receive it. A perfect example is our *Yamim Tovim* (festivals): we are not commemorating an event of our past, but rather re-experiencing the miracle that gave rise to the particular Yom Tov. Moreover, we are stepping into that time once again and receiving the same quality of light that was emanated at that moment in order to enhance our Yom Tov for our sakes as well as for future generations. To that end, we are given *mitzvot* – things to do that are going to help us draw this same type of light down for ourselves.

When we do not have the merits to receive a light, we cannot do anything to receive it. Such was the case of King Hezekiah when surrounded by the enemy warriors of Sennacherib.[3] He said to Hashem:[4] "I don't have the power to run after them and kill them, and I can't even sing a *shira* (song)! I'm just going to go to sleep and You do it, Hashem." And that is what happened. All Hezekiah did was to hang on to his full *bitachon* in Hashem and a miracle happened that saved them all. However, there was no festival instituted to commemorate this miracle, because it was a miracle meant uniquely for that moment; in future generations we would not have the ability to bring about the revelation of that same light.

In contrast, on Passover, for instance, we have to recite special prayers in the evening and then participate at a seder in which we

---

3. II Kings 19:35.
4. *Sefer Beit Genazai al haTorah: Shemot*, vol. 1, 428; in the names of Rabbenu Bechaye and Rabbi Chaim Benatar, the Or Hachayim Hakadosh.

recount all the miracles of the Exodus. We even try to stay up all night long because the light coming down is so lofty that we want to be there to receive it – consciously – and not miss a minute of it. On Purim, the Jews from Persia were saved by a hidden miracle, and since it is in our hands to receive down here the same divine *hashpaa*, we are given specific *mitzvot* to do on the day of Purim. On each festive day we are asked to do specific things connected with the festival, so we can merit bringing down to ourselves the heavenly light that is counterpart of the festive day.

The seventh day of Passover is the night in which the Sea of Reeds split miraculously before the People of Israel. And we do hold a Yom Tov – we may not do *melacha* as on any other Yom Tov. However, there are no special *mitzvot* to mark the special character of this festival. The seventh day of Passover is really part of the Passover festival. As the verse says:[5] "For a six-day period you can eat matzos and on the seventh day shall be an assembly *(atzeret)* to Hashem." The light is there, but we cannot bring it down. That is why it is called *atzeret* (general gathering) – a word stemming from the word *"atzor"* (stop). The light is there on that day, just as it was there at the splitting of the sea, but it is not connected with anything we have to do. It is there because that is divine will.[6]

We may see a similar phenomenon on Shabbat. In the evening, we have *mitzvot* from the Torah that sanctify the Shabbat at its onset: we light the candles, say a Kiddush over the wine, etc. In contrast, after morning prayers, when the Shabbat light stems from the concealed divine will – a much loftier light than that which was revealed to us in the previous evening – we are not asked to say Kiddush over the wine! We do say Kiddush, but it is a *mitzva* that the Rabbis of the Great Assembly instituted; it is not mentioned in the

---

5. Deut. 16:8.
6. Still, the Sages of the Inner Torah, Rabbi Moshe Luria among them, teach that one who remains awake all night on the Seventh Day of Passover and reads the Zohar teachings relating to Redemption – as included in modern Sephardic *machzorim* (festival prayer books) – is connecting to the awesome illumination we receive at this time. The *machzor* published by Rabbi Mordechai Eliyahu, *Machzor Kol Yaakov* (Jerusalem: *Darkhei Horaa lerabanim*, [n.d.]), includes the verses related to the crossing of the sea and a prayer in which one contemplates divine names related to the splitting of the sea, to be read at the point of dawn on the Seventh of Passover.

Torah. On Shabbat eve, since it is a smaller light and we do have the ability to bring about its revelation here below, the Torah gives us specific *mitzvot* to do, but in the morning, this is not the case. However, we do have an allusion to the radiant light coming through on the Shabbat day in the name *Kiddusha Rabba* (Great Kiddush) which is given to the morning kiddush.

The space on High associated with the level of divine revelation called *Atika Kadisha* is the original light of Creation before its constriction. If we understand that Hashem's *hashpaa* comes down to us like a heavenly ladder made up of many rungs, the concealed divine will that gave rise to Creation is like a crown on top of this ladder – much like a king's crown stands above his head, and is not included within his head. The function of this level of divine revelation is giving – directing the highest form of divine sustenance onto the world below.

Many *siddurim* (prayer books) for laymen include, before the Shabbat evening Kiddush, a statement in Aramaic starting with the word "*Atkinu*," which identifies the aspect of Hashem that we are honoring in this *seuda*. Next comes a prayer in Aramaic in which we ask that the *shefa* may come from *Atika Kadisha* all the way down to us.[7] We refer to this prayer as *Vihei Raava* after its beginning words:

> May it be the will *(vihei raava)* of Atika Hadisha, holiest of all holy, most hidden of all hidden, concealed from all, that the heavenly dew be drawn from him to fill *Zeir Anpin* and *Chakal Tapuchin Kadishin* (the Field of Holy Apples) with the light of His countenance, with desire and joy for all. May there be drawn from *Atika Kadisha*, holiest of all holy, most hidden of all hidden, concealed from all, desire and compassion, grace and lovingkindness, with a radiant light, with desire and joy, upon me and the members of my household, upon all those who dependent on me, and upon all the Children of Israel, His people. May He redeem us from all the evil troubles that

---

7. The teachings on this prayer are adapted from "Tefilat Vihei Raava" *Sefer Pitchei Tefilla*, vol. 3, 252ff.

befall the world. May He bring us and all our souls grace and kindness, long life, ample nourishment, and compassion from Himself. Amen, may such be His will. Amen and Amen.[8]

Human parents judge how much their child needs, and out of their love for him, only give him what they think he can benefit from. As below, so Above. During the weekdays, the *shefa* comes down to us only to the extent that we have worked on ourselves to improve our *midot* (character traits) and Torah observance. The higher levels of divine revelation judge who deserves to receive divine flow and direct this flow accordingly toward different channels and then to us. In contrast, Shabbat is a gift; that is why the Talmud brings us the message that Hashem sent us through Moses: "I have a good gift in My house of treasures and Shabbat is its name. I want to give it to the Children of Israel; go and inform them."[9] A gift comes to us whether we deserve it or not; if we have to be worthy of it, then it is no longer a gift but a reward!

Rabbi Luria stresses that in the *Vihei Raava* prayer we are expressing the yearning to be at the stage of maturity in which our divine service will no longer require the scrutiny of strict justice. According to the Ari z"l, we should say it before each of the three Shabbat meals, although most layman prayer books only print it before the first *seuda*.

The *tal* (dew) mentioned in the prayer is the heavenly *shefa* coming down to us. The Zohar reveals to us that the manna we received in the desert was really a heavenly dew whose source on High was at the level of unconditional mercy associated with the Source of divine will. In *Vihei Raava*, we are asking that this *shefa* should go directly to the heavenly *Shekhina* and from there it should go to all of *Knesset Yisrael* and then personally down to us.

Some are frustrated at feeling the need to have a rest after the second *seuda* and wish they had the energy for Torah study, for our ability to study is enhanced on Shabbat. Indeed, it is important not to sleep after a prayer before we have the *seuda* that completes that prayer,

---

8. "*Vihei raava*" in Aramaic with a linear translation into English may be found in the Appendix.
9. Shabbat 10b.

because at the *seuda* we internalize the lights we have drawn down by means of our prayer, even on the weekdays. However, when we sleep after the second *seuda* of Shabbat, it is as if we ourselves are putting in Hashem's hand an unspoken request that He complete from Above what we cannot do on our own to internalize the light that has been flowing during the *seuda*. Moreover, sleeping after this *seuda* is part of the *oneg* (delight) of the Shabbat day.

Chapter 8

Second *Seuda* – Above Time

When *Hakadosh Barukh Hu* acts through *Atika Kadisha*, the Source of divine will – i.e. from the higher levels of divine revelation, from the highest heavenly world – we below become aware of divine action.[1] An example of this is the Exodus from Egypt. As we read in the Haggada on Passover, *Hakadosh Barukh Hu* promised to get us out of Egypt Himself, not involving any of His messengers: "I, and not an angel […] I, not a seraph […] I, and not a messenger."

Another example is the situation of the Children of Israel right after the Exodus, in which they needed a miracle from the top of the ladder, a miracle that would undo all the rules of Creation that led to the constriction of Creation. The divine flows directed to men through the intermediary of the lower worlds come down by means of heavenly messengers and are concealed within the cloak of nature, so that we are not aware of their action. But when there is a miracle breaking the rules of nature – an open miracle – we are seeing *Hakadosh Barukh Hu* acting Himself, so to speak, without going through all the divine crew, without listening to all the accusers who say we do not deserve it.

---

1. The teachings about the descent of divine *shefa* in this chapter are based in the explanations of Rabbi Jacob Hillel in *Binyan Ariel*, 40-81.

Key to the Locked Garden

The preceding brings to light Hashem's puzzling utterance, "Why do you cry to Me?"[2] When we make a request from *Hakadosh Barukh Hu*, our prayer has to go through all the levels of divine messengers who will decide whether we deserve what we are asking for. However, there are times of divine favor when we are able to bypass their scrutiny and get help straight from the top of the ladder.

In the second *seuda*, somehow, we are above time – or more precisely, above the sense of time we have in this world.

Let us revisit the morning prayer that precedes the second *seuda*. Particularly at the time of *Mussaf*, the level of divine revelation in which Hashem acts as our King – known in Aramaic as *Zeir Anpin* – is imbued with a light stemming from a higher dimension than on the weekdays. According to Rabbi Luria, "there – i.e. in that space – we are above and beyond compassion."[3] What is revealed on High at this time is not even compassion but pure good will and favor toward *Knesset Yisrael*. And the same thing happens at the time of the reading of the Torah in synagogue, for then we are receiving the light of *Chokhma* (divine wisdom).

Thus, in the Shabbat morning *Amida*[4] and the *Mussaf Amida* which follows it,[5] we say *veyanuchu bo* (they shall rest on it, i.e. the Sabbath referred to by the masculine pronoun), whereas at the first Shabbat *seuda*, which corresponds to the *Shekhina*, we said *veyanuchu ba* (they shall rest on it, i.e. the Sabbath referred to by the feminine pronoun).

During the reading of the Torah, whose Source stems from *Chokhma*, we are drawing down the light of *Chokhma*. However, the Ari z"l teaches something amazing: it is not only when the Torah is read to us on Shabbat morning, but also when we participate in the second *seuda* that we draw to ourselves the lofty light of *Chokhma*, the light of the Torah.

And still more astonishingly, the lights of Torah that we absorb by participating in the morning *seuda* are even higher than those at the

---

2. Ex. 14:15
3. *Sefer Pitchei Tefilla*, vol. 3, p. 357.
4. In the paragraph of the Shabbat Amida in which we are asking Hashem *"retze na bimenuchateinu,"* to regard our Shabbat rest with divine favor.
5. See chapter 7, "Heavenly Dew."

time of morning prayer. Rabbi Luria clarifies that we are talking about the level of the little crowns over the letters in a Torah scroll.

One who is appointed to read the Torah scroll has to learn the words with their correct signs of punctuation as well as their *taamim* (cantillation notes), for both of these affect the reading of the words. However, one who looks at a Torah scroll will see that there are little crowns drawn over some of the letters. These crowns do not affect the reading in any way. Called *tagin*, these small crowns over the letters evoke the light of *Keter*, which is the root of everything. The *tagin* are the counterpart of the heavenly roots of the letters, and this level of divine revelation does not come through to us at the reading of the Torah but only at the *seuda* that follows it.

The Ari z"l wrote three songs, one for each of the Shabbat *seudot*; each word of the *piyyutim* is pregnant with the meaning of what is happening in the spiritual dimension throughout the *seuda*. Rabbi Luria wrote detailed essays on each of these songs. When we study these essays before Shabbat, just by reading the song at the time of the *seuda* we are reminded of its teachings.[6] We may see, for instance, two stanzas of the song composed for the second *seuda*.

May [the light of *Atika*, whose] radiance [is too lofty to be enclosed into vessels], rest upon her [that is, Shabbat] through the Great Kiddush and the good wine [of the Torah mysteries stemming from the light of the *ketarim* (crowns) that shine down on us in this *seuda*,] in which the soul rejoices.	נְהוֹרֵיהּ יִשְׁרֵי בָהּ. בְּקִידּוּשָׁא רַבָּא. וּבְחַמְרָא טָבָא. דְּבֵהּ תֶּחֱדֵי נַפְשָׁא:

---

6. See my translation with Rabbi Luria's interpretation of the Ari z"l's songs in Appendix III: Mystical Readings for the Shabbat Table.

May He direct upon us His splendor and may we gaze upon His radiance [through the perception of the intellect]. May He cause us to perceive His mysteries that are transmitted in a whisper [alluding to the unification, for our experiential perception of the unification is a transmission rather than a study].

יְשַׁדֵּר לָן שׁוּפְרֵיהּ. וְנֶחֱזֵי בִּיקָרֵיהּ. וְיַחֲזֵי לָן סִתְרֵהּ. דְּאִתְאַמַּר בִּלְחִישָׁא:

Moreover, there are short Zohar texts which may be read at each of the *seudot*, so as to internalize the light of the Holy *Ein Sof*.

These Zohar texts tell us repeatedly how these *seudot* give joy to Hashem, for this is the time when He can reveal Himself to us. We are thus grateful that by reading a text, even if we do not fully understand it, we may enact our awareness of the revelation, for a revelation from Above is only complete when received below.[7]

Although in our times it is unusual to hear of a woman who reads the Zohar, a Torah scholar of our time writes:[8]

> Even women, who are exempted from the *mitzva* of studying Torah and are only asked to learn the laws regarding the *mitzvot* that they are responsible to fulfill, if they want to read every day in the Zohar in order to merit the awesome levels of holiness mentioned in it and to have the *Shekhina* dwell in their homes, they are encouraged to do so.[9]

---

7. See these Zohar readings with a linear translation in the Appendix III: Mystical Readings for the Shabbat Table.
8. Rabbi Benayahu Yissachar Shemueli, *Parashat Haketoret; Seder Hakorbanot* (non-profit publication for the protection of *Klal Israel* distributed by Yeshivat Nahar Shalom, Shilo Street, no. 6, Jerusalem), 17. The text of this teaching of Rabbi Shemueli is available upon request by e-mail; tel. 02-6241622.
9. Yeshivat Nahar Shalom in Jerusalem has prepared soft cover booklets under the title *Sefer HaZohar Hakadosh Hayomi, Hamevoar Belashon Hashave Lakol Nefesh Betosefet Iyunim Ufarparot* (Hotsaat "Heikhala Derashbi," [n.d.]), containing daily selections of the Zohar in which the Aramaic text is followed, phrase by phrase, by its Hebrew language translation. Each daily selection covers two pages of the Zohar, with the

The writer adds that he discussed this matter with Torah leaders of the generation, and many of them confided that their mothers had the practice of reading Zohar in addition to their daily prayers. There are even women, he says, who finish the entire Zohar throughout the year, and when they do, prepare a *seuda* for Torah scholars to celebrate it and then say Kaddish, which is a prayer causing much joy on High.

The unification taking place in *Mussaf* continues throughout the second *seuda*. At this time, we are absorbing a divine flow whose lofty essence is not enclosed in the finite letters.

The lights of Torah stemming from *Chokhma* really stem from the *tagin* over the letters. When Moses went on High, he saw *Hakadosh Barukh Hu* binding these little crowns to the letters of the Torah. Hence at this *seuda*, we are drawing to ourselves the light of the Torah mysteries, associated with the idea of crowns over the letters; the light above the letters, a light without vessels to contain it.

In the first *seuda*, we rejoice together with our beloved *Shekhina* who is out of the weekday darkness and is together with *Hakadosh Barukh Hu* where she belongs.[10] As we say the Kiddush over the wine in the first *seuda*, the *Shekhina* receives light from the level of divine revelation in which Hashem acts as a King. This level of revelation is called *Zeir Anpin* (reduced countenance), in contrast with the level of the second *seuda* which is known as *Atika Kadisha* or *Arikh Anpin* (extended countenance).

At the beginning of Shabbat, the *Shekhina – Knesset Yisrael –* is just coming back from her weekly exile. The unification with *Hakadosh Barukh Hu* is thus the lower unification which brings together two separate entities. This is comparable to the stage of *kiddushin*, the first stage of marriage which precedes the closer union of *nissuin*. On Shabbat morning the *Shekhina* continues to ascend. As mentioned, when we pray the silent *Mussaf Amida*, the level of divine revelation in which

---

intention that after seven years the person will finish the entire Zohar. To purchase copies, a Hebrew speaker may call the publisher in Jerusalem: 02-6221039; 02-6251451; 02-6222560.

10. The teachings that follow are adapted from "Seudata DeAtika Kadisha," in *Sefer Pitchei Tefilla*, vol. 3, 355ff.

Hashem acts as a King is imbued with a light stemming from a higher level, in which there is no constriction or strict justice.

In the repetition of *Mussaf*, in the *Kedusha* section, through our participation at this time, the *Shekhina* is higher in the range of the divine revelation than on the weekdays; we thus echo the cry of the angels on High: *"Ayye mekom kevodo* (Where is the place of His glory)?"

"The place of His glory" alludes to the *Shekhina*. The angels ask where the *Shekhina* is, because she is now higher than her usual weekday space. It is at that moment that we receive the higher soul level called *neshama*: the *Shekhina* is higher than her usual space, and hopefully we are as well. Rabbi Chaim Vital teaches that it is at the time of *Mussaf* that the *Shekhina* is referred as *eshet chayil ateret baalah* (a woman of valor who is a crown for her husband),[11] for she is receiving directly from the higher level of divine revelation – that of *Chokhma*.

This is a unique time, for at no other time except on Purim does the *Shekhina* receive directly from the higher level of *Chokhma*. Hence at this time Creation is in a higher state of completion than ever, and we are able to receive and integrate more than ever before. Now Hashem may direct divine flow down to us –*Knesset Yisrael Themselves* – straight from the top of the ladder; therefore we rejoice that Hashem is relating to the world below without having to deal with any constriction.[12]

That is what we are requesting when we say that Aramaic prayer *Vihei Raava* just before the three *seudot*. We are asking for the divine flow to come from the Source of divine will (*Atika Kadisha*) to Hashem as King (*Zeir Anpin*), Who will give it to the *Shekhina on High* and then to *Knesset Yisrael Themselves*. Then we will be able to receive the good gift of Shabbat from the *beit genazai* (hidden house of treasures) at the top of the structure of divine revelation. We should never lose track of this thought when we say this Aramaic prayer: the divine flow stems from the Source of all blessings and goes through the different levels of revelation before it reaches us.

---

11. Prov. 12:4.
12. See "Maamar Shalosh Seudot beShabbat," in *Sefer Beit Genazai: Maamarei Shabbat*, 1st ed., vol. 2, 492ff.

Second Seuda – Above Time

The situation may be likened to one in which a king owes us money. We do not receive it directly from the king. We have to go through his government, and it is up to us not to confuse the two. Alternatively, it is as if we are talking to the king on the telephone: it is up to us not to confuse the telephone receiver with the voice coming from within.

The good gift of Shabbat first goes to the *Shekhina* and only then to us.

Even though the *Mussaf* of Shabbat is such a unique time for the *Shekhina on High*, still at this time, we, *Knesset Yisrael Below*, are unable to receive directly from the lofty level of divine revelation which imbues the *Shekhina on High*.

As we shall see, this situation is reversed at the Shabbat afternoon Mincha, and our potential for ascent is greater at Mincha than during *Mussaf*.[13] Nevertheless, most of us will find it easier to enter the inner space of the prayer at the time of *Mussaf* than during Mincha, in which we are able to play a prime role. At *Mussaf*, the heavenly unification is with the *Shekhina on High*: the *Shekhina* is in a state of spiritual perfection at this time, and we are just "joining in." In contrast, at Mincha the unification is with the complete spiritual entity of *Knesset Yisrael Themselves*, made up of human beings covered by physical matter like ourselves, and not everyone merits being part of this union.

Charged with the energy of the morning *Amida* and that of the Torah reading, we are able to enter deeply into the *Mussaf* prayer. Although we are not consciously aware of this, our souls may attach themselves to the truly righteous of the past and present. We may then ascend to the height of our spiritual being, at the point in which the barrier preventing us from internalizing divine revelation thins considerably.[14] In contrast, at the Mincha *Amida* prayer, each one of us has to rely on

---

13. In Mussaf the *shefa* flows down to us from a lower place on high than in Mincha. Since the *Shekhina* is unable to go that high in our times, we fill in at the time of Mincha. However, in Mussaf, although we are not consciously aware of it, we can ascend together with the tzadikim of past and present. In Mincha we are on our own, so only one who is spiritually ready to do so actually ascends.
14. See in *Sefer Beit Genazai: Maamarei Shabbat*, 1st ed., "Maamar Ahavah Rabbah Veahavat Olam BeShabbat" (12-13), "Maamar Tzaddik Ketamar Yifrach BeShabbat" (348-49), and "Maamar Amirat Keter be Mussaf Shabbat" (561-563).

Key to the Locked Garden

his own merits to ascend – and that is always more of challenge! At the end of each of the Shabbat prayers we thus beg Hashem with particular intensity, *"Retze na bimenuchatenu* (May You look with favor upon our *menucha*, i.e. please want us as Your soul companion!)."

At the heavenly Source of divine will there is unconditional *rachamim* (compassion), which is a gift and not dependent on what man deserves. Thus, whenever *rachamim* is present the joy is not complete, because we have a feeling of eating what is called "the bread of shame." Shir Hashirim hints at this shame, voicing *Hakadosh Barukh Hu's* call to the *Shekhina* who hides in exile, reluctant to show herself to the King in all His greatness.[15] *Hakadosh Barukh Hu* tells her:[16]

Open [your heart] to Me, My sister, My love, My dove, My perfect twin, for My head is filled with dew and My locks with the drops of the night!	פִּתְחִי לִי אֲחֹתִי רַעְיָתִי יוֹנָתִי תַמָּתִי שֶׁרֹּאשִׁי נִמְלָא טָל קְוֻצּוֹתַי רְסִיסֵי לָיְלָה:

On weekdays, according to Rabbi Luria's teaching, the King as it were removes His crown so that the unification of prayer can be at the present level of the *Shekhina*, for on weekdays the *Shekhina* cannot receive light from the lofty level of divine revelation of *Keter*. In contrast, the *Mussaf Amida* is the time when Hashem brings to fruition His initial intention for Creation.[17] It is in the *Mussaf* prayer that the collective soul of His earthly companions rises to meet with Him at the height of their spiritual structure, for only at this point can Hashem reveal Himself.

It was at the Giving of the Torah that the People of Israel became the single individual of His soul companion, each one of whom was so aware of the highest bond with the Creator that s/he felt like the phrase in the Song of Songs, "My soul departed as He spoke." We lost this lofty

---

15. As taught in "Amirat Keter BeMussaf Shabbat," *Sefer Beit Genazai: Maamarei Shabbat*, 2nd ed., 569, at the end.
16. Paraphrasing Song 5:2.
17. The following material on the "Light of the Crown" is reproduced from my book *Living the Kabbalah*, (New York: Continuum, 1999), 27-35.

state due to the sin of the Golden Calf, but recovered it partially through Moses' intervention, if only for the duration of Shabbat, as well as on the festivals. Although Shabbat leaves its mark on us, we lose a significant part of our Shabbat consciousness during the week.

Hence on the weekdays, the collective soul of Hashem's earthly companions is unable to rise to Him at the time of the *Amida* prayer. The King of the world hides His Crown in order to lower Himself and become One with His people despite their present deficiency. In other words, during the week our union with the Creator takes place in the lowest points of contact of our soul-roots, as opposed to Shabbat, in which the union takes place in the highest point of meeting.

On Shabbat the divine energy radiates with renewed power and the spiritual worlds return to their Source. Hashem removes our mental obstructions, not just for the duration of the morning prayers as He does during the week, but for the entire day. We can now ascend to the "Crown," and, if it can be said, we give Hashem back His Crown in the *Mussaf Amida* of Shabbat. In technical terms, as taught in the Torah's inner dimension, we do not actually reach the level of Crown in the *Mussaf Amida*; but as Rabbi Luria explains, the light of the Crown is radiating throughout the entire Shabbat, and it is at this time that we most feel its luminous energy. We fully accept His Kingship over us and cleave to Him at this level of closeness.

In the repetition of the *Amidah*, it is divine will that we should lift our eyes to Heaven in the *Kedusha* and elicit the divine response described by the *Sefer Heikhalot*:[18] "For I have no greater pleasure in the world than the moment that they lift their eyes to Mine while My eyes are on theirs." The hidden meaning of "lifting the eyes" is Israel's ascent to the Crown, high enough, as it were, for "eye contact."

When two people in love with each other look into each other's eyes, there is no need for words. Each one of them has an experiential perception of the deepest recesses of the beloved's being; each one of them knows what the beloved desires without needing to be told.

---

18. *Sefer Heikhalot* (Book of Palaces) is an ancient book of Kabbala purported to have been written in the 2nd century C.E.

Key to the Locked Garden

"Ascending to the Crown" brings us back to Sinai, when we were close enough to perceive the Torah and yearned to receive it as a product of the unification of the soul with the Beloved. We now understand this wording of the *Kedusha* section of the *Mussaf* prayer:

| A Crown will they give You, O Hashem, our God – the angels of the multitude above, together with Your people Israel [who are assembled] below.[19] | כֶּתֶר יִתְּנוּ לְךָ ה' אלֹהֵינוּ מַלְאָכִים הֲמוֹנֵי מַעְלָה. עִם עַמְּךָ יִשְׂרָאֵל קְבוּצֵי מַטָּה: |

In the unification of the *Mussaf Amida*, the King is wearing His Crown while Israel, His earthly companions, wear their own spiritual crown. For the duration of the *Mussaf Amida* we are transported back into time, to the giving of the Torah, when the Almighty and His soul companion spoke "face-to-face." In the *Mussaf Amida*, Hashem elevates the spiritual structure of our collective souls, so that we can become One with Him in a union of the higher levels of our soul.

It is divine will that we learn about these mysteries; our awaited Redemption depends on this. Now, in this second *seuda*, we have a higher type of illumination stemming from *Atika Kadisha*, the heavenly Source of divine revelation in which the action stems from *Hakadosh Barukh Hu* without the constriction of Creation. We have to understand what a great illumination this is: the Sages teach that *Knesset Yisrael* was the last creation in deed, but she still was the first in divine thought, and this is the light coming through at this moment.[20]

At the time of the second *seuda*, Hashem is remembering how we were the first thing in His thought together with the Torah. In the constriction of light that led to Creation, this divine thought was hidden; and this led in turn to judgment and the execution of justice. As long as this purpose of Creation is concealed there will be judgment and execution of justice in the world, but from the moment that it is revealed we will find ourselves above judgment and justice. At the root

---

19. *The Complete ArtScroll Siddur: Nusach Sefard*, 503.
20. Cited in the name of the work *Avodat Yisrael*.

of the concealed divine will it is revealed that all is good, for in that space the driving purpose of divine thought is *Knesset Yisrael*; and no matter what the situation is, no matter in what state they find themselves, this driving purpose will come to fruition. It will be revealed that everything was created for the sake of *Knesset Yisrael* and that this purpose is higher than compassion. As the verse puts it, "behold, it was very good." [21] Although this is above our ability to comprehend fully, it remains clear that all that transpired from the beginning of Creation until now goes toward the fulfillment of the purpose of Creation – for the sake of *Knesset Yisrael*.[22] Hence the time of this *seuda* is a great time of favor towards *Knesset Yisrael*, and it does not come from a space of compassion but rather because it is all good. We stay in this space for the remainder of Shabbat.

Rabbi Luria reminds us that at this moment we are above time. The concept of time only came to be after the creation of the physical world, and the concealed divine will is above Creation. We thus have the faith that in time, when Hashem wills it, we will see the fulfillment of the purpose of Creation "for the sake of Israel." However, since in the lofty space of the second Shabbat *seuda* we are above time, it is already happening that "behold it was very good," and so it is a time of great favor toward the People of Israel. At this time we are receiving an illumination – a foretaste – of the promise made to the *Shekhina* and hinted at in the words we say to Her at the onset of the first Shabbat *seuda*: "a woman of valor is the crown of her husband."[23] During this second *seuda* we receive one of the levels of the additional Shabbat soul.[24] It is as if we were already at the time of the Ultimate Future, and the *Shekhina* is receiving directly from the higher level of divine revelation as she will then.

As the Ari z"l teaches, the words *"az titanag al Hashem"* which occur in the Shabbat noon Kiddush prayer refer to the fact that the divine

---

21. Gen. 1:31.
22. As Rashi expounds on the first verse of Genesis: the world was created for the Torah, which is called "the beginning of His way," and for Israel, who are called "the first of His crop."
23. Prov. 12:4
24. See Appendix I: Soul Levels.

flow is now pouring down toward the *Shekhina* directly from the Source of divine will. As a result, this is a special time of delight for the *Shekhina*, who is receiving sustenance directly from the higher level of revelation. As long as the *Shekhina* is distanced from the Source, there is no *oneg* (delight) for her; that is why we have to comfort her at the beginning of Shabbat when we sing *Lekha Dodi*. At the end of *Lekha Dodi* we say, "Your God will rejoice over you like a groom is rejoicing over his bride."

In the Shabbat afternoon Mincha prayer the bride's joy is not mentioned, for at this point she has nothing of her own, and there is an expression of *hachnaa* (submission to the higher divine will) more than of joy. In contrast, on Shabbat morning the *Shekhina* goes to a higher level, to the state of *simcha* (joy) and *taanug* (delight), for now she is fulfilled and in her own essence. She and *Zeir Anpin*, her divine counterpart, are now receiving together, as equals, from the higher levels of divine holiness. Hence in the Kiddush prayer we say *az titanag* (she will delight), noticing that *titanag* is a feminine grammatical form. She is in a state of *oneg*, for she is receiving divine flow.[25]

---

25. See *Sefer Beit Genazai: Pitchei Tefilla*, vol. 3, 358.

Chapter 9

Soul Companions

At the third *seuda* we are above emotions.[1] In the afternoon Shabbat prayer we say, "You are One and Your Name is One, and who is like Your people Israel – one nation on earth."[2] These words lead us to the apex of the Shabbat experience.[3]

The Midrash allows us to glimpse a scene in which Shabbat – in other words, the *Shekhina* –complains to *Hakadosh Barukh Hu*, "You gave each one of the weekdays a soul companion, and to me You did not give any!"[4] So Hashem told her, "*Knesset Yisrael* will be your soul companion. And I will be their soul companion, for I also do not have one."

This midrash gives us insight into the spiritual makeup of our relationship with Hashem. The relationship switches back and forth between our acting as soul companions for the *Shekhina* and *Hakadosh Barukh Hu* acting as our soul companion. At the onset of Shabbat the People of Israel sanctify it, thus acting as soul companions of the Shabbat,

---

1. See Chapter 14, "You will call Me *Ishi*."
2. Opening words to the *Kiddushat haYom* blessing of the Shabbat Amida at the time of Mincha.
3. The following teachings are adapted from "Ata Echad veShimcha Echad umi keAmecha Israel," *Sefer Beit Genazai, Pitchei Tefilla*, vol. 3, 371ff.
4. As Rabbi Luria notes, Midrash Rabba expounded by *Machzor Vitri*, 371 side a.

for by means of their divine service at this time they contribute to the *Shekhina*'s ascent from the lower spiritual dimensions. Through our divine service – the Shabbat prayers, the Kiddush over the wine and the *seudot* – we draw light onto the *Shekhina* and bring about her ascent until the moment of the repetition of the *Mussaf Amida* prayer. It is at this point that *Hakadosh Barukh Hu*'s relationship to us as our soul companion leaves the state of potential and becomes actual. In the merit of our efforts, which contributed to the unification of the *Shekhina on High* at the time of *Mussaf*, *Hakadosh Barukh Hu* will now come together with the Community of Israel Themselves.

At the time of Mincha, the unification is not with *Knesset Yisrael* at the level of our collective soul roots on High, but with the collective souls of the People of Israel below. Consequently, it is important for each one of us to have this in mind as we attend Mincha early on Shabbat afternoon.

As mentioned, *Knesset Yisrael Themselves* refers to all of us in the world below in a state of spiritual togetherness under our physical form. We can now think of the words of the Shabbat afternoon *Amida* in the light of the preceding. We say, "You are One, and Your Name is One." And since this came to fulfillment through Israel's participation, when we say "Who is like Your people Israel – one nation on earth," what we are really saying is: "Israel is now Your soul companion!" Hashem's awesome closeness to *Knesset Yisrael Themselves* that comes about at this time will remain vibrant, for it will not be used as an opportunity to ask for our needs, but rather for the mere sake of *devekut* (clinging to Hashem).

In Rabbi Luria's own words:

> This unification will continue until Arvit when we say "You graciously endowed man with knowledge," as is explained in the work *Machberet haKodesh, Shaar haShabbat,* and also in the siddur of Rabbi Shabtai [although the focus of his teachings is different]. The logical argument is that, as the Ari z"l teaches, [the heavenly unification] taking place on Shabbat is alluded to in the expression *shalhevet Yud-Heh* (flame of the Divine). The letters of this expression may be rearranged to form *Shabbat for Hashem*, for

as alluded to in the verse "Many waters cannot extinguish love,"[5] the unification is not meant to provide for our needs, but rather to intensify the *devekut*. As soon as we voice our first request [in the evening *Amida* as Shabbat ends, when we say] "You graciously endowed…," the unification ceases to be. This is then the time in which we ask for Hashem's *noam* (pleasantness) to flow upon us – namely, that the unification with the Community of Israel Themselves, which is the *noam* we are referring to, may continue throughout the weekdays as well.[6]

Rabbi Luria explains elsewhere:[7]

> The divine will to delight in Israel is likened to water, which flows downward and extinguishes fire. Israel's arousal from below is likened to fire that leaps upward. In our present dimension, water douses fire. When the divine will becomes overwhelming in its desire to descend and give to Israel, the result is that we begin to relate to Hashem solely as Provider of our needs. The fire of passion that compels us to rise up to our Beloved and to give pleasure to Him is then doused by materiality. At this level, fire and water are contradictory and cannot exist together. But at the highest level, these two aspects are complementary to the point of becoming one.

Rabbi Luria continues:

> The very pain of the estrangement from Hashem arouses our fire once again, and we become even more inflamed by the desire to cling to Him. We now long to cause Hashem delight by observing His commandments and weaving the consciousness of God into

---

5. Song 8:7.
6. *Sefer Beit Genazai: Pitchei Tefilla* vol 3, 371b.
7. Adapted from Rabbi R. M. Luria, "Maamar Mareh Haseneh," *Sefer Geulat Mitzraim, Kollel Maamarim Ubiurim al Derekh Haavoda Meyusadim al Derekh Ha Ari z"l Luria Be'inian Gezerat Brit Bein Habetarim Veyetziat Mitzraim*) Jerusalem: privately published, 5749), 138-144. See "Introduction: Fiery Coals" in my book *Living Kabbalah*.

our way of life. This consummates in a soul-union at the level of our heavenly souls that arouses the overwhelming divine desire to give. This water then puts out the new fire[.]

However, Rabbi Luria continues, when Israel's arousal from below reaches the point at which "love's sparks become fiery coals," then water cannot put out the fire. The thirst for passionate attachment becomes permanent, so that "many waters cannot extinguish love, nor can rivers drown it." Alas, we are not there yet; and as soon as we voice our first request ("You graciously endow man with knowledge") in the evening *Amida* after the close of Shabbat, the many waters of sustenance that we are requesting will dim the fiery coals of our love sparks.

Even though this first request is of a spiritual nature, still, it will always result in the extinguishing of our fire, until we reach the time of the permanent Shabbat. That is why we say, upon finishing that first weekday *Amida* at the conclusion of Shabbat:[8]

May *Adonai* our God's pleasantness be [i.e. flow down] upon us; May He establish our efforts above in eternity; May He establish our efforts [below in the world].   וִיהִי נֹעַם ה׳ אלקינו עָלֵינוּ וּמַעֲשֵׂה יָדֵינוּ כּוֹנְנָה עָלֵינוּ וּמַעֲשֵׂה יָדֵינוּ כּוֹנְנֵהוּ

We are asking that the intimate closeness with the Community of Israel Themselves may continue throughout the weekdays.

The switching of roles in which we sometimes act as givers and at other times as receivers underlies the divine service of the People of Israel. Every day we help infuse the *Shekhina* with the light she became depleted of when she went down. We do that in different ways; every willing heart sustains her in a particular way. There are men who get up before midnight, the time when, as our sages have expressed it, "*Hakadosh Barukh Hu* delights with the souls of the *tzaddikim* who are studying Torah." At this time the members of the Community of Israel

---

8. Ps. 90:17.

act as soul companions to the *Shekhina,* who went down to the lower spiritual dimension. We thus say in the Midnight Prayer:

> Hashem roars from on High, and from the place of His holiness He lets out His cry. He roars and roars over His habitation[9]
>
> ה׳ מִמָּרוֹם יִשְׁאָג וּמִמְּעוֹן קָדְשׁוֹ יִתֵּן קוֹלוֹ שָׁאֹג יִשְׁאַג עַל נָוֵהוּ

Thus we voice the cry of the *Shekhina* when she is below her level, deprived of her soul companion. The righteous people who are up at this time studying Torah or reading psalms act as soul companions, and in return *Hakadosh Barukh Hu* promises, "And I will be their soul companion."[10]

During the weekday morning *Amida*, particularly when it is recited at the exact point of *netz* (sunrise), by means of our effort to cleanse our souls of past mistakes, we are helping to give back to the holy *Shekhina* the light she left behind upon going down to the lower dimensions. *Hakadosh Barukh Hu* created the world in a way that would enable us to take an active part in the holy task of restoring the *Shekhina's* light in order to give us a share in the running of the world with the light of our Torah observance.[11] With each of the *Amida* blessings we fill the *Shekhina* with the light she became depleted of. As the Talmud teaches,

> Torah scholars increase peace in the world, as it is said:[12] "And all your children will be students of Hashem, and your children will have peace" – do not read "your children *(banayich),"* but "your builders *(bonayich)."*[13]

---

9. Jeremiah 25:30. Translated by Abraham Greenbaum in *The Sweetest Hour: Tikkun Chatzot*; New York, Breslov Research Institute, p. 14.
10. "Ata Echad Veshimcha Echad Umi Keamekha Israel," *Sefer Pitchei Tefilla*, vol. 3, 372b.
11. Rabbi Yaakov Moshe Hillel, *Binyan Ariel* (Jerusalem, Hotzaat Chevrat Ahavat Shalom, 2006), 36, 57.
12. Is. 54:13.
13. Berakhot 64a; cited from the *ArtScroll Siddur*, 185.

Key to the Locked Garden

Yet another way to infuse the *Shekhina* with light in our weekday divine service is to follow the practice of the early chasidim, who, as the Talmud teaches,[14] "would prepare themselves for an hour, pray for an hour, and then wait another hour."

Many have wondered about this statement. One can understand the hour before prayer as a process of divesting themselves of physicality, and even the hour of prayer itself, but why an hour after prayer? And yet, this is when the divine promise of being our soul companion is being fulfilled. After the weekly morning prayer, the *Shekhina* has to descend once again to the lower spiritual dimension until the next prayer – the afternoon *Amida* – and then again till the evening *Amida*. It is at the time of the evening prayer that the *Shekhina* goes down to the lower dimensions to gather the holy particles fallen from her children's souls.[15] When we say the weekly evening prayer, we are participating in the process of elevating the particles. Rabbi Luria thus teaches that in the evening prayer, the heavenly unification is with *Knesset Yisrael Themselves*. *Hakadosh Barukh Hu* comes to be with them in a unification that will protect them throughout the night:[16]

The morning and afternoon prayers [said] in the daylight indicate the *Shekhina*'s closeness at the time of Her plenitude, but the evening prayer alludes to the unification with the Community of Israel at the time of darkness in the nighttime.	תפלת שחרית ומנחה כשיש עוד אור היום מורה על השראת השכינה בעת אורה אבל תפלת ערבית מורה על יחוד [...] עם כנ"י גם בעת חושך ולילה [...]

By saying the weekday evening prayer, we are thus activating divine protection at the time we need it the most!

At the time when the *Shekhina* goes down after the morning prayer, those who are able to stay involved with Torah – whether through Torah study, reading of psalms, preparing the Shabbat *parasha* or other

---

14. Berakhot 32b.
15. "Vayima'asu beEretz Chemda [Beit]," in *Sefer Bet Genazai: Eretz Israel*, vol. I, 57ff.
16. "Jacob Tikken Tefilat Arvit," *Sefer Beit Genazai al haTorah*, 685ff.

such involvement – are acting as her soul companion.[17] Hence Torah sages merit receiving an additional soul every day at the time of prayer just as on Shabbat. Some even merit to retain it during the time of their Torah involvement after morning prayer, with something like the fiery closeness we delight in throughout Shabbat afternoon. Moreover, with every single *mitzva* we fulfill, we are helping build up the holy *Shekhina* and unify her with her Beloved, and in recompense we will merit being part of Hashem's promise, "I will be their soul companion."

---

17. After the Morning Prayer is thus the optimum time to read the verses of the daily section of *Chok LeIsrael*.

Chapter 10

We are the *Kalla*

We have seen that at the time of Mincha, the level of revelation in which Hashem acts as King – *Zeir Anpin* – becomes imbued with a light which is even higher than that of the morning. But in our times, the *Shekhina – Malkhut*, who acts as Queen – is unable to go that high on Shabbat, and so *Malkhut* is not actually imbued with that light.

At the moment when the doors of the Ark are opened to remove the Torah scroll, we say the following verse twice:

| As for me, my prayer to You Hashem in this moment of divine favor, O *Elokim* (just God), in the abundance of Your lovingkindness, answer me with the assurance of Your deliverance. | וַאֲנִי תְפִלָּתִי לְךָ ה' עֵת רָצוֹן אֱ-לֹ-הִי-ם בְּרָב חַסְדֶּךָ עֲנֵנִי בֶּאֱמֶת יִשְׁעֶךָ |

As Rabbi Luria teaches,[1] the Ari z"l explains that in repeating this verse we are voicing the *Shekhina*'s plea for a time of favor.[2]

The first time we say this verse, we are asking that the *Shekhina*, from where she is now, may also receive this lofty light of divine *ratzon* (will). We want to show that, in contrast with the weekdays, this moment of Shabbat is a time of favor and loving compassion, for the concealed divine *ratzon* that gave rise to Creation is now revealed. Rabbi Luria notes that we may see this verse as a continuation of our prayer. The name *Elokim* is one of the holy divine names ascribed to the *Shekhina*: at this highest moment of favor, the *Shekhina* asks that it be divine will to renew Creation for another seven days.[3] The second time we say this verse, we voice her plea: "Answer me with the truth of Your deliverance."

After the reading of the Torah, we recite the Mincha *Amida* prayer. It is then that we merit the awesome closeness in which the *Shekhina* is our soul companion, for the souls of all those praying Mincha now form the spiritual entity of *Knesset Yisrael Themselves*. At this point, we are acting as a *merkava* (vehicle) in which the *Shekhina* ascends to a higher level of divine revelation than at *Mussaf*. The Sages thus teach that on Shabbat our soul ascends together with the heavenly worlds, and at the time of Mincha is the highest ascent of Shabbat.

The question has been asked: "Do we ever see that man's body ascends on Shabbat, [to the point that] at the time of Mincha [we ascend up to] *Arikh Anpin* of *Atzilut*? In fact, it does not move from where it is standing!" And the question is answered: "The refinement of our *mochin* (consciousness) constitutes our ascent."[4] That is, after we merited being instrumental to contribute (to the *Shekhina*'s ascent), we have a renewed ability to cleave to Hashem and Hashem will extend to our consciousness a lofty spiritual influx.

---

1. The teachings that follow are adapted from "VaAni Tefilati lecha H' Et *Ratzon*," *Sefer Pitchei Tefilla*, vol. 3, pp. 364ff.
2. Ps. 69:14. Translation of the first half of Psalm 69:14 is my own, to fit the meaning Rabbi Luria is ascribing to this verse; translation of the second half stems from Avraham Sutton, *Yearning for Redemption*.
3. "Shinuy Tefilot chol veShabbat [dalet]," *Sefer Pitchei Tefilla*, vol. 3, pp. 139ff.
4. The above cited question was quoted in the name of the anonymous work *Tevuot Shemesh* (Jerusalem: Makhon Yam Chokhma, Jerusalem, 5245), 53n63, 53n64.

We are the Kalla

The Ari z"l stresses the important of our reading the prayer "*Uva Letzion*" during the Mincha Prayer on Shabbat afternoon:

Before the Torah scroll is removed from the Ark, we say *Uva Letzion* with the intention of drawing heavenly light toward the world of *Beriya* (Creation), before [the *Shekhina*] receives the light of the Torah scroll. Through the light consequent on our reading *Uva Letzion*, the *Shekhina* will be able to receive as well the loftier light of the Torah scroll.[5]	אנו מקדימין קודם הוצאת ס"ת לומר קדושת ובא לציון אשר ענינה הוא 'המשכת אור אל עו' הבריאה בתחל טרם שתקבל אור הס"ת כנז' כדי שע"י המשכת האור הזה תוכל אחר כך לקבל הארה העליונה של הס"ת [...]:

We also participate in the elevation of the *Shekhina* during Shabbat Mincha when we say the three verses beginning with the word "*tzidkatekha*" (Your righteousness). As we read these three verses, we must have the intention to receive the final level of the Shabbat additional soul.

In the Shabbat afternoon *Amida* we say the words "*tiferet gedulah*" (a splendor of greatness). These words allude to Hashem's pride in us, His special people, for our efforts to be there for Hashem on Shabbat, in general, and our *avodat Hashem* (divine service) in the *Amida* of *Mussaf*, in particular, have contributed to the heavenly unification in the *Mussaf Amida*. The prophet Isaiah expresses this pride in the verse: "Israel, in whom I take glory (*etpaer*)."[6] The word "*etpaer*" (אתפאר) contains three of the letters of the word "*tiferet*" (תִּפְאֶרֶת) and is from the same root. Hashem now considers us what we say next, "*ateret yeshua*" (a crown of salvation). Here again, if we look past the literal translation, we immediately notice the word "*ateret*" (crown), and it brings us back to the *eshet*

---

5. Rabbi Chaim ben Yosef Vital, "Inyan Minchat Shabbat," *Shaar haKavanot: Chelek Sheni* (Jerusalem: Rabbi Tzvi M. Vidavski, 5746), 102b.
6. Is. 49:3.

chayil, who is the *ateret* of her husband. This moment, when we, *Knesset Yisrael* here below, are called *ateret yeshua*, is the height of Shabbat.

We then say, "A day of rest *(menucha)* and holiness you gave to your people." The word *"menucha"* is repeated several times times in this paragraph.[7] This *menucha* does not only refer to restraint from creative activity, for that is only the outer *menucha* which helps us penetrate in the inner recesses of the Shabbat experience. The fruit within the shell is the inner *menucha* of the unification, namely, the higher space of harmony only found in a state of togetherness with the soul companion. We discussed how a woman only attains true *menucha* in her husband's home. The word *"menucha"* thus alludes to that special fiery closeness whose apex is in the Shabbat afternoon *Amida*. And we say: "*menucha shlema sheAta rotze bah* (a perfect rest which You desire)," for if it can be said Hashem desires this as well and so this moment is brought about from Above.

We conclude this paragraph with the words:

| May Your children recognize and know that from You comes their *menucha*, and through their *menucha* they will sanctify Your Name. | יַכִּירוּ בָנֶיךָ וְיֵדְעוּ כִּי מֵאִתְּךָ הִיא מְנוּחָתָם וְעַל מְנוּחָתָם יַקְדִּישׁוּ אֶת שְׁמֶךָ: |

By this time, we are ready to die for *Kiddush Hashem* (sanctification of Hashem). Upon saying the final words of the paragraph about sanctifying Hashem's Name, we may imagine that we are in the hands of an enemy who is compelling us to perform an act of idolatry, and that rather than fall into idolatry, we are surrendering our life in *Kiddush Hashem*.

When we show our total commitment to *avodat Hashem* so that not even our life stands in the way, we are able to receive the divine flow of *Atika Kadisha* at the level of *Keter* that Hashem is directing downward at this point.

---

7. See on this topic "Yom Menucha Ukedusha," *Sefer Beit Genazai: Maamarei Shabbat*, 2nd ed., 597ff.

In the light of this, we understand why we were called earlier *goy echad* (one nation) in the *Amida* of Mincha ("You are One and Your Name is One; and who is like Your people Israel, one nation on earth"). The word "One" *(echad)* alludes to the light of *Atika Kadisha* as revealed in the Thirteen Attributes of Mercy that are thought of as one single entity. At that level, divine lovingkindness is as unconditional as it is complete, and this is where we are now. It is at this moment of the Shabbat experience that we can fully say: "Hashem, Your children will know that *meitkha* (from you) stems their *menucha*." If we pay attention to the Hebrew letters of *meitkha* (מֵאִתְּךָ), we first notice *me et* (מֵאֵת), meaning 'from' and then the letter *kaf* (כ), the initial letter of *Keter* (כתר). That is where our *menucha* stems from at this time.

Three steps backward: the spiritual delight of closeness to Hashem is no longer as vibrant as during the *Amida* prayer. However, its impression remains with us throughout the ensuing the third Shabbat meal, the highest of Shabbat, for at this time *we, Knesset Yisrael, are the kalla*.

The quality of time on Shabbat afternoon is reflected in the verse about the Patriarch Jacob just before he had his dream of the heavenly ladder:[8]

| He encountered the place and spent the night there because the sun had set.[9] | וַיִּפְגַּע בַּמָּקוֹם וַיָּלֶן שָׁם כִּי בָא הַשֶּׁמֶשׁ |

Rashi expresses difficulty in understanding this verse because, according to the rules of Hebrew grammar, it should have said that the sun was sinking in the horizon and so Jacob had to spend the night there. However, that is not what the verse says. The words *"ki ba hashemesh"* (because the sun had set) imply that the sun set *for him*, suddenly, not in its normal time, so that he should spend the night there.

---

8. Gen. 28:11.
9. Based on "Vayalan Sham ki Ba Hashemesh," in *Sefer Beit Genazai al HaTorah: Bereshit*, vol. 2, 692ff.

Key to the Locked Garden

The Midrash teaches that Jacob tried to go forward on his journey; but all of a sudden the world stood like a wall before him, for the sun had set. The Hebrew words *"ki ba"* (had set) should thus be read as one single word – *kiba* (extinguished) – as if Hashem had turned off the lamp of the sun prematurely, not in its normal time, in order to speak with His beloved Jacob in privacy. The Midrash likens this to a king who receives the sudden visit of a beloved friend and requests, "Extinguish the lanterns, for I want to speak to my friend in privacy." In a similar way, *Hakadosh Barukh Hu* extinguished the sunlight in order to speak to Jacob privately.

It seems challenging to understand this Midrash; it is not clear how the presence of others may detract from the quality of a meeting, since the others are unable to hear the conversation. Similarly, we have mentioned how a non-Jew who keeps Shabbat is liable to the death penalty, and the severity of the punishment is explained by the analogy of a king who is together with his wife the queen and a person comes and puts his head in between them. Again, it is not evident how a non-Jew who observes Shabbat is interrupting the togetherness between *Hakadosh Barukh Hu* and Israel.

We have to discuss two concepts in this context: one is *daat* (intimate knowledge) and the other one is *hasachat hadaat*. *Daat* is the intimate knowledge of divine love; its essential feature is *hasachat hadaat* (total exclusivity). When such a bond is present, there is no room for anything else. The bond of *daat* between the Holy One and the Children of Israel is expressed by the prophet:[10]

You alone have I loved (*yadati*) among all the families of the earth.	רַק אֶתְכֶם יָדַעְתִּי מִכֹּל מִשְׁפְּחוֹת הָאֲדָמָה:

As soon as there is any other element present, the intimate knowledge of *daat* no longer applies.[11] We thus find that Moses Rabbenu asked

---

10. Amos 3:2; my translation based on Rabbi Luria's teachings.
11. The following explanation stems from Rabbi Luria's essay "Yikavu haMayim el Makom Echad," in *Sefer Beit Genazai 'al haTorah: Bereshit I*, p. 51ff.

Hakadosh Barukh Hu that His *Shekhina* should dwell exclusively upon the People of Israel: "I and Your people should be set apart from all the people who are on the face of this earth."[12] Rashi explains his request: "That You should no longer rest Your *Shekhina* upon the other nations of the world."[13]

Here too, Moses's prayer seems difficult to understand, for what wrong would there be if the *Shekhina*'s Presence would dwell on righteous members of the world nations if they are worthy of it? The answer is that the word "*Daat*" really points to the unification on High between *Hakadosh Barukh Hu* and the collective souls of Israel. Moses was thus asking that the unification should only be between the Holy One and the Community of Israel. If the *Shekhina* were to dwell with the nations as well, the quality of *devekut* between Israel and *Hakadosh Barukh Hu* would diminish.

We have seen how, in contrast with all other *mitzvot*, keeping Shabbat has the special purpose we state in the Shabbat afternoon *Amida*: "May Your children realize that their rest [and all that their rest involves] really comes from You." This "rest" alludes to a time of intimate knowledge of love demanding exclusivity. We have to be totally engrossed in this time of closeness and oblivious of any reason for sadness or worry, as if we had finished all we ever had to do. We have to focus on our love and attachment to *Hakadosh Barukh Hu* to the exclusion of everything else.

In the light of the preceding, we may reconsider the Midrash's story of the king and his visitor. The king wants total privacy with his beloved; he wants no one else around so he can focus on his bond with the beloved, without diverting his attention to anything else. And that is what Jacob's encounter is trying to teach us. The sun set in order to indicate the quality of bond that Hashem wants with all the Children of Israel who were to descend from Jacob: an intimate bond of love and attachment in which there is nothing that could distract our attention from this bond.

This silent divine request may seem a challenge, particularly in our times, in which there are so many distractions. However, equipped with the consciousness of the additional Shabbat soul, we may aspire

---

12. Ex. 33:16.
13. Berakhot 7a.

to such a bond... if that is what we aim for, if that is what we yearn for with every fiber of our being. Our Sages have pointed out that while the Patriarch Abraham referred to as the Temple site as *har* (mountain), and Isaac referred to it as *sadeh* (field), Jacob referred to the Temple site as *bayit* (home). "Home" is a defined and limited space in which no outside presence is allowed. Shabbat is called *nachalat* Jacob *avikha* (an inheritance of our father Jacob)[14] because these words convey the significance of Shabbat: an innerspace of total union, of total privacy from outside interference.

The statement of the Sages that Jacob received a boundless inheritance may thus refer to that type of *devekut* not limited by a foreign element that detracts from the full revelation of the intimate bond. And Hashem's closeness with *Knesset Yisrael*, as it manifests during the afternoon Shabbat prayer, whose *reshimu* (impression) remains with us throughout the Third Meal, has the same quality of totally focused attachment as that we see in Jacob's encounter with Hashem at dusk.

There is a second reason why Jacob is the one to show us this intimate bond with Hashem that we have mostly on Shabbat. The unique love that Jacob and his beloved wife Rachel shared helped arouse the love of Bride and Groom on High. This heavenly love was then extended to *Knessed Yisrael Below*.

A man who relates to his wife the way that Jacob related to Rachel does not speak of loving his wife; what he feels for her is more than love. It is as if his wife is part of his very being; in this sense, his love is beyond emotions. The emotions may be seen as a type of light in the sense that we know where we are – we are able to identify our feelings. There are times in which we may be past emotions, however, and one who looks within at this time of Shabbat may realize that it is not love of Hashem that s/he finds, but rather the infinite yearning to fuse with the Source. In a similar way, by the time we sit down to have the third Shabbat *seuda*, we ourselves are beyond the level of emotions.

---

14. Is. 58:14.

Chapter 11

A Tunnel under the Throne of Glory

By the time we are ready to sit down to the third *seuda*, we should have already said Mincha, and so the lofty light from the concealed divine will is coming down. With the help of the coming *seuda* we are now able to draw it down to ourselves; that is why this is the highest point for us. (For the *Shekhina on High,* the highest moment was during *Mussaf* when she was getting divine flow directly from the Source.)

When we sit down to the third meal, after the special meeting of the afternoon *Amida* when we were called goy echad (one nation), we are acting as the *eshet chayil* who arouses divine pride. It is important to sit together to partake of the third Shabbat *seuda,* for only when we do so, representing *Knesset Yisrael,* are we acting as soul companions sharing in the joy of the Beloved by enjoying a special *seuda* together.

On a practical level, one who wants to act as a soul companion will make sure s/he eats less at the second *seuda* so s/he can be there to honor Hashem at the third meal. What is more, whenever it is possible, s/he will try to say the morning prayer earlier so that s/he can have the second *seuda* earlier as well.

The Ari z"l notes that at the third *seuda* we do not say Kiddush over the wine as in the other two *seudot*. We are encouraged to drink wine after reciting the appropriate blessing, but toward the middle of the meal and not at the beginning as at the other *seudot*.[1]

At the third Shabbat meal, we may have in mind that we are eating from the divine flow coming downward from the space of the concealed divine will.[2] This is the highest moment of Shabbat, and yet we do not say the paragraph *yismechu beMalkhutekha* (we will rejoice in Your Kingship) at Mincha. In a similar way, it is not joy that we are experiencing at the Third Meal; we have entered a state which is beyond joy, and we are quietly savoring it.

In order to understand, let us consider the Patriarch Isaac, who went to Mount Moria to pour out his soul in prayer, asking for his wife Rebecca to have a child. The sages tell us that Rebecca was barren and it is forbidden to pray for a miracle that would involve changing the laws of nature. For instance, a man whose wife is pregnant may not pray for his wife to have a boy: the baby is already in her womb, and if it be a girl, praying for a boy would be a request for a miracle.

We thus see that the Patriarch Abraham did not pray for his wife Sarah to have a child. When he was speaking to Hashem, he just made a statement of fact: "See, to me You have given no offspring."[3] And we may surmise that this was one reason why Jacob did not pray for Rachel to become pregnant.

Now let us look at the situation regarding Isaac. The verse says: "Isaac entreated Hashem in the presence of his wife."[4] This, according to the Midrash, is as if he were digging a tunnel under the Throne of Glory from within and she from without. Digging a tunnel under the Throne of Glory may be understood as attaining such a deep level of *teshuva* (repentance) that one reaches the first emanation of *teshuva* before the Creation of this world. When a person repairs his past to that extent, s/he

---

1. Rabbi Chaim Vital in the name of his teacher, the Ari z"l. See *Pri Etz Chaim: Shaar haShabbat*, Perek 24 (Jerusalem: Rabbi Tzvi M. Vidavski, 5748), 444.
2. Adapted from "Et Ratzon Beseudat Shlishit," in *Sefer Pitchei Tefilla*, vol. 3, 377ff.
3. Gen. 15:3.
4. Gen. 15:3.

A Tunnel under the Throne of Glory

is distanced from our dimension and somehow may possibly bypass the system of justice that Hashem established in the world.

Although it is forbidden for us to pray for a change in the laws of nature, there is a dimension on High in which the *hanhaga* (divine conduct of affairs) is above the laws of nature. In that space, there is no clear distinction between "within nature" and "above nature." A seventeenth-century commentator, Rabbi Menachem Recanati, points out that the Bible uses the expression *al Hashem* (literally: above Hashem) when speaking of prayers for sustenance as well as offspring. Sustenance and offspring are "above" the aspect of Hashem acting as King and Judge which is revealed to us on the weekdays, and which is referred to as "Hashem" i.e. The Name spelled with four letters, because they come to us from that dimension on High. Thus when asking for a child, Hannah prays *al Hashem*,[5] and King David tells us: "Cast what you conceive as your destiny *al Hashem* and He will sustain you."[6]

We may wonder how the Midrash arrived at the comparison of Isaac and Rebecca's prayer to the digging of a tunnel into higher dimensions. Evidently this is based on the word *vayeatar* (וַיֶּעְתַּר), translated above as "entreated."

To understand what a Hebrew word is trying to convey, we always look at the three-letter root from which the word stems. The root of וַיֶּעְתַּר is made up of the letters ע, ת, ר – which can also be read as the word *eter*, meaning "shovel" or "pitchfork." The Talmud explains that the prayer of the righteous is sometimes likened to a shovel, for just as the shovel moves the grain from one place to another, so the righteous turn divine decrees from strict justice to compassion.

The verse states that Isaac entreated Hashem *lenochach* (לְנֹכַח) his wife. The Zohar tells us that he dug a channel for his prayer to reach the space known in Aramaic as *mazala* – in Hebrew *mazal elyon* – meaning the lofty dimension on High, at the level of the concealed divine will, from which stems the divine decision to bestow offspring.[7] The numeric value of the word *mazala* is the same as that of the word *"nochach* (in the

---

5. I Samuel 1:10.
6. Ps. 55:23.
7. Zohar, *Toldot* 137b.

Key to the Locked Garden

presence of)".[8] Thus by saying that Isaac "dug a tunnel," the Midrash is suggesting that he ascended to the dimension on High in which there is no difference between something which is in accordance with nature and something which breaks the laws of nature.

The Hebrew word *"mazal"* is usually rendered as "destiny." It refers specifically to the influence of the constellations. Thus the Sages emphasize: *ein mazal le Israel* (the People of Israel are not influenced by the constellations). Still, in our context, the word *"mazal"* may be related to *"yizal* (flow)*"*, as in the verse[9] "the water shall flow *(yizal)* from his wells," thus indicating that what man sees as 'destiny' really flows down from a lofty space on High.[10] The expression *"mazal elyon"* links us back to the concept of *teshuva* that was created before the world itself. Moses attained this primordial level of *teshuva* before he could receive the Second Tablets that Hashem transmitted to him.[11]

Neither Abraham nor Jacob asked for offspring; and in the case of Isaac, there is a very interesting verse: "The man became great. He continued to grow until he became very great."[12] This is usually interpreted as referring to his growing wealth. However, we could also read it as saying that Isaac may have been allowed to ascend to this higher dimension in which Providence is not limited by nature.

In a similar way, when the Children of Israel were sandwiched between the Sea of Reeds and the angry Egyptians, their first reaction was to pray. However, it became known to them that the normal channels of prayer would not lead them to the type of salvation they needed, which was a miracle breaking the laws of nature.

In truth, the very existence of the People of Israel is above nature in every way, and they are guided by a divine flow in which what is "within nature" and what is "above nature" merge into one. For instance, in the time of the prophet Isaiah, King Hezekiah incurred a

---

8. From the Kabbalistic work *Machane Ephraim*.
9. Numbers 24:7.
10. The teaching about the Thirteen Attributes stems from Rabbi Jacob S. Kassin, *Till Eternity: With explanations of the underlying reasons for the commandments and their esoteric significance* (Lakewood, N.J.: Orot Publications, 2006), 377.
11. Tractate Rosh Hashana 17b; cited in Rabbi Kassin, op. cit., 377.
12. Gen. 26:13. Literal translation my own.

dangerous illness, and as he felt his life coming to an end, he asked that the prophet be summoned.[13] Isaiah arrived and told the king that his death had been decreed on High – as a divine reaction to his conscious decision to transgress the commandment to procreate. The Talmud explains that the righteous Hezekiah had seen in a prophetic trance that his child would be a wrongdoer and had not wanted to increase evil in the world.[14] King Hezekiah entreated the prophet to pray on his behalf. The prophet, unmoved, stated that the king's death warrant had already been signed. The king, according to the Talmud, then told the prophet: "It was handed down to me from the house of my father's father *(avi aba)* that even if a sharp sword is pointed at a man's neck, he should not despair of mercy." As the chasidic master from Ruzhin taught, the expression *avi aba* designates the world of divine will which is above that of *Atzilut*.

Let us try to understand what that high dimension relates to in terms of our divine service. Relating to Hashem through love, fear, or even attachment, may be seen as garments or veils whose effect is to diminish the intimate connection with the Beloved. Above that is the total surrender to divine will. One who is at that level – in which s/he has no will other than what Hashem wants – is able to connect to that lofty dimension.

After the Shabbat Mincha prayer, we *are* at that lofty space. It is at this moment of Shabbat that we are able to connect to Hashem at the lofty level we are referring to. We have gone through love and awe of Hashem on Shabbat eve, love and delight during the morning of Shabbat. Now, after the Mincha afternoon prayer, we are ready to make that last climb to the space in which we want passionately what Hashem wants.

We thus silently echo the *Shekhina*'s plea that Creation be renewed for another seven days, that we may once again taste the honey of this closeness on the following Shabbat,[15] and more still, that we may draw it to our relationship on the weekdays.

---

13. See Kings II, ch. 20, and Isaiah, ch.38.
14. Tractate Berakhot 10b.
15. *Sefer Beit Genazai: Pitchei Tefilla*, vol. 3, 140.

Key to the Locked Garden

TAKING LEAVE OF THE SHABBAT QUEEN

The Ari z"l teaches that as Shabbat comes to an end, at the moment of sunset, we should say the verse referred to as *"Vihi noam"*:[16]

May *Adonai* our God's pleasantness be [i.e. flow down] upon us. May He establish our efforts above in ternity. May He establish our efforts below in the world. וִיהִי נֹעַם ה' אלהינו עָלֵינוּ וּמַעֲשֵׂה יָדֵינוּ כּוֹנְנָה עָלֵינוּ וּמַעֲשֵׂה יָדֵינוּ כּוֹנְנֵהוּ

Rabbi Chaim Vital explains[17] that two kinds of flows of holiness come to us on Shabbat: one kind comes through the Shabbat *seudot*, while the other comes through the Shabbat prayers. We draw the Shabbat lights to us as an inner light by means of the three Shabbat prayers, and as a surrounding light by means of the Shabbat *seudot*. We want to draw these two types of holiness to ourselves for the coming weekdays. By saying the verse *Vihi noam*, we will draw Shabbat's inner light into our souls; by means of the *Melave Malka* (Shabbat conclusion meal), we will elevate all the meals that we will have throughout the weekdays.

We note that we do not say *Vihi noam* at the close of the three festivals, even though we also receive a supplement of holiness during the festivals. A brief aside on the difference between the festivals and Shabbat will help us understand this difference:

The *Rishonim* (Early Sages) teach that Shabbat is different from the festivals in that it carries an obligation of *oneg* (delight), whereas when it comes to the festivals our obligation is one of *simcha* (joy). What is the difference between *simcha* and *oneg*?

The Sages teach that one who prays *Arvit* at the onset of Shabbat and says *Vaychulu* is considered Hashem's partner in the work of Creation.[18] Rabbi Luria explains that when you say *Vaychulu* on Shabbat eve you are stating your belief that Hashem created the world as if you had seen the Creation

---

16. Ps. 90:17.
17. *Shaar Hakavanot Chelek Beit*, 17.
18. See Chapter Two, "Fiery Coals of Love."

with your eyes. Not only that, but you are also affirming your belief that the world was created out of kindness. You are transmitting your consciousness that all that Hashem did was for Israel's benefit and that there is nothing bad in it. You are making this statement as if you yourself had participated in the work of Creation, and you are not dismayed at anything that happens in the world. This is *oneg*, delight. It is the state of one who is content with all that surrounds him and sees lovingkindness in all that happens to him.

Joy, however, is possible without this state of total contentment. A person can be joyful when happens that causes him to forget about what he is lacks, though the lack may be causing him anguish and a broken heart. If it were not that joy filled his entire being, he would look around and realize that there were many things to mar his joy.

Joy thus comes from an exterior thing that causes your enthusiasm, leading you to forget everything else, whereas delight is within you: your entire being is permeated with delight and you feel that all is well.

This helps us grasp the difference between the festivals and Shabbat. On each of the festivals we have a specific cause of joy. At Passover our joy stems from liberation from bondage, at Shavuot from the giving of the Torah, and on Sukkot our heart swells with a spiritual elevation derived from direct contact with the lights of the Clouds of Glory, to the point that we forget our sorrows.

On Shabbat, however,[19] there is a special illumination enabling man to say *Vaychulu* as if he had been made a partner to Creation and he were able to see that all that goes on in the world is good. Everything that happens is an act of lovingkindness and there no evil whatsoever; we feel that had we been active partners in Creation we would have done things in the same way. Everything is very good – whether for the collective or for each individual soul.

This state of mind stems from the bright faith in the closeness between the Holy One and the Community of Israel which is the precious gift that is revealed on Shabbat. The special closeness between Hashem and the Community of Israel that we experience on Shabbat makes us give Him everything we have – our joys, our worries, our

---

19. Rabbi Luria cites the teaching that follows in the name of the commentator known as *Kol Bo*.

Key to the Locked Garden

sorrows, our lacks – much as a wife gives all she has to her husband in the inner trust that he is going to do his best to fulfill her every need.

The Ari z"l thus tells us that before the impression left by the lofty Shabbat *yichud* – referred to as *noam* (pleasantness) – has left us, we should say, "May Hashem our God's pleasantness be [i.e. flow down] upon us." That is, on the weekdays we should also be inspired by *devekut* to our Maker, and the Shabbat *noam* should not cease after *Arvit*, when we must come back down to the world of *Asiya*, referred to as *maase yadeinu* (our efforts).

Ten minutes before the end of Shabbat, we should say *Petichat Eliyahu* (see the appendix "Mystical Readings," page ___.) This is a composition in Aramaic, written by the prophet Elijah, which includes the main elements of the "divine plan." Many laymen begin their morning as well as afternoon prayers by reading Petichat Eliyahu, for it sensitizes the reader to the situation of the *Shekhina* and is said to open one's heart, thus improving the quality of the coming prayer. At the end of *Petichat Eliyahu* we can hear the loving voice of *Hakadosh Barukh Hu* comforting the *Shekhina*:[20]

| Hakadosh Barukh Hu said: Do you think that since the Temple was destroyed I have gone back up to My Temple on High? Not so! I have not been there ever since you were exiled. | אֶלָּא אָמַר קֻדְשָׁא בְּרִיךְ הוּא. אַנְתְּ חָשַׁבְתְּ דְּמִיּוֹמָא דְאִתְחֲרַב בֵּי מַקְדְּשָׁא דְּעָאלְנָא בְּבֵיתָא דִילִי וְעָאלְנָא בְּיִשּׁוּבָא, לָאו הָכִי, דְּלָא עָאלְנָא כָּל זִמְנָא דְאַנְתְּ בְּגָלוּתָא. |

Five minutes before the end of Shabbat, we should start *Arvit*.

ATA CHONANTANU (YOU HAVE GRACED US WITH INTELLIGENCE)

In the *Amida* for Motzaei Shabbat we add a paragraph to the fourth blessing (*Ata Chonantanu* [You have graced us with intelligence]). The added paragraph praises Hashem for separating light from darkness and the seventh day from the six weekdays. Why do we have to add a blessing to our *Amida* prayer addressing the transition from a day of light

---

20. Cited from Rabbi Avraham Sutton's unpublished translation of *Petichat Eliyahu* (available from the author on request).

and holiness to a time of darkness and weekday consciousness? The same question, Rabbi Luria notes, can be asked about the blessing we pronounce in our Havdala ritual, *"Baruch Ata Hashem... Hamavdil ben kodesh lechol* (Blessed are You Hashem [...] Who separates between holy and secular)." Why would we make such a blessing? Wouldn't it be good if Shabbat remained for a longer time?

On every Shabbat, we complete a spiritual structure that we began to build on the preceding Sunday, the first day of the week. Therefore, at the end of every Shabbat there is a renewal of our divine service, and the blessing we recite during Havdala does not address the Shabbat which just ended, but rather our new beginning. Even though our spiritual building begins with darkness and weekday consciousness, its purpose is precisely to lighten this darkness. Our endeavor thus warrants a blessing praising the Master of the world for permitting us to have a new spiritual beginning, as if we were born anew. The difference between Shabbat and the weekdays is like that between light and darkness; there is a complete concealment of the Shabbat light. But the purpose of the concealment is to enable us to begin anew; for as long at the preceding light continues to shine, there is no point trying to build it once again.

Psalm 30 ("A chant song for cutting away the barriers that prevent the dedication of the Temple")[21] shows a similar development: "Hashem, I will exalt You, for Your have raised me up from the depths." The Hebrew expression *ki dilitani* (for You have raised me up from the depths) stems from the word *"dal* (poor)," indicating that whenever we are facing a new spiritual enterprise we must convey our grateful awareness that we able to participate in this new beginning.

In light of the preceding, we may understand why after each of our festivals there is a day called *Isru Chag,* in which the *reshimu* (impression) of the festival's light remains on the day after the close of the festival. After Shabbat there is no *Isru Chag.* According to the Ari z"l, the reason is that the light of Shabbat is so high that it does not leave a *reshimu.* Rabbi Luria explains that our festivals are days in which we receive a new spiritual flow that will enrich our divine service in the days to come; the *reshimu* is thus an essential part of

---

21. Rabbi Avraham Sutton, *Yearning for Redemption: The Psalms of King David.* (Jerusalem, self-published, 2011), 36-37.

Key to the Locked Garden

the festival in which we will integrate the new spiritual flow. For instance, on Pesach (Passover) we receive the light of *geula* (Redemption) and on Shavuot we receive the Torah anew. On each of the festivals, the light we integrate will help us to continue growing in the direction of what we have received.

In contrast, Shabbat marks the end of the structure we have been working on all week long; and so there must perforce be a total absence of light at the close of Shabbat, in order to permit us to begin gathering a totally new light in the days to come. The six weekdays after Shabbat are thus a time of building. (After each Rosh Hashana we face a similar time of renewal.) Our Sages have taught that having hot liquids on Motzaei Shabbat strengthens us; for at this time when we are planning a new beginning, we are presently facing lack and darkness and need healing and support.

MOTZAEI SHABBAT PRAYERS

Upon finishing the *Amida* prayer on Motzaei Shabbat, before reciting Psalm 121 to conclude our *Arvit* (evening prayer,) we insert our prayers for the coming week. Before the beginning of these prayers, according to Rabbi Mordechai Eliyahu, we should say the following:

I hereby prepare myself to receive the light of the Shabbat supplement for the weekdays. With the help of Hashem I will thus become sanctified during the weekdays from the Shabbat holiness, as Hashem our God commanded us in His holy Torah: "Sanctify yourselves and be holy." May it be Your will, Hashem, my God and God of my ancestors, to accept [our prayer] as if we had in mind all the *kavanot* (intentions) one should have at this time.	הֲרֵינִי מֵכִין עַצְמִי לְקַבֵּל אוֹר תּוֹסֶפֶת קְדֻשַּׁת שַׁבָּת לִימֵי הַחֹל, וְאֶתְקַדֵּשׁ בְּעֶזְרַת ה' יִתְבָּרַךְ בִּימֵי הַחֹל מִקְּדֻשַּׁת הַשַּׁבָּת, כְּמוֹ שֶׁצִּוָּנוּ ה' אֱלֹקֵינוּ בְּתוֹרָתוֹ הַקְּדוֹשָׁה: וְהִתְקַדִּשְׁתֶּם וִהְיִיתֶם קְדֹשִׁים. וִיהִי רָצוֹן, מִלְּפָנֶיךָ ה' אֱלֹקֵינוּ וֵאלֹהֵי אֲבוֹתֵינוּ שֶׁיַּעֲלֶה לְפָנֶיךָ כְּאִלּוּ כִּוַּנּוּ בְּכָל הַכַּוָּנוֹת הָרְאוּיוֹת לְכַוֵּן בָּזֶה:

We recite the following verses while standing up:

Return Hashem, how much longer will Your anger last? Reconsider, and think favorably about Your servants. Saturate us every morning with Your lovingkindness; when we know that You love us we will be able to sing with happiness and rejoice throughout all our days and even the dark nights of our suffering. Grant us joy corresponding to the number of days of our affliction; grant us years for every day we saw trouble.

שׁוּבָה ה׳ עַד מָתָי וְהִנָּחֵם עַל עֲבָדֶיךָ: שַׂבְּעֵנוּ בַבֹּקֶר חַסְדֶּךָ וּנְרַנְּנָה וְנִשְׂמְחָה בְּכָל יָמֵינוּ: שַׂמְּחֵנוּ כִּימוֹת עִנִּיתָנוּ שְׁנוֹת רָאִינוּ רָעָה וִיהִי נֹעַם ה׳ אלקינו עָלֵינוּ וּמַעֲשֵׂה יָדֵינוּ כּוֹנְנָה עָלֵינוּ וּמַעֲשֵׂה יָדֵינוּ כּוֹנְנֵהוּ:

May *Adonai* our God's pleasantness be [i.e. flow down] upon us. May He establish our efforts above in eternity. May He establish our efforts below in the world.

We then recite Psalm 91 in its entirety, repeating the last verse.[22]

We then sit down and recite the latter part of the prayer *Uva leTzion*, beginning with the words "*VeAta Kadosh.*" We conclude the *Arvit* service with Psalm 121 and the *Aleinu*.

---

22. *The Complete ArtScroll Siddur, Nusach Sephard*, notes in the name of the commentator Abudarham, that Psalm 91 contains 124 words and a repetition of the psalm would yield 248 words, a number equivalent to the number of our body parts, thus symbolizing Hashem's protection of every part of those who serve Him. Rather than repeating the entire psalm it has become the custom to repeat the last verse, *orech yamim* (with long life). *The Complete ArtScroll Siddur, Nusach Sephard*, 640-641. Women should thus repeat this last verse twice, for a woman has 252 body parts.

Key to the Locked Garden

After saying *Vihi noam* and the prayers that follow it,[23] we say Havdala, the Shabbat conclusion service.[24]

In his chapter on the Havdala service,[25] Rabbi Luria emphasizes the correlation between Shabbat and our Holy Temple. On Shabbat it is as if the Temple was rebuilt and standing on its premises. We thus sing in one of the *zemirot* (holy songs):[26] "Those who love Hashem and anticipate the rebuilding of the *Ariel* [holy Temple], celebrate and rejoice on the Shabbat day as at the Giving of the Torah." *Malkhut*'s elevation on Shabbat is pitted against her impending descent at the close of Shabbat. At her root on High, *Malkhut* remains connected to a lofty level. However, *Malkhut* accepted the divine request to distance herself from her Source and go down to the worlds below every night for the sake of her children, for the sake of all the souls who benefit greatly from her intervention.

In the Hallel, the sequence of psalms of praise which we recite on Rosh Hodesh and festivals, there is the verse "The stone the builders despised has become the cornerstone."[27] The stone stands for *Malkhut*, who will eventually ascend to her Source on High. In the Ultimate Future she will become what we sing about her at the beginning of her *seuda* meal: the *eshet chayil* (woman of valor),[28] who, as King Solomon says elsewhere and we sing in *Lekha Dodi*, is "a crown for her husband."[29]

Inside the Temple there were elements whose light was very lofty: the Holy of Holies, the Cherubs, the holy Ark, the Menora, etc. The outside of the Temple, in contrast, was made of stones. How could it be, asks Rabbi Luria, that all these lofty lights were surrounded by mere stones? The makeup of the Temple building is alluded to in the verse "the stone the builders despised." While the Temple was standing on its premises, the lofty source of *Malkhut* was revealed, for there were many open miracles. Alas, after its destruction, all we have left is the Western

---

23. See *The Complete ArtScroll Siddur, Nusach Sephard*, 639-643.
24. The teaching that follows is adapted from Rabbi Moshe Luria, "Havdala al Hayayin Betzet HaShabbat," *Sefer Pitchei Tefilla*, vol. 3, 391-394.
25. Ibid.
26. *Kol Mekadesh Shevii.*
27. Ps. 118:22.
28. Prov. 31:10-31.
29. Prov. 12:4.

A Tunnel under the Throne of Glory

Wall, a wall of stones, and *Malkhut* – our *Shekhina* – is in concealment. It is as if we had returned to "the stone the builders despised." Our prayer is that *Malkhut* should go back to being the cornerstone, with the light shining on her as on the Temple days.

In a similar way, when Shabbat begins, we celebrate with wine and song as we look forward to being part of the *Malkhut's* ascent. However, there is also a special value in *Malkhut's* descent on the weekdays, for the holy purpose of this descent is that *Malkhut* gathers and collects the fallen holy lights, in order to benefit us. Furthermore, *Malkhut's* ability to ascend on High on Shabbat is due precisely to her descent to the lower worlds in the weekday and her gathering all the fallen lights of holiness that she will elevate on the following Shabbat. The inner purpose of the Havdala prayer is thus to show that *Malkhut's* descent to the lower worlds is a preparation for the following Shabbat.

Just as we brought in the Shabbat with wine and song, we take leave of Shabbat in Havdala with wine and song, celebrating *Malkhut's* descent in order to prepare the lights of holiness of the Shabbat to come. She goes down from her present greatness, but it is all for the sake of the holiness of the next Shabbat. Hence she is still referred to as *Malkhut* in her descent, for its purpose is building Hashem's Kingship with the intention that it should be complete.

After the blessing on the wine, we breathe in the scent of fragrant herbs to revive our *nefesh*, comforting it for its loss of the additional Shabbat soul supplement. Then we recite the blessing *Borei meorei haesh* (who creates the illuminations of fire) on a lit candle with intertwined wicks. The creation of fire was in the divine thought; but it only materialized after the first Shabbat, when the Holy One inspired Adam to rub two stones together. Rabbi Luria tells us how, according to the Ari z"l,[30] upon reciting *Borei meorei haesh,* we should have in mind that the verse, "For Hashem your God – He is a consuming fire,"[31] refers to *Malkhut*. At the end of Shabbat, the *gevurot* (forces of strict justice, which is associated with fire) are in the ascendancy. We say *Borei meorei haesh* with the

---

30. Cited from "Birkat Meorei HaEsh," *Sefer Pitchei Tefilla,* vol. 3, 390.
31. Deut. 4:24.

inner intention to convey that we have no connection with the *gevurot*. Our bond is only with the Creator, for He is our God.

Rabbi Luria points out the seeming contradiction in this blessing: why are we reciting a blessing which celebrates the *gevurot* that are now in the ascendancy, but on the other hand affirms that we have no connection with them – only with the Creator? He explains that the *gevurot* fulfill a purpose in the world and benefit our divine service; we thus recite a blessing over them. However, because the outside forces attach themselves to them, we emphasize that our blessing is to Him Who creates the illumination of fire, and that in their Source the *gevurot* are a divine creation to further the forces of holiness in the world.

As we brace ourselves for the week to come, we must attempt to retain the consciousness that was with us during Shabbat. We thus ask that Hashem's pleasantness – namely, the light of the *yichud* – flow down upon us, that the consciousness that the purpose of Creation is the attachment to our Maker may remain with us during the week. We then say Psalm 91, the purpose of which is to protect us from difficult occurrences.[32]

Our request that the *noam* of Shabbat remain upon us is not merely a prayer for spiritual delight. During the weekdays the impulse for evil is ever arousing in us temptations for the pleasures of this world. We thus ask to remain inspired by the spiritual delight of Shabbat so that we do not risk falling as we are drawn to physical pleasures. We also ask, "May He establish our efforts below in the world"; for as the holy chasidic master Baal Shem Tov taught, the soul of the People of Israel stems from the world of *taanug* (delight). It is thus while inspired by spiritual delight that it distances itself from the temptation of material pleasures.

According to Rabbi Luria, there is another interpretation of the blessing over fire in the Havdala closing service, based on the inner dimension of the Torah.[33] We begin Shabbat by igniting two candles, and we end with a blessing over the ignited multiple wicks of the Havdala candle.

---

32. The paragraph that follows is adapted from *Sefer Beit Genazai: Maamarei Shabbat*, 2nd ed. p. 619.
33. The following teaching is adapted from Rabbi Moshe Luria, "Birkat Meorei Ha'esh," in *Pitchei Tefilla*, vol. 3, 389-391.

Shabbat enters as well as leaves with a blessing over fire. The difference is that the initial fire is that of a candle, while the end fire is more like that of a torch.

We find these two images of fire at the Giving of the Torah. Prior to the giving "there was thunder and lightning";[34] after the giving "the entire people saw the thunder and the flames."[35] Lightning (*berakim*) has the quality of light; flames (*lapidim*) resemble the quality of a torch. The use of fire at the inception as well as at the close of Shabbat may be an allusion to the teaching of the Sages that the Torah was given on a Shabbat. It is for this reason, according to the commentator Abudarham, that when they open the Ark on Shabbat morning in order to remove the Torah scroll, the congregation recites the verse, "You have been shown to know that Hashem, He is the God…"[36] Every Shabbat we thus re-experience the Giving of the Torah. Therefore at its inception we ignite candles that resemble the image of lightning, and when it ends we ignite a form of torch, perhaps reproducing the fire left with us after the Giving of the Torah.

A verse from Proverbs says,[37] "A man's soul is the lamp of Hashem, which searches the chambers of one's innards." The process of igniting a candle emulates the action of man's soul; our Shabbat candles may thus represent the greatness of our additional Shabbat soul and mirror our spiritual being. On Shabbat, however, our physical involvements are also imbued with holiness. Our physical being becomes permeated with holiness as we eat and drink the Shabbat delicacies served at the three *seudot* of Shabbat. Hence at the end of Shabbat, our material being also reaches a lofty expression, and we ignite a multiple-wicked candle whose torch-like flame reflects the spiritual elevation of our physicality that we merited to acquire on Shabbat. The peak of our physical ascent takes place at the end of Shabbat; while our Shabbat lights may reflect our soul, the torch-like flame of our Havdala candle may mirror the spiritual burning of our materiality and elevation of our physical being.

---

34. Ex. 19:16.
35. Ex. 20:15.
36. Deut. 4:35.
37. Prov. 20:27.

Therefore just as we need to thank our Maker for our additional Shabbat soul, the *Melave Malka* meal is a token of our appreciation for the elevation of our physical matter.

The candle's reflection of the soul's light and the torch-like flame reflection of our physicality may also be a mirror image of what happens on High, for our physical being is an extension of *Malkhut*, whose ascent on Shabbat is unparalleled. The spiritual quality of our physicality is concealed, however, in the model of *Malkhut*, who has nothing in and of herself, but whose Source on High is loftier than that of the soul. When Hashem's light illuminates our body parts as vessels to contain the light of our soul, the illumination is thus greater than when the light is directed onto our soul itself. Thus during the weekdays *Malkhut* – our *Shekhina* – is below her beloved counterpart, but on Shabbat, she is above all other levels. This is a preview of what will happen in the Ultimate Future, in which she will become *eshet chayil ateret baala* (a woman of valor, who is a crown for her husband),[38] as she is during the Shabbat *Mussaf*. At the close of Shabbat, many thus sing – while others read – holy songs about the messianic times, honoring Elijah the Prophet and the Mashiach descending from the Davidic line, for as Shabbat is coming to an end we have an illumination of the Ultimate Future. In a way, the end of Shabbat is higher than its inception, for it has the quality of *lapid* (flame) and *avuka* (torch) while its beginning has the quality of *ner* (candle).

Toward the end of Shir Hashirim we read "For love is strong as death... Love's sparks are fiery coals, a flame of the Divine."[39] At its inception Shabbat has the quality of "love is as strong as death," as it reveals the love between *Hakadosh Barukh Hu* and *Knesset Yisrael* whom He elevates to Himself. As the Ari z"l taught in the name of the Zohar, at the time of candle lighting, the *Shekhina* is "face to face." Afterward, on the Shabbat day, *Malkhut* ascends considerably, until the time of Mincha, when the *yichud* takes place between *Hakadosh Barukh Hu* and *Knesset Yisrael Themselves*. This *yichud* continues uninterrupted until we say *Ata chonantanu* (You have graced us with intelligence) in the *Amida* prayer of Shabbat night. And after becoming distanced from the Shabbat

---

38. Prov. 12:4.
39. Song 8:6-7.

illumination, our longing for divine closeness burns within us like a flame, as in the above verse "Love's sparks are fiery coals, a flame of the Divine." As noted by the Ari z"l, *Shalhevet Yud Heh* (a flame of the Divine) has the same letters as *Shabbat l'Hashem* (Hashem's Shabbat day).

The blessing *Borei meorei ha'esh* (Who creates the illuminations of fire) thus represents the longing that remains in the heart of *Knesset Yisrael* toward *Hakadosh Barukh Hu*.

Again, the process on Shabbat is similar to that at the Giving of the Torah. At the Giving of the Torah the people initially requested "We want to see our King," and their arousal could be likened to the candlelight of the Shabbat inception. About the experience of the Giving of the Torah, we are told, "Face to face Hashem spoke with you."[40] Then after the unification the desire for remaining in that state of closeness burned within them like *lapidim* (flames), or the torch of Shabbat's closing.

This process is alluded to in the Song of Songs, for at the beginning of the Song the verse reads,[41] "O that He would kiss me with the kisses of His mouth [O that He would reveal the secrets of His Torah to me as He began to do at Sinai]. Your spiritual love is far more precious to me than wine [all the pleasures of this world]." This may be likened to our entering the Shabbat experience with the Shabbat lights. Then, toward the end of Shir Hashirim, we have "for love is strong as death … Love's sparks are fiery coals, a flame of the Divine," similar to the quality of torch we are left with at the end of Shabbat.

In his *Sefer Shulchan Melakhim*, the late Kabbalist Rabbi Shmuel Darzi, zt"l stated in the name of Rabbi Eliezer that after a person drinks all the wine from the Havdala cup it is a praiseworthy to put a small amount of water in the Havdala cup and drink it, in order to show how beloved the *mitzva* is to him. Then, he should pour out what is left of that water into the wine that has already spilled from the cup, and douse the Havdala candle in it. He may then dip his fingers into that wine-water mixture and pass his fingers over his eyes.[42]

---

40. Deut. 5:4.
41. Song 1:2.
42. Communication with Rabbi Avraham Sutton, who studied with Rabbi Darzi.

His *talmid* (disciple) Rabbi Avraham Sutton explains how he puts this teaching to practice:

> I use 2 *kosot* (glasses). I fill the first *kos* with wine to overflowing, so some spills over unto the plate. I put a little bit of water in the second one. I completely finish the wine in the first *kos*. Then I pour that little water from the second *kos* into the first *kos*, drink a small sip, and then pour the rest of the water on the wine that already spilled from the first *kos*. Then I douse the candle in that mixture.[43]

After Havdala many have the custom of reading the verses in the Torah that contain blessings for the Community of Israel.[44]

THE MELAVE MALKA

At the close of Shabbat, we are asked to have a special meal called *Melave Malka* to accompany the Shabbat Queen as she leaves us until the next week. This fourth meal may be likened to the *sheva brachot*, the festive meals we hold after our weddings. For a wedding, it is the custom to invite a sizeable number of the bride and groom's acquaintances. For the *sheva brachot* we just invite some close relatives and intimate friends to whom we feel particularly attuned, for we want them to be part of our *simcha*.

In order to make the *Melave Malka* an important occasion, when cooking for Shabbat, we may prepare a dish containing meat for the sake of this meal at the conclusion of Shabbat. Then, when Shabbat finishes, we may set the table so that it is clean and appealing and light two candles without pronouncing a blessing. By showing the importance we attribute to the act of escorting the Queen, we help imbue her with light as she prepares for the coming week. In order to bind the Shabbat light with that of the weekdays, we may even take the flame to light these two candles from the candle of the Havdala service. Moreover, as mentioned

---

43. Oralc.
44. *The Complete ArtScroll Siddur, Nusach Sephard*, pp. 660-667.

by Rabbi Isaac Yosef,[45] it is praiseworthy to abstain from doing *melacha*, except for the preparation of what we need for the *Melave Malka* meal, until the conclusion of this meal.

Even though after Shabbat it may be a challenge, we should make a point of having bread for *Melave Malka* and have two whole loaves (rolls) available to recite the blessing on them. Each loaf should contain a *kezayit* ("like an olive," or 28 grams). We must have two minimum measures of bread. We may therefore weigh the bread we plan to have to make sure we do not eat more than the 52 grams we need to eat at this time, but still eat enough to enable us to say the Grace after Meals. Our recitation of the Grace after Meals is important to the *Shekhina*; for as we say it, she is able to receive *shefa* from on High to give to Her children. Before the *Melave Malka* meal, we should say the *Petichat Eliyahu* again; this time, however, we only read the first two or its three sections, ending with the words *"kum Rebbi Shimon."*

We must remember that we do not *have* to do any of this. Unlike the three Shabbat meals, which are commanded, the *Melave Malke* is optional. However, we help to reveal Hashem's Kingship in this world by engaging in Hashem's service with eagerness, rather than with the passivity with which we usually relate toward a government. As we shall see in following chapter, when we go out to receive the Shabbat Queen before the time in which the commandment of Shabbat is incumbent upon us, we are showing that we accept Hashem's kingship upon ourselves with total willingness. The same is true when we engage in the *Melave Malka*. These are part of the teachings that are too lofty to be enclosed in letters, so that there no halakha that tells us that we must do them.

---

45. *Yalkut Yosef* (Jerusalem: Eliyahu Shitrit, 5754).

Chapter 12
Ascending with the *Tosefet Shabbat*

Like the *Melave Malka*, the *Tosefet Shabbat* (addition to Shabbat) is not a commandment. It is rather a practice stemming from our eagerness to serve God, so that we do more than is required. In the chapters to come, we will learn about the lofty divine service that goes hand in hand with this quality of relationship with the Holy One.

These teachings about how to prepare for Shabbat are not new; they originated with the teachings of the Ari z"l, drawn from his understanding of the holy Zohar. The advice proffered in the next few chapters describes how kabbalists prepare for Shabbat. In our time, Hashem is making these teachings available to all Torah-observant Jews in order to help us speed our desired Redemption.

It may seem that the type of Shabbat expounded throughout this book, and especially in the remaining chapters, is not within the reach of the ordinary person. However, equipped with the consciousness of the additional Shabbat soul, we may aspire to such a bond...if that is what we aim for, if that is what we yearn for with every fiber of our being. Shabbat is called a day of desire. We say in the Shabbat morning *Amida*, "*Chemdat hamim oto karata* (most desired of days You called it)," suggesting that the essence of the day is that it is a desired day. Rabbi Luria teaches in his books on *Eretz Yisrael* that when man below feels the *chemda* (desire) to get close to his Maker, his *chemda* activates *chemda* on High, and it becomes divine will to help man below to attain his/her desire.

Rabbi Luria clarifies that the root of *chemda* is in the light of the *neshama* (higher soul).[1] Here we need to speak briefly about the dimensions of the soul.

There are three inner dimensions of the soul.[2] These are the *neshama* from *neshima* (breath), the *ruach* (literally, wind), and the *nefesh* (from *nafash* (rested).[3] The *neshama* rests upon the brain; the *ruach* dwells in the heart; the *nefesh* is attached to the liver. The *nefesh* and the *ruach*, which are responsible for human emotions, are directly connected with the body. However, because of its lofty origin, the *neshama* is not completely attached to the body; body and *neshama* are two separate entities dwelling together.

At the moment of death, the *neshama* leaves the body. The *nefesh* remains, and the *ruach* fluctuates back and forth, returning annually on the anniversary of the death to dwell on the body for that day.

The *nefesh* is bound to the body's material needs and tendencies. It is an animating force, the motivation behind our basic life forces such as eating and drinking. The *neshama* deals exclusively with matters of the spirit. It is an intellectual soul longing to serve the Creator; its goal is to teach man how to make his life a constant fulfillment of the will of God.

The *ruach* is in constant movement between the *nefesh* and the *neshama*. On weekdays, the *ruach* attaches itself to the *nefesh*; on the Shabbat, in which the *ruach* is not involved in any mundane activity, it separates from the *nefesh* and attaches itself to the *neshamah*. In addition, for the duration of the Shabbat, each Jew receives a *neshama yetera* (additional soul). (Besides the inner dimensions of

---

1. See "Eretz Chemda MiTechilat Haberia," *Sefer Beit Genazai: Eretz Israel*, vol. I, 33-37.
2. Adapted from Rabbi R. M. Luria "Maamar Neshama Yetera BeShabbat," *Sefer Beit Genazai: Maamarei Shabbat*, 1st ed. 85-89.
3. The following material on the levels of our soul is reproduced from my book *Living Kaballah*.

the soul, there are two further dimensions – the "surrounding lights" of the *chaya* and the *yechida* – which we will discuss briefly at the end of the nect chapter.)

The *neshama yetera* does not come all at once; different levels arrive at different times on Shabbat (see Appendix I). When Shabbat departs, the *ruach* returns to the *nefesh,* and the *neshamah yetera* returns to Heaven.

When a person is aroused to feel the *chemda* to get close to his Maker at the approach of Shabbat, his *ruach* and his *nefesh* also become attached to his *neshama.* Man then has more spiritual energy to achieve what his soul thirsts for.

Not only the dimensions of the soul, but the spiritual worlds are affected by the onset of Shabbat. Above us, as mentioned earlier, there are spiritual dimensions – heavenly worlds – preventing us from experiencing divine closeness on the weekdays as we do on Shabbat or Yom Tov. The lowest of them is called *Asiya* (Action), and it is the spiritual interface with our physical world. Above *Asiya* is a dimension called *Yetzira* (Formation); then comes *Beriya* (Creation), and finally the dimension of *Atzilut* (Closeness), which is closest to Hashem.

In honor of Shabbat these dimensions start ascending beginning Thursday night. Rabbi Chaim Vital, writing in the name of his teacher the Ari z"l, revealed to us that with each of our prayers we elevate the spiritual dimensions above us, linking one within the other. He stressed that attending Mincha early on Friday is an important contribution to this elevation.

Particularly on Fridays, it is often the case that one does not make it to the synagogue on time. It is important to realize, however, that when a man prays in his own at home it is questionable whether he even fulfills the basic requirement.

Although Friday is a challenge, still it is a very important day for us. The Ari z"l guided us as to what to do on Fridays in order to participate in the ascent of the heavenly dimensions, thus bringing about the ascent of souls of others as well. We may also bring about the ascent of parts of ourselves that may still be enmeshed in the lower world, waiting to be released and ascend to the light.

Even when people are caught in the relentless race of modern life and their souls are unable to ascend to the spiritual world on their own merits, they can still experience an *aliyat neshama* (ascent of the soul) on Shabbat by taking part in the additional ascending element called *Tosefet Shabbat* that Hashem provides for His people. Without the *Tosefet Shabbat*, they will not.

It is important to understand that if one comes into Shabbat at the last minute, after a mad race to finish everything, the way in which one will experience Shabbat is going be different than if one had come into it with inner harmony and eagerness, after being ready to receive it for a significant amount of time. The way we relate to Shabbat experience depends on our faith, however. It is part of *emunat Yisrael* (the faith on which our *avodat Hashem* is based), to believe that if we follow the Sages' teachings on Shabbat observance, our souls will gradually ascend throughout the different times of the Shabbat day.

As Rabbi Luria teaches, however, the Shabbat feeling is more than merely faith: if we feel elated by the sweetness of Shabbat, if our heart and mind respond to it, we know that Hashem takes pleasure in our deeds. If we do not feel the joy of Shabbat, it is a sign that we need to examine our conduct.[4]

We will now focus on the Shabbat elevation from the divine perspective. As mentioned, on week nights the *Shekhina* goes down to the lower worlds to gather the holy particles from her children's souls; these particles fell when they transgressed the divine will. At the onset of Shabbat, the *Shekhina* ascends with all the particles she gathered on the week nights. (Because of the *Shekhina*'s descent, we have an advantage over the people of Temple days, when the *Shekhina* was not compelled to go down to the lower worlds because of our sins. In Temple days, if a person became involved in serious sin and a great part of his soul fell to the lower world, it stayed there until the person was able to repent.)

---

4. Adapted from Rabbi R. M. Luria's "Maamar Giluy HaShekhinah beMishkan, Bait Rishon uSheni," *Sefer Or Hamikdash, Kolel Maamarim Ubiurim al Derekh Haavoda, Meyusadim al Divrei haArizal Luria, Beinyanei Hamikdash…Vimei bein Hameitzarim* (Jerusalem: Makhon Shaarei Ziv, 5753), 40-42.

Consequently, at this time, anyone who has sincerely expressed regret for past mistakes and taken upon him/herself to rectify them in the near future will be able to tune in to the inner dimension of his bond with Hashem, at the point where his past mistakes do not cloud the light of his *neshama*, and sense that this is a day of delight. This in turn will gird him with strength to avoid falling into material temptations in the coming week and to face the task of rectifying his/her past.

Thus on weekdays the *Shekhina* helps our souls when, as the Zohar puts it, her feet go down to the space of death. At the onset of Shabbat, we go to the field to welcome our holy *Shekhina* returning from the lower world, and we say, "Come O Beloved! Let us go toward the Bride!"

In his discussion as to how to welcome Shabbat, the Ari z'l tells us to focus on the initial letters of the first verse of Psalm 92 – *lamed* (ל), *mem* (מ), *shin* (ש), and *heh* (ה) – forming the word "*leMoshe* (of or for Moses)."[5] On Friday afternoon, Moses exercises great care to elevate sparks of departed souls that are enmeshed in the lower worlds of impurity, unable to ascend from there on their own. We mentioned that on Erev Shabbat the heavenly worlds ascend, each one becoming included in the world above it.

The souls dwelling in the lower words ascend as well, together with the heavenly worlds; but they are unable to distance themselves from the lower worlds *Beriya, Yetzira,* and *Asiya,* and rise to *Atzilut.* Moses also helps the souls of people in this world who do not have the merits of Torah observance that would permit them to go up with the power of their additional Shabbat soul.

On Erev Shabbat, as the lowest dimension of holiness goes up, Moses as well as thousands of other *tzaddikim* (righteous) who are dwelling in *Gan Eden* (the blessed afterlife), go down to the world of impurity and then come back up again. Each of them brings up with him souls of the departed who are permitted to participate in this ascent at this time, and souls of living people who are unable to make this ascent on

---

5. "Derush Alef: Inyan Mizmor Shir leYom haShabbat," *Shaar haKavanot, Chelek sheni,* 49b.

their own. They escort these souls on High, thus reenacting the Exodus every single Erev Shabbat.[6]

The Ari z"l teaches that at the onset of Shabbat there is a time of *din* (strict justice), for although every soul wants to ascend to the dimension of holiness, each soul has to wait until it is ready and receives permission to ascend.[7] The souls have to be judged by a heavenly Court at this time, and only those who merit it will be able to ascend, while others will have to descend. It is thus at this time that we, the Children of Israel below, recite Psalm 92, which alludes to the lawless flourishing like grass while they are truly generating their own eternal desolation. In contrast, the righteous flourish like date palms.[8]

Rabbi Luria derives from this teaching of the Ari z"l that this judgment is not only for the souls on High but also for the souls of people living in this world. It is important to understand that each soul is part of a larger soul that includes other physical and spiritual beings within it.

A kind of migration of souls thus occurs every Erev Shabbat:[9] some souls who dwell in the lower Gan Eden ascend to the higher Gan Eden, while other souls come down to this world in order to facilitate the ascending process of *Tosefet Shabbat* for the sake of the souls of people dwelling in this world as well as for their own sake.[10]

When the Shabbat light begins to flow, on Thursday night, Hashem emits a light from Above which, like a magnet, attracts these spiritual dimensions back up to the Source. Those who are ready to "join the ride" are able to take advantage of this time for their own selves as well as for any fragments of soul – wherever these may be – connected with other beings and with all the People of Israel.

---

6. See Rabbi Moshe Luria's discussion of this topic: "Mizmor Shir leYom haShabbat leMoshe," *Sefer Beit Genazai: Pitchei Tefilla*, vol. 3, 190ff.
7. The teachings that follow are adapted from "Mizmor Shir leYom haShabbat Zman Din," *Sefer Beit Genazai: Pitchei Tefilla*, vol. 3, 197ff.
8. Paraphrasing Rabbi Avraham Sutton's translation of Psalm 92:8 and 92:13.
9. Noted by Rabbi Chaim Vital in *Shaar Hakavanot*, 50a. See Zohar, *Terumah* 136a and *Saba deMishpatim* 91a.
10. The different elements included in the ascending process of *Tosefet Shabbat* will be explained in chapter 15, "On the Sixth day."

It is important to note that although this elevation is initiated from Above, still we must aim to be part of the process, primarily by being ready on time. We show that we are ready on time by saying the *Kabbalat Shabbat* (welcoming Shabbat) prayers eighteen minutes, at the very latest, before sunset. True, according to halacha, if something happens and a person is late, s/he can even say it later than that. But if we do not manage to be ready and say *Kabbalat Shabbat* eighteen minutes before sunset, we miss the "ascending train" of *Tosefet Shabbat*. And in truth, we should say it much earlier than that.

With the *Tosefet Shabbat* Hashem extends His Hand down to us, but we have to be able to take it. We have to be in a state of spiritual cleanliness in which we can take this help. The Zohar helps us understand how our sins block the spiritual conduits of *shefa*.[11]

> Whenever a person transgresses, it affects him in two different ways. On the one hand, it affects his inner being, for because of sin his *neshama* leaves him and the vacant space is occupied by a force of impurity that is going to stay there until the person gets his *neshama* back by repenting. On the other hand, it has repercussions for the soul root of his being on High, as well as on all the souls connected to his soul.

The effective repair of our past requires two steps. First of all, we have to fix the blockage in our inner being. Second, we must repair the damage inflicted upon our greater soul on High.

The Sages speak about the help coming from Above to repair our inner being at the onset of Shabbat. Upon our saying the verse *"vaychulu hashamayim vekhol tzvaam* (the heaven and earth were finished, and all their array),"[12] two angels come and put their hands on one's head and say, "Your iniquity has gone away and your sin shall be atoned for."[13] This does not literally mean that the sin is expiated, but rather that the film of impurity it leaves behind is taken away. However, the second part of our

---

11. Zohar, *Naso* 122b. Cited in *Chok leIsrael*, 514.
12. Gen. 2: 1-2.
13. Paraphrasing Is. 6:7.

repair – in which we aim to rectify the flaw caused on High – remains to be done. We initiate the process of the higher repair at this time by participating in the elevation of the spiritual dimensions at this time; we complete it in the coming week, or as soon as we are able, by undergoing whatever *tikkun* (rectification) our particular error may require.

The Ari z"l explains that an essential aspect of the ascent of the heavenly dimensions takes place during the saying of Psalm 29 in *Kabbalat Shabbat*. As we recite the words of the psalm, each of the lower dimensions becomes included within the dimension above it until they are all included within the highest one. Our awareness of this process helps it to take place.

As mentioned, Hashem emits His powerful help from Above to help us bridge the distance. The spiritual dimensions ascend back to their Source by divine command. But the effort we supply through our eager involvement in the prayers we say at this time, as well as through all the preparations that we will have done before that at the beginning of the sixth day of the week, helps us to join these dimensions and ascend together with them to the highest of all. Again, this can only happen through our active involvement in the process of their ascent.

Erev Shabbat begins after the evening prayer on Thursday night. We begin to receive the additional ascending element of *Tosefet Shabbat* by consciously accepting it at the times it comes down to us, from the fifth hour on Friday (that is, five hours by our modern clock after *netz* [sunrise], whenever that is). The end of Erev Shabbat is when we consciously accept Shabbat. The woman then proceeds to kindle the Shabbat lights and after that to say the *Kabbalat Shabbat* service. A man who has no wife must kindle Shabbat lights and recite the appropriate *bracha* (blessing) himself and then say *Kabbalat Shabbat*.

We will now discuss how the concept of *Tosefet Shabbat* works within the time we have available on Erev Shabbat. According to the Ari z"l's teachings in *Shaar haKavanot*, we should try to join a Mincha service early on Friday afternoon. Then any time between the end of the Mincha prayers and the beginning of *Kabbalat Shabbat*, we should read Shir Hashirim. After that we should say the *Kabbalat Shabbat* service three times. The first time is what we call *Kabbalat Shabbat basadeh* (welcoming Shabbat in the field). In the time of the Ari himself, they would actually go outside the city limits, where the forces of impurity prevail.[14]

During the weekdays, the outside forces hover in the vicinity of the realm of holiness.[15] On Shabbat, as the heavenly worlds ascend, there remains an empty space between the realm of impurity and that of holiness. The three branches going upward of the Hebrew letter *shin* — ש – initial letter of the word *sadeh* (שדה) represent the three full levels that the *Shekhina* ascends at the inception of Shabbat.

These three levels are represented by the concepts of *midbar* (desert), *sadeh* (field), and *bayit* (home). A *midbar* is a place in which one cannot plant anything nor settle in it. A *bayit* is a place of holiness – a home in which a married couple unite in fulfillment of their divine service. Intermediate between *midbar* and *bayit*, a *sadeh* is a place appropriate for planting, but not for a human dwelling.

The *sadeh* is seen belonging to *reshut harabbim* (public domain). This domain was formerly occupied by the forces of impurity; however, there were also forces of holiness accompanying the *Shekhina*'s presence. These forces of holiness have just vacated the *sadeh* at the *Shekhina*'s ascent on High. However, there remains an impression – a trace – of the holiness that was there a moment ago, just like when we go to sleep, our soul goes up on High but a trace remains in our body as we sleep. Whereas the *sadeh* contains impurity intermingled with forces of holiness, the *bayit* is the *reshut hayachid* (the private domain), a place of holiness permitting the dwelling of the Divine Presence.

Rabbi Chaim Vital stresses that upon going to the *sadeh* one should actually go out of town, rather than saying the *Kabbalat Shabbat* service in one's own private courtyard. Nowadays cities are larger, and one can no longer walk out of town. However, it is preferable if we can find a place nearby from which we can see into the distance, in the direction of the setting sun. For instance, the late kabbalist Rabbi Yehuda Getz

---

14. See Rabbi Chaim Vital, "Derush Alef: Inyan *Kabbalat Shabbat*," *Shaar Hakavanot, Chelek Sheni*.
15. Rabbi Chaim Vital, "Hakdamah Leshaar Hashabbat," *Sefer Pri Etz Chayim* (Jerusalem: Rabbi Tzvi M. Vidavski, 5748).

Key to the Locked Garden

zt"l, who lived in the Old City of Jerusalem, would go to the steps behind Yeshivat Bet El, from whence he could gaze into the distance while saying the *Kabbalat Shabbat* service. The *talmidim* (students) who knew him well say that Rabbi Getz would always shed tears at this holy moment of welcoming the *Shekhina* in honor of Shabbat. After his demise the government named the steps leading to the Western Wall after him.

It is true that some people work on Fridays and are unable to devote time to spiritual involvements on this day. However, one who is at the level in which all he does is an extension of his desire to serve his Maker will be inspired from Above as to how to "make the time" and free himself of obligations on Friday, even it means that his budget may slightly suffer as a result.

It is therefore up to us to designate a place as *sadeh* and go to this place, after reading Shir Hashirim, with the intention of welcoming the *Shekhina*, who is now leaving behind the impurity she is in contact with during the weekdays and is on her way back Home. This should be our sole intention, for Shabbat is not for us; it is Hashem's day of joy and we are asked to participate in this joy, each one of us according to his preparation. It is with this intention in mind that we recite the *Kabbalat Shabbat* service. When finished, we are now ready for our second recitation of the *Kabbalat Shabbat* service. Rabbi Vital teaches:

> After that, go back home. Come inside and enwrap yourself in your *tallit* (prayer shawl) with its prescribed *tzitzit* (fringes). Wrap it around your head as mentioned in Tractate Shabbat 82b and in the teachings of Maimonides, Chapter 30 in the section "Laws of Shabbat." Now go to the table, already set and laden with the challa rolls for the coming Shabbat meal; go around the table as many times as needed till you repeat all what you said in the *sadeh*.[16]

By going around the Shabbat table, we are defining the boundaries of a space in which the outside forces may not enter. That was the mystery of the *machane Yisrael* (the encampment in the desert): they were protected from the outside forces when within the encampment. And in a similar

---

16. This second time, we only need to say the words *Boi Kalla* (Come oh Bride) three times after saying Psalm 29; we do not need to repeat the entire *Lecha Dodi*.

Ascending with the Tosefet Shabbat

way, by going around this defined space we are spiritually marking the boundaries of the place which will be fit for *hashraat haShekhina* (the indwelling of the *Shekhina*) for the duration of Shabbat. Only holiness will be permitted within this space.

The Ari z"l then teaches:

> Afterward, read the first four Mishna chapters in the tractate Shabbat, having in mind that each one is counterpart of one of the letters of the *Shem Havaya*. This is the mystery of the adornments of the heavenly Bride.[17]

The tractate Shabbat has twenty-four chapters, corresponding to twenty-four *kishutim* (ornaments) of the Shabbat *Kalla*. We usually read another four after the first Shabbat meal and the other sixteen on the Shabbat day, around the second and third Shabbat meals.

After we have finished singing the *Kabbalat Shabbat* service while walking around the table, we go to the place in which the housewife ignited the Shabbat lights and recited a blessing over them. We contemplate the lights for a moment, having in mind that the *Shekhina* is now ascending Home and that we want to do all we can to help this happen in the best way.

We then go to synagogue with the intention of saying the *Kabbalat Shabbat* prayers for a third time, this time in synagogue together with the congregation. However, if the congregation is not yet doing *Kabbalat Shabbat* at this moment, we do it for this third time on our own, for again, time is of essence: in order to receive the *Tosefet Shabbat* supplement – the levels of additional soul that come down on Erev Shabbat – we have to be finished saying the *Kabbalat Shabbat* prayers at least eighteen minutes before *shekia* (sunset). We must remain in synagogue until the end of the service even if we have prayed on our own, so that we may hear and respond to *Barekhu* and to the Kaddish.

In order to facilitate the understanding of this chapter, a brief discussion of the structure of the Jewish day will be helpful. The Jewish

---

17. *Shaar Hakavanot*.

day starts from the evening onward; it begins at sunset and continues until the next day at sunset.

From 96 to 72 minutes before the first ray of sun comes over the horizon is *alot hashachar*, which is usually translated as "dawn." The first ray that comes over the horizon is called *netz hachama* (sunrise). The day from *netz* to *shekia* (sundown) is divided into twelve hours.

Chatzot hayom (midday) is when a person stands in an open area and has no shadow at all. Half an hour after that, one can say the Mincha prayer; it it is then called Mincha Gedola (early Mincha). Somewhat later (the calculation is complicated, and it is best to check a timetable for today's time[18]) is Mincha Ketana (late Mincha).

In the Temple days, it was considered that night started nine and a half hours after sunrise and continued until *alot hashachar*.[19] When we Jews sinned and went into exile, we were asked to take half the time between Mincha Ketana and the last ray of sunset – that is, ten hours and forty-five minutes after sunrise, calling it *Plag Hamincha*; according to the school of thought of Rabbi Yehuda, this *Plag Hamincha* is actually the last time one can pray Mincha. On the other hand, according to the Talmudic sages one can pray Mincha till sunset (defined as the moment when the last ray of sun leaves the horizon), and then one can pray *Arvit* from sunset and onward.

However, some Kabbalistic sages, basing themselves on the Zohar, hold that all prayers must be said while the sun is still shining on the earth. This view derives from the verse: *yiraukha im shamesh* (so that they may fear You as long as the sun shines).[20] By this view one should finish saying the *Amida* prayer of *Arvit* before sunset, which means before the last ray of sun leaves the horizon.[21] If we are guided by this opinion, we accept Shabbat before the last ray of sun leaves the hori-

---

18. For instance, the Website myzmanim.com does not initially show the time for Mincha Ketana. However, one has the option to click All Zmanim at the bottom of the screen and the time for Mincha Ketana appears.
19. Halakhot for the Temple differ from those that apply outside the Temple.
20. Ps. 72:5; see Berakhot 7b.
21. See the last Ran of Chapter Two in Tractate Shabbat. The correct time for sunset may be checked in any trustworthy Jewish calendar, such as the Website www.myzmanim.com.

zon. The man accepts Shabbat by praying *Arvit*, and according to this opinion he should finish praying *Arvit* by *Plag Hamincha*; the woman accepts Shabbat upon herself by lighting candles and therefore lights at *Plag Hamincha*.[22]

It is important to note, however, that not all Kabbalists agree with this opinion. For instance, according to Rabbi Jacob Sofer, author of *Kaf haChayim*, the compendium of halakhot based on kabbalistic teachings, accepting Shabbat before *Plag Hamincha* is not valid.[23]

It would thus be good to join a synagogue in which they pray according to the time of Plag haMincha. However, one who is unable to do this should at least say *Kabbalat Shabbat* – in which he will receive the *nefesh*, *ruach* and *neshama* supplements as well as the *Tosefet Shabbat* supplement – even if has to pray on his own.[24]

A word about receiving the different levels of the additional soul on Shabbat. We receive the additional level of *nefesh* when saying *boi kalla* (come O Bride), at the end of the song *Lekha Dodi* during *Kabbalat Shabbat*; we receive the additional *ruach* as the congregants in synagogue say *Barekhu*; and we receive the additional level of *neshama* just before the *Amida* when saying *ufros aleinu sukkat shlomekha* (extend upon us Your canopy of peace). Hearing *Barekhu* before Arvit is thus essential, and we must have in mind the intention of receiving the *ruach* aspect of the additional Shabbat soul as we hear it. Right after we say the Shabbat evening *Amida*, we must say the verse *vaychulu hashamayim vekhol tzvaam* (the heavens and earth were finished, and all their array).[25]

The Ari z"l urges us:

And if you forgot to [have in mind] to receive the additional level of *ruach* as the first *Barekhu* [is said in synagogue before *Arvit*] or if you did not hear it, have in mind at [the end of the Shabbat

---

22. According to Rabbi Yehuda, on the Shabbat during Chanuka, the Chanuka lights are ignited an hour before *shekia* and the Shabbat lights immediately after that.
23. Rabbi Jacob Chaim Sofer, *Kaf haChayim* (Jerusalem: private publication, 5775).
24. See the Ben Ish Chai on *Parashat Vayera*, in *Chelek Hahalakhot* (Jerusalem: Merkaz Hasefer, 5754).
25. Gen. 2:1-2.

evening prayer as the congregants are saying] the last *Barekhu* that you are receiving together the additional level of *ruach* and that of *neshama*. The reason is that if you did not receive the additional level [of *ruach*] it is impossible [for you] to receive the additional level of *neshama* at *ufros aleinu sukkat shelomecha* (extend upon us Your canopy of peace), as mentioned above. Therefore, you may now [in the second *Barekhu*, just before *Aleinu*] have in mind to receive together the additional soul levels of *ruach* and of *neshama* together.[26]

The woman who wants to avail herself of the *Tosefet Shabbat* supplement may say Shir Hashirim early enough so that she will finish saying it before *Plag Hamincha*. Her husband is likely to start much earlier if he wants to do the *Kabbalat Shabbat* service three times as explained. However, for the woman, who is entrusted with the responsibility for home management, being ready at the time of *Plag Hamincha* will already be a challenge for her. If she is free to devote the time immediately following *Plag Hamincha* to welcoming Shabbat, she may say the *Kabbalat Shabbat* prayers three times just like her husband. However, she has to keep track of time even more than he does in order to make sure to finish saying the Shabbat evening *Amida* on time.

A woman is allowed to light the Shabbat candles at *Plag Hamincha* even if her husband and children are not ready at this early hour, because the woman accepts Shabbat upon herself by lighting candles whereas her husband and sons accept it by saying the prayers to welcome Shabbat.[27]

Rabbi Luria teaches about the *Tosefet Shabbat*:[28]

> Even though this gift of ascending on High is a gift and does not depend on man, still the Ari z"l explained in *Shaar HaKavanot* concerning Shabbat that each soul of Israel receives an

---

26. Rabbi Chaim Vital, "Derushei Arvit Leil Shabbat, Derush Beit," *Shaar Hakavanot*.
27. As taught by Rabbi Israel Avichai, Rosh Yeshiva of Yeshivat haMekubalim Beit El.
28. Rabbi Moshe Luria "*Tosefet Shabbat*," *Sefer Beit Genazai: Maamarei Shabbat*, 2nd ed., 302b.

Ascending with the Tosefet Shabbat

additional Shabbat soul stemming from the Collective Soul of Israel. In contrast, one who strives to prepare himself [through his involvement in all that is required to be part of the *Tosefet Shabbat*] receives his own personal additional Shabbat soul. [...] And the more he strives [to involve himself] in the *Tosefet Shabbat* long before *shekia*, the more he will personally benefit, even though [by now] he already has his personal additional Shabbat soul. Consequently, [from the point in which he accepts Shabbat upon himself] it is forbidden for him to do *melacha*, for as Rabbi Moses Alshikh writes, the prohibition of doing *melacha* on Shabbat stems from the additional Shabbat soul, whose lofty nature is above the concept of *melacha*.

Two verses stand out among those in which we are asked to observe Shabbat. The first was given to us in the First Tablets:[29] *zachor et yom Hashabbat lekadsho* (remember the Shabbat day to sanctify it). The second was part of Moses's final message to the Children of Israel:[30] *shamor et yom haShabbat lekadsho* (observe the Shabbat day to sanctify it). Observing Shabbat entails fulfilling all its laws. Remembering Shabbat, according to the disciples of the Ari z"l, involves taking advantage of the *Tosefet Shabbat* supplement and ascending to the Source of *kedusha* (sanctity).[31] We may achieve this ascent by joining a *minyan* who say Mincha at the earliest possible time, aiming to join the elevation of the heavenly worlds which occurs at this time. Remembering Shabbat is understood by these Kabbalists as meaning that we involve ourselves in all the steps of the *Tosefet Shabbat* procedure, which will be detailed further on.[32] Rabbi Luria tells us:[33]

---

29. Ex. 20:8.
30. Deut. 5:12.
31. See Rabbi Moshe Luria, "Zachor et Yom haShabbat lekadesho [Alef]," *Sefer Beit Genazai al haTorah: Shemot*, vol. 1, 653-655.
32. See Chapter 15, "On the Sixth Day."
33. Rabbi Moshe Luria "Zachor et Yom haShabbat lekadesho [Alef]," *Sefer Beit Genazai al haTorah: Shemot*, vol. 1, 654.

> We may fulfill what the Torah asks us – "Remember the Shabbat day to sanctify it" – when we draw an additional measure of *kedusha* onto the Shabbat by ascending to the Source of all holiness – Hakadosh Barukh Hu. We were thus asked: *vahaya bayom hashishi vehekhinu et asher yaviu* (and it shall be on the sixth day when they prepare what they bring).[34] In so doing we will adding to the measure of *kedusha* that Hashem provides for Shabbat and we will be able to infuse the coming weekdays with some of the Shabbat holiness.

Those who miss the *Tosefet Shabbat* will receive their reward for their Shabbat observance, but they will miss the inner elevation they could have attained by striving to be ready on time and participating in all that is required to avail themselves of the *Tosefet Shabbat*.

The holiness derived from the *Tosefet Shabbat* is a gift; but we have to "be there" to take it, having done everything else so that we are free to say all the indicated prayers. These prayers are like our "ticket" to get onto this "sky-train" Hashem is providing for many who may not rise on their own.

It is important to note that the reception of the additional soul levels is not something of which we become consciously aware. However, Rabbi Luria says that you can verify "how you are doing" on Shabbat by whether or not you feel happy.

Rabbi Vital teaches that upon finishing *Arvit,* the man leaves the synagogue and comes back home. Upon entering his home, he should say "Shabbat Shalom!" out loud, with total joy, like a groom welcoming his bride with intense joy and a radiant countenance.[35]

---

34. Ex. 16:5.
35. Rabbi Chaim Vital, "Drushei Arvit Leil Shabbat, Drush Beit," *Shaar Hakavanot,* 73.

Chapter 13

Growing with the Additional Soul

We have three main soul aspects that are accessible to us: the *nefesh*, *ruach* and the *neshama*. During the week, the *ruach* is affected by the *mitzvot* done by the *nefesh*; but on Shabbat the *ruach* enables us to receive more from the lofty *neshama*, thus opening us to receive the Shabbat holiness. Therefore, technically it is not that man receives a new soul on Shabbat but rather that within the aspects of soul already in him, his lofty *neshama* soul overcomes the *nefesh*'s tendency to physicality. This appears to challenge the Talmudic teaching that we receive a new soul from Above for the length of Shabbat, not just part of our own;[1] however we shall see that there is no contradiction.

    The basic aspects of our soul are inner lights that enclose themselves within man, respectively within the *kelim* (spiritual body parts) that correspond to his brain, heart and liver. There are also higher lights which are too lofty to be contained within our *kelim*. These thus remain as surrounding lights standing above man's head and directing their illumination upon him.

---

1. Tractate Beitza 16b.

When we get to the point that all our physical tendencies are refined, then the organs in which the different parts of our soul are dwelling are considered to be vessels, like spiritual containers that can hold more and more divine light. At this point we may have reached the level in which our surrounding soul may come into us. If that happens, we now have the benefit of our surrounding soul as inner light; and then we will receive new, loftier lights as surrounding soul. This enables us to receive on a higher level.

The additional soul we receive on Shabbat was a surrounding soul all week long and only illuminated us at a distance. As long as it was only shining down on us as a surrounding soul, we could enjoy its influence but could not consider it our own soul. Only when we work on the quality of our fulfillment of *mitzvot* to the point that Hashem allows it to come into us, casting light onto our *kelim*, only then can we call it our soul.

There are Torah sages who receive an additional soul every morning during their morning prayer, for they have improved their levels of awe of divine greatness and love of Hashem to such an extent that they are able to receive their surrounding lights as inner lights and have the additional soul within their *kelim*.[2] And that is what we all have to aim for, even if we are far away from that goal; for really, on the weekdays, our *kelim* are unable to stand the intense light of the additional soul unless we have worked on ourselves to refine them considerably.

The Sages teach that one who did not exert himself prior to Shabbat will not eat on Shabbat, even though Shabbat is "a good gift."[3] Besides the literal sense, Rabbi Luria offers an additional understanding. The idea of exerting ourselves prior to Shabbat may refer to the preparation of the *kelim* in order to make them worthy of receiving the lofty Shabbat soul, which is an additional level of soul stemming from our soul on High.[4]

---

2. Cited in the name of the Ari z"l (*Sefer Olat Tamid*) in "Tosefet Shabbat," *Sefer Beit Genazai: Maamarei Shabbat*, 2nd edition, 301b.
3. Shabbat 19a, Beitza 16a.
4. Rabbi Luria cites this teaching in the name of the work *Ohev Israel: Parashat Ki Tisa*, in "Tosefet Shabbat," *Sefer Beit Genazai: Maamarei Shabbat*, 2nd edition, p. 302a.

When a person's *avodat Hashem* on Shabbat itself is very high, then the lofty lights that s/he received for that Shabbat may remain with him/her even after the day is over, and then s/he can receive new surrounding lights loftier than the former ones. As a result, on the next Shabbat those surrounding lights may also become part of his/her inner soul for the weekdays.[5] It is thus up to us to aim to grow on each and every Shabbat.

The Talmud[6] mentions the practice of Rabbi Yehuda bar Ilai (a fourth generation Tana, student of Rabbi Akiva, and the most frequently mentioned sage in the Mishna): on Friday afternoon someone would bring to him a basin filled with hot water so the rabbi could wash his face, hands and feet. Rabbi Yehuda would then wrap himself in his linen garments and sit down with the appearance of an angel. Rabbi Luria explains that Rabbi Yehuda was availing himself of the *Tosefet Shabbat*. By receiving Shabbat (at the earliest possible time before sundown) "he drew within himself already at that moment the lights that had surrounded him during the weekdays." These lights then became his inner soul, and as a result he had the appearance of an angel.

As mentioned, on the eve of Shabbat – that is, early on Friday afternoon – the heavenly worlds begin their ascent, and the Torah gives each individual soul of Israel the power to receive the *Tosefet Shabbat* already at that time. Rabbi Luria highlights:

> Any individual who receives Shabbat long before sunset ascends [together with the spiritual dimensions] [...]. As the Ari z"l explains, on the eve of Shabbat the heavenly worlds begin their ascent, and each individual [soul of Israel] can then sanctify the Shabbat and ascend to the sources of light.[7]

This ability our soul has to go up before Shabbat to the spiritual dimension together with the heavenly worlds is a gift from Heaven. As such, it

---

5. "Tosefet Shabbat," in *Sefer Beit Genazai: Maamarei Shabbat*, 2nd ed. 302b.
6. Shabbat 25b. The following quotation refers to Rabbi Yehuda Bar Ilai, whose *yortzeit* (anniversary) is on the 14th of *Iyar* (Pesach Sheni) and whose tomb is a half hour south of Safed in Israel.
7. "Tosefet Shabbat," *Sefer Beit Genazai: Maamarei Shabbat*, 2nd ed. 302b.

Key to the Locked Garden

is not dependent on man's deeds. The Ari z"l explained that each soul of Israel receives an "additional level of soul stemming from the collective Soul of Israel." And Rabbi Luria adds: "In contrast, one who prepares himself has [in addition to that general soul stemming from *Knesset Yisrael*] his own personal additional soul."[8]

It is thus important to have all our Shabbat needs ready by the fifth hour on Friday morning so that we may devote the rest of our Friday to the spiritual involvements that have to do with Shabbat. However, we may still do *melachot* as we do on weekdays. But from the moment when we accept Shabbat early according to *Tosefet Shabbat*, we have to keep all the Shabbat laws.

Concerning the time for receiving the *Tosefet Shabbat*, it is taught:

| It is a great thing to add to the *Tosefet Shabbat* practiced in the place you live, according to the yearning of your heart. According to most Torah Sages in Israel, it is commendable to add at least ten minutes, and one who is able to add half an hour – fortunate is his lot. However, one should not accept Shabbat earlier than *Plag Hamincha*, which in the summertime is about an hour and a quarter before sundown, and in the winter is about an hour before sundown.[9] | יש ענין גדול שאדם יוסיף תוספת שבת, יותר ממנהג הרגיל במקומו, כפי אשר ידבנו לבו, וטוב וראוי על פי גדולי ישראל, להקדים לפחות בעשר דקות, ומי שיכול להקדים חצי שעה אשרי לו, אבל אין להקדים יותר מפלג המנחה, שבקיץ זה כשעה ורבע קודם השקיעה, ובחורף זה כשעה לפני השקיעה. |

This study also tells us the various ways in which we may convey our early acceptance of Shabbat:

---

8. Ibid.
9. "Likrat Shabbat: Segulat Tosefet Shabbat," anonymous article (by a scholar known to a scholar known to the author) handed out in synagogue.

It is possible to accept the *Tosefet Shabbat* by igniting the Shabbat lights, or by saying the psalm "A Song for the Shabbat Day,""[10] or by saying "Come O Beloved," ending with the words "Come O Bride! Come O Bride! Shabbat Queen!" or at least by saying the words "Shabbat Shalom," while having in mind that upon saying these words, the Shabbat holiness will dwell upon one. From then on, *melacha* is forbidden.	אפשר לקבל תוספת שבת על ידי הדלקת הנרות, או באמירת "מזמור שיר ליום השבת" או אמירת לכה דודי, ומסיימים בואי כלה! בואי כלה! שבת מלכתא! או לפחות לומר המילים "שבת שלום" ולכוין שבאמירה זו יחול עלי קדושת השבת. ומאז אסורה במלאכות שבת...

The essence of drawing down the additional Shabbat soul and retaining it throughout the first three days of the week is through the *Birkat HaMazon* (Grace after Meals). We should say the *Birkat HaMazon* with all our heart, with the intention of giving *nachat* (joy) to the *Shekhina*.

The only thing that gives joy to the *Shekhina* on the weekdays is our recital of *Birkat HaMazon*.[11] Giving sustenance to us below is difficult for the *Shekhina*; for the root of human sustenance comes from a lofty space on High called *Mazal Elyon*, and if she does not receive sustenance from this space on High, she has nothing to give to the Children of Israel below. However, when we eat and recite *Birkat HaMazon*, the *shefa* resulting from the *Birkat HaMazon* goes all the way up to the *Shekhina on High*, and from this *shefa* she gives to humans below. The reason why she derives joy from our *Birkat HaMazon* is that all the words of *Birkat HaMazon* that we recite on weekdays with joy are a spiritual energy that we are sending up to the *Shekhina*. And on Shabbat the effect of our eating bread with each of the three Shabbat meals so that the meal is considered a *seuda* is even higher than this; the *Shekhina* derives joy from the food

---

10. Ps. 92.
11. Zohar, *Vayakhel* 218a.

itself that we eat on the *seudot mitzva* (the meals we are commanded to eat) and not just from the *Birkat HaMazon* as on weekdays.

It is thus important to recite the *Birkat HaMazon* not with sadness, which comes from the outside forces, but rather with joy, as one who gives with a good eye. In return, Hashem will bestow His goodness upon us with a good eye.

The inner dimension of the Torah teaches how the actual *Birkat HaMazon* text helps us retain the additional Shabbat soul on the first three weekdays and open ourselves to receive that of the following week. In the third blessing of the *Birkat HaMazon*, there is a practice of visualizing the respective divine names connected with the weekdays spelled out in full. When a person is ready to do this *avodat Hashem*, he or she should acquire a siddur a siddur that spells out these divine names in a simple manner that is intended for beginners.[12]

Rabbi Luria studies the interconnection between Shabbat and our desired Redemption, pointing out two rabbinic statements which seem to contradict each other. One statement posits that if all the People of Israel would observe two Sabbaths they would immediately be redeemed; elsewhere it says that it would be enough for them to keep one Shabbat.

These two teachings can be reconciled in the following manner: As mentioned earlier, when a person's *avodat Hashem* on Shabbat itself is very high, then the lofty lights that he received for that Shabbat may remain with him even after the day is over, and he then receives new surrounding lights loftier than the former ones; and on the next Shabbat those surrounding lights become part of his inner soul for the weekdays. Now on the first Shabbat it is the surrounding light of the *chaya* (living soul) that comes into the person; if he continues growing, on the next Shabbat it is the aspect of *yechida* (unique soul) that comes into him. When this occurs, the person has the five soul lights within him, and this is a *geula shelema* (a total redemption) for him. The two Shabbatot on which this took place are considered to be one single Shabbat because one completed the other.

---

12. See "Sod haYichud," *Siddur HaRamchal* (Jerusalem: Ramhal Institute, 2006), 522.

Chapter 14

You Will Call Me *Ishi*

In an earlier chapter we discussed the midrash, cited by Rabbi Chaim Vital, in which Shabbat complains to *Hakadosh Barukh Hu*, "You gave each one of the weekdays a soul companion, and to me You did not give any!" and Hashem replies, "*Knesset Yisrael* will be your soul companion. And I will be their soul companion for I also do not have one."[1]

The Ari z"l explains that Shabbat is *Matronita deMalka* (the King's Royal Queen), thus implying that wherever there is a king, there has to be a queen as well. The very word "king" implies the existence of a kingdom, an entity made up of subjects relating to this king as sovereign ruler and accepting his decrees over themselves with eagerness. The Ari z"l tells us that the word "king" conveys an aspect of constriction within the divine revelation. Thus even if the king is beloved by his subjects, still he has to judge them according to the system of justice that he established.

The ideas of "constriction" and "revelation" may sound incongruous, but we must remember that without several levels of constriction, the light of *Ein Sof* (the Infinite Being) cannot be perceived. A revelation means that the Holy *Ein Sof* condenses His light at different levels

---

1. Rabbi Chaim Vital. *Shaar Maamarei Rashbi,* citing Midrash Rabba 11:8. Cited from "Tov Lehodot l'Hashem," *Sefer Beit Genazai: Maamarei Shabbat,* 2nd ed., 346a.

of constriction and allows us to call Him by His Names.[2] The levels of revelation that are closest to us are those that we have described as the King and His *Shekhina*. The *Shekhina*, who is even closer to us than the King Himself, is on the one hand the "revelation of divine majesty" and on the other, the body of all the King's subjects as one. We may regard all the levels of divine revelation as a structure consisting of levels that are interconnected like the links of a chain, and the light flows constantly from the Source of all blessings to the end of the structure.

The *Shekhina on High* is the heavenly root of the collective souls of Israel. She is referred to in the feminine gender because she is a receiver of the divine flows and is revealed in the Children of Israel. One of the ways in which the *Shekhina* is revealed to us is as the Shabbat Queen, for on Shabbat there is a revelation of Hashem's Kingship. During the weekdays, the light of *Ein Sof* is concealed. The weekdays are referred to in Hebrew as *chol*, which literally means "sand," for like the grains of sand, each one is separate from the next.[3] We can also see the weekdays as branches of a tree, each of which seems like tree in and of itself.

On Shabbat, however, the root of Creation is revealed, and one can see that all Creation is in a state of unity and nothing has an independent existence. The spiritual worlds ascend, and with them all the heavenly beings dwelling in them, and all elements of Creation yearn to cleave to the Source. That is the meaning of what *Hakadosh Barukh Hu* said to the Shabbat: "*Knesset Yisrael* will be your soul companion." And to Israel He said: "Remember the Shabbat day to sanctify it (*lekadsho*)"[4] – that is, remember what I said to Shabbat! The Hebrew word *lekadsho* has a connotation of separation: we have to distance ourselves from anything that is not divine will.

Rabbi Luria explains that there is a revelation of Hashem's Kingship on Shabbat when the People of Israel sanctify the Shabbat in an expression of total faith that *Hakadosh Barukh Hu* created the world

---

2. Different divine names are applied to different ways in which Hashem interacts with the world: as noted above in Chapter Three, in Psalm 55 we may see how King David call upon a certain name when he desires to draw downward the type of divine interaction or providence associated with the name.
3. *Sefer Beit Genazai: Maamarei Shabbat*, 346.
4. Ex. 20:8.

and supervises it, directing onto them a divine sustenance that will be their *chayut* (life-force) for the coming week. Their sanctification of Shabbat – their leaving aside all worldly occupations to become involved in Shabbat observance – is like a body language with which they are proclaiming that there is no reality other than His Presence. This answer silences Shabbat's claim "You gave a soul companion to all the weekdays and to me You did not!" A weekday might well need a companion, since each of the weekdays is separate from the rest. But when Shabbat comes and all the People of Israel sanctify Shabbat – distance themselves from weekday consciousness, enwrap themselves in the spiritual garments of the additional Shabbat soul, and gather together in synagogues to sing in honor of Shabbat – it is revealed that all is One, that there is One Source unifying everything from Above. Hence there can be no complaint about the lack of soul companion.

Hashem thus said to the Shabbat that we are her soul companion because we are part of the revelation of His Kingship. Furthermore, there is something else we are doing at this time, for in Psalm 92 we say, "It is good to thank Hashem." In reciting this Psalm, we are part of the revelation of a main purpose of Creation; we acknowledge that Hashem created the world in order to bestow His goodness upon His creatures.[5] On the weekdays we are under the motto "By the sweat of your brow you will eat bread."[6] The notion of "bread" includes the divine flows of material as well as spiritual nature. On Shabbat, however we receive a gift from Hashem, a day of delight for body and soul, in which we recharge our batteries with all kinds of divine flows stemming from the Source of all blessings.

People look different on Shabbat. The shining countenance of each and every Jew shows a desire for closeness to *Hakadosh Barukh Hu*. This is because the radiance of the Shabbat light breaks through all our barriers, sensitizing us to the wavelengths of divine love flowing down at the onset of Shabbat. Man then becomes aroused to respond in kind, "like

---

5. Rabbi Chaim Vital citing the teachings of the Ari z"l in *Shaar Haklalim*; cited in "Tov Lehodot l'Hashem," *Sefer Beit Genazai: Maamarei Shabbat*, 2nd ed., 346b.
6. Gen. 3:19.

Key to the Locked Garden

waters reflecting a loving look,"[7] and it is precisely at this time that we are asked to read Shir Hashirim which is a total outpouring of the soul, expressing infinite yearning to cleave to Hashem.[8] As we read it, we feel as if we are being welcomed in the House of Treasures on High where we may attain an experiential perception of the verse "See, Hashem gave you Shabbat."[9]

The rest of Psalm 92 alludes to the way in which Creation's purpose of benefiting the creatures is revealed on Shabbat as we recharge our souls with delight for the body and soul – a delight coming from the Source on High and manifesting here below. There is a direct relationship between our acceptance of Hashem's Kingship over ourselves and our ability to receive the goodness He wants to give us. One is intertwined with the other; for it is when we show Hashem's Kingship by fulfilling divine will as spelled out in the Torah that we are rewarded with an illumination from the holy *Ein Sof*. Without our fulfillment of divine will, in receiving Hashem's goodness we would be "eating the bread of shame."

Furthermore, in commanding Israel to "sanctify" Shabbat *(lekadsho)*, Hashem uses the verb that is used in the marriage ceremony, when the groom says to the bride "*At mekudeshet li* (you are consecrated to me)." Similarly, Ezekiel has Hashem say to *Knesset Yisrael*, "*Vatihyi li* (and you became mine)."[10]

The People of Israel thus act as soul companion to Shabbat whereas *Hakadosh Barukh Hu* is seen as soul companion to *Knesset Yisrael Themselves (Knesset Yisrael Atzmam*, an expression coined by Rabbi Luria to designate the collective entity of our inner souls dwelling in this world under physical garments, empowered by our Torah observance).[11] Hence, as soul companions to Shabbat, we sanctify Shabbat at its beginning, in a process whose outcome occurs when we recite the Kiddush over the

---

7. Paraphrasing Prov. 27:19.
8. It was the practice of the late Rabbi Meir Yehuda Getz, zt"l, to say Shir Hashirim on Friday afternoon before the early Mincha and then say it again in synagogue before the evening prayer.
9. Ex. 16:29.
10. Ezek. 16:8.
11. The teachings that follow are adapted from "Veshav H' Elokecha et shevutecha," in *Beit Genazai al haTorah: Devarim*, vol. 3, 1656ff.

wine, much as a man goes through the process of *kiddushin* with his bride just before the *nissuin* stage of the marriage ceremony.

Hashem tells us through His prophet: "At that time you will call me *Ishi* and no longer will you call me *Baali*."[12] The word *baali*, which literally means "my master" but is used as "my husband," implies a unification of two separate entities whose goal is transmission of *shefa* from the Giver (*Hakadosh Barukh Hu* to the Receiver (the *Shekhina*, who will receive it for us). In contrast, the word *ishi* – untranslatable – implies such a level of closeness that we may refer to it as "the love of One."

As mentioned, on Shabbat, the heavenly dimensions begin to ascend and become included one within the other until Shabbat morning and the more they ascend the more it becomes revealed that all the emanated beings come from the same identical root on High. We do not have a revelation of this closeness on the weekdays, which is why the unification of the weekdays is like that of two separate entities.

The revelation of "the love of One" occurs at the peak of the Shabbat day, when all the heavenly worlds have completed their ascent; in the world below, that is at the time of *Mussaf*. However, from the very beginning of the process, during the Sabbath evening *Amida*, the overwhelming feeling of Oneness already pervades.

The Zohar expounds on the source of this bond in a text we refer to by its first word, *Kegavna*. This text has been incorporated into the Sefardi prayerbook. It is a very important text, especially for those who are unable to go to synagogue for the Shabbat evening service, for its reading takes the place of *Barekhu*, the joint blessing of Hashem that can only be said with a *minyan*. Those praying in a *minyan* say *Barekhu* at the beginning of Arvit while receiving one of the layers of the Shabbat additional soul.[13] The *Kegavna* passage discusses the Shabbat Arvit prayer as the beginning of the process leading to the total togetherness of our joint soul roots with *Hakadosh Barukh Hu* during *Mussaf*.

The body of this text alludes to the Shabbat mystery: the *Shekhina* is called "Shabbat" when she begins the process of the heavenly unification at the time of our Shabbat evening *Amida* prayer, having

---
12. Hos. 2:18.
13. Personal communication with Rabbi Luria zt"l.

divested herself of the *sitra achra* (the "other side"), or the forces of evil. The concluding paragraph is the most relevant because it is by saying it that we state our readiness to receive the aspect of the additional soul it represents. The point of the final paragraph is that our intention must be to infuse the *Shekhina* with blessings from Above. The word *"barukh"* (blessed) alludes to the light of *Chokhma* or divine wisdom, the Source of all blessings and of life itself.

In synagogue, when the prayer leader calls *"Barekhu et Hashem hamevorakh* (Bless Hashem, the blessed One)," the congregant answers: *"Barukh Hashem hamevorach leolam vaed* (Blessed is Hashem, the blessed One, forever and ever)." In place of this, one who is alone at home can say the following Aramaic statement:

Velomar barekhu et Hashem Hamevorakh. Et daika da Shabbat demaalei Shabeta: Barukh Hashem Hamevorakh. Da apiku debirkhaan mimekora dechayei veatar denafik mineh col shakiu leashkaa lekhola uvegin de'ihu mekora beraza deat kayama kerinan leh hamevorakh ihu mabua debera vekivan demetaan hatam ha kulehu leolam vaed. Veda ihu Barukh Hashem hamevorakh leolam vaed.

וְלוֹמַר בָּרְכוּ אֶת ה' הַמְבוֹרָךְ. אֶת דַּיְקָא דָּא שַׁבָּת דְּמַעֲלֵי שַׁבְּתָא: בָּרוּךְ ה' הַמְבוֹרָךְ. דָּא אַפִּיקוּ דְבִרְכָאָן מִמְּקוֹרָא דְחַיֵּי וַאֲתַר דְּנָפִיק מִנֵּיהּ כָּל שַׁקְיוּ לְאַשְׁקָאָה לְכֹלָּא וּבְגִין דְּאִיהוּ מְקוֹרָא בְּרָזָא דְּאַת קַיָּמָא קָרֵינָן לֵיהּ הַמְבוֹרָךְ אִיהוּ מַבּוּעָא דְבֵירָא וְכֵיוָן דְּמַטְאָן הָתָם הָא כֻּלְּהוּ לְעוֹלָם וָעֶד. וְדָא אִיהוּ בָּרוּךְ ה' הַמְבוֹרָךְ לְעוֹלָם וָעֶד:

What this passage says is that when the prayer leader says, "Bless *et* Hashem, the blessed One," the word *et* (a word that is usually a particle preceding the object of a verb but that can also mean "with") alludes to the *Shekhina*. We are asking that all *shefa* should flow down until it reaches the *Shekhina*, infusing all the heavenly words in the process.

One who knows the inner meaning in this prayer and has worked and yearned for it all week long, connects in a very strong way and grasps why Shabbat is often identified with the idea of *taanug* (delight) in divine closeness. From the time in which we receive the additional level of soul of Erev Shabbat, in the evening prayer, the Shabbat delight begins to spread within us.

The lofty level of closeness called "the love of One" (*bechina shel kechad,* as Rabbi Luria refers to it) is a bond in which the essence of one is attached to that of the other. As Rabbi Luria points out, the words "*echad* (one)" and "*ahava* (love)" have the same numeric value:[14] In the *Shema,* the declaration of faith that we read every day, we first say, "Listen Israel, God is our Lord; God is One."[15] Then we whisper, "Blessed is the Name of His glorious Kingship forever and ever." And then we say: "*Love God your Lord with all your heart, with all your soul…*"[16]

Our first statement – "Listen, Israel"– is an expression of understanding and internalizing that Hashem is One: and upon saying the word One we are transported to the "love of One," reminded us that we are part of His essence, in a love which is too lofty to be expressed by emotions. Unlike the love bringing together two separate beings, this is the bond of one single entity become complete. As Rabbi Luria says:

> And nothing can be greater than the love with which *Hakadosh Barukh Hu* elevated Israel to the level [in which they are] One with Him, which is similar to the love of self that every person has. Although there is no love greater than this, still it is not an emotional love but rather – a love of one who is one with himself.[17]

Rabbi Luria gives examples that help us grasp the expression "one who is one with himself." When the verse tells us that the Patriarch Jacob loved Yosef more than all his other children it does not mean that his emotional love for Yosef was stronger than that for all the others, but rather that Yosef was an extension of him. This relationship between Jacob and Yosef is hinted at in the verse "*Ele toldot Yaakov Yosef* (These

---
14. Rabbi Moshe Luria, "Jacob tiken tefilat arbit," in *Sefer Beit Genazai al haTorah: Bereshit,* vol. 2, 680b.
15. Deut. 6:4. Translation: *The Living Torah.*
16. Deut. 6:5. Translation: *The Living Torah.*
17. *Sefer Beit Genazai al haTorah: Bereshit,* vol. 2, 680.

are the chronicles of Jacob: Joseph),"[18] suggesting that Jacob's relationship to Yosef was like that to his own self, which is above a relationship measured by emotions. In contrast, Jacob's love for the brothers was an emotional love, similar to his love for Leah, whereas his love for Rachel was like the love of self. Rabbi Luria summarizes:

> And this is the root that the People of Israel must know, namely that Israel was first to arise in the divine thought – the love directed toward them is thus the "love of One." We thus find that the Torah says to all Israel:[19] You must love your neighbor *kamokha* (as [you love] yourself). The word *kamokha* means "as if he were part of you," unlike the emotional love. Rather, you must realize and know that all Israel are one complete structure and each soul of Israel is like one body part of this structure and so it follows that there has to be a "love of One" between them. The verse [about loving your neighbor] thus ends: "I am God." Namely, the same type of love at the Source between *Hakadosh Barukh Hu* and Israel has to [interconnect] all the souls of Israel.

After saying "Listen, Israel, Hashem our God, Hashem is one," we say, "Blessed is the Name of His glorious Kingship (*Malkhuto*) forever and ever." These words, which we must say in a whisper, bring us back to the reality that we fell from the higher level we had all attained at the Giving of the Torah. We are now taking it upon ourselves to sanctify Hashem in every way that we can – in the spiritual as well as the physical, aiming to bring about the revelation of Hashem's Kingship in the world below, in places where there is no consciousness of divine Kingship.

The purpose of the descent imposed upon us is to elevate the particles of holiness which fell into the dimension of impurity in an early stage of Creation and still remain there. Among the fallen lights were the heavenly sources of love and fear. As Rabbi Luria

---

18. Gen. 37:2.
19. Lev. 19:18. Translation: *The Living Torah*.

teaches, the goal of our divine service is that "instead of using these traits for material concerns, we elevate them to the dimension of holiness. Consequently, we then say: 'You will love Hashem Your God with all your heart…'" This is the love of emotions elevating the particles of divine love to their heavenly Source. Our divine service will continue bringing about the rectification it is aimed to achieve until the time of Redemption comes, in which all the fallen divine particles will be elevated to their Source. At that time we will go back to the bond alluded to by the words "Hashem is One," and with it to the "love of One."

The Midrash tells us that when the patriarch Jacob felt that his end was near he called his sons and asked them to honor the Holy One as his fathers had honored Him. His sons responded, "Hear O Israel, Hashem our God, Hashem is One." Reassured, Jacob whispered, "Blessed be the Name of His glorious Kingship forever and ever," hinting to them that the Redemption would come about with the completion of the task of elevation alluded to by these holy words.

Moreover, the word *Malckhuto* (His Kingship) alludes to the *Shekhina* in her heavenly mission to go down to a lower world and collect the divine particles of our souls that we lost by transgressing the Torah in this as well as other generations of our history. The *Shekhina* does not have access to her lofty consciousness while she goes to the lower worlds; this is in order to safeguard it from the outside forces who would be quick to attach themselves to this light. Since we are the souls included within the *Shekhina*, when we reconnect to our roots and show eagerness to participate in her "return home" also on Shabbat, it has a beneficial effect on High.

On every Shabbat we have a new perception of the Love of One: as we bring in Shabbat, the *Shekhina* leaves the lower world, and her gradual ascent back Home continues with the three Shabbat prayers and their corresponding *seudot*. The *Kegavna* passage that may be read just before saying Arvit on Shabbat evening, tells us that the *Shekhina* is also called Shabbat because on Shabbat she becomes united with the holiness above. We are told that "the Holy King does not sit onto His Throne of Glory until she is also perfected in the mystery of Unity, just as He is."

At every prayer and its following *seuda* we attain a higher perception of the Love of One. In the first *seuda* we experience the emotions of love and joy (simcha). About the second *seuda*, we are told: "Then you will delight in Hashem."[20]

Delight (*oneg*) is higher than joy *(simcha)*, but we are still within the realm of emotions. Then in the Shabbat afternoon prayer we say: "You are One and Your Name is One, and who is like Your people Israel, one nation on earth" – and at the third *seuda* we are above emotions.

---

20. Is. 58:13-14.

Chapter 15
On the Sixth Day

Each of the weekdays was created with one of Hashem's lights or *Sefirot*: *Chesed* (lovingkindness), *Gevura* (restriction), *Tiferet* (harmony), *Netzach* (dominance), *Hod* (empathy), and *Yesod* (foundation). On Fridays the light of *Yesod* is shining down to us; its counterpart is *taanug* (delight), meaning the spiritual delight of closeness to Hashem.[1]

A special feature of the light of *Yesod* is that if we divide it into thirds, its first third is concealed and the other two revealed. In order to understand, one can think of the Holy Temple, which permitted the ultimate spiritual delight – our closeness to Hashem – to come to fruition. Two thirds of the Temple were revealed; but the innermost third, the *Kodesh Kodashim* (Holy of Holies) was concealed, separated from the main Sanctuary by a special curtain, the *parochet*. No one was able to enter except the High Priest, and only once a year, on Yom Kippur. The *menora* (candelabrum) was in the *Heikhal* (main Sanctuary), and it was here that divine revelation began. The people did not have access to the *Heikhal*, but only the *kohanim*; however, the people could see the

---

1. The teachings that follow are adapted from "Maamar Erev Shabbat Shaah Chamishit," in *Sefer Beit Genazai: Maamarei Shabbat*, 2nd ed., 219ff.

menora's center light glowing, for it remained permanently lit as testimony that Hashem's Presence dwelt among the Jewish people.

As will be remembered, the day from *netz* (sunrise) to sunset is divided into twelve hours. Until the end of the fourth hour on Friday morning, the light of *Yesod* is concealed. When the fifth hour begins, the Shabbat light begins to extend its glow of *taanug*, of delight in our closeness to Hashem – the energy of spiritual delight, which is so difficult to reach on weekdays.

Kabbala teaches that when we say the psalm of the day on Friday at the end of our morning prayers, we allude to the fifth hour on Friday. To introduce the psalm of the day on other weekdays we say, "*Hayom yom rishon/sheni/shelishi*.... (Today is first day/second day/third day...)." However, when it comes to Friday, we say "Hayom yom hashishi [הששי] (today is *the* sixth day)," adding the letter *heh* (ה) as definite article. The numeric value of the letter *heh* is five. It is at the fifth hour that the revelation of our special closeness to Hashem begins. Hence when we say the psalm of the day at the end of morning prayers, we are being reminded that the light of Shabbat will soon begin to shine. We internalize it by having in mind to accept the first part of the additional Shabbat soul at the fifth hour on Friday.

Rabbi Luria states that already at the beginning of the fourth hour the outside forces begin to separate from holiness as the Shabbat light begins to shine. However, at its beginning, the light is in a state of concealment. All the levels of Creation, the heavenly dimensions, begin to ascend to the Source of all blessings on High. The actual ascent begins on Friday at the point of *chatzot* (midday), and the process of elevation continues until its point of culmination on Shabbat morning.

A warning is in order, however. It is impossible to experience the spiritual delight of closeness to Hashem unless we distance ourselves from physical pleasures. The definition of "physical pleasures" is subjective, for it interconnected with each person's level of closeness to his Maker. It is up to each one of us to distinguish between what gives us energy to accomplish our work and what could be a physical gratification that we do not need to indulge in.

From the beginning of Friday, we have to start thinking of distancing ourselves from all that connects us to self-indulgence and physicality, which we call our garments of skin. The goal of our Friday afternoon *avoda ruchanit* (spiritual service) is to deserve the garments of light – the additional Shabbat soul – and to be able to experience *oneg* on Shabbat.

Rabbi Luria teaches that the concentration of the light we will receive on Shabbat will be in proportion to the intensity of the desire we show on Friday, as the Shabbat light begins to pour down in a concealed form:

> According to the intensity of the longing one feels on Friday, the lights will come with double intensity on Shabbat. We are referring to the preparations in honor of Shabbat that are done on Friday in bright daylight, for such attitude reveals the longing there is – if it can be said – between *Hakadosh Barukh Hu* and Israel.[2]

We can show the desire we feel by aiming to have ready all the elements of Shabbat which, together, blend into Shabbat experience – the meals cooked, the house cleaned, the table set – already on Thursday. This is undoubtedly challenging; but it is important, for one whose attention is pulled in every direction while engaged in the many tasks of cooking and cleaning will find it difficult to identify any feeling of longing within. In contrast, when everything is ready early on Friday morning, we are able to concentrate on the elements of the spiritual preparation – which we will delineate in the pages to come. Since the deeper purpose of each of these practices is to distance us from the "other side," our involvement with their fulfillment helps our desire to surface.

On Friday the outside forces are eager to "trip" us in any possible way, for they know that we are about to receive a great concentration of light on Shabbat and that they must distance themselves from us. Whether you are a man or a woman, if you are involved in cooking or shopping you will not be able to give yourself to the spiritual preparations which would allow you to distance yourself from the outside forces. Furthermore, on Friday afternoon, at the time when your soul could have been ascending with the *Tosefet Shabbat* supplement, you may be in need of a rest from the morning's activity and unable to participate.

---

2. Ibid., 221b.

Key to the Locked Garden

The effort of having the Shabbat needs ready on Thursday evening is our way of showing our eagerness to receive the additional Shabbat soul, which will enable us to experience a special degree of closeness to Hashem.

It is important to understand that these elements of spiritual preparation are not a commandment, but rather an expression of our desire. From the moment we engage in any activity as a commandment, we are following the King's orders and no longer showing desire.

The first stanza of Rabbi Masud's *piyyut* sets the tone of the Shabbat day from the start:

A psalm: song for the Shabbat day. I too will state my piece.[3] To arouse my heart to love the Rock Who made me and established me.[4] To serve Him always with joy. [To express my awareness of] the infinite kindness He bestowed upon me. To praise Him with my mouth and tongue. The mystery of Shabbat is *zachor* (remember) and *shamor* (guard). It is a sign of the covenant between Him and me.[5]	מִזְמוֹר שִׁיר לְיוֹם הַשַּׁבָּת. אֲעֶנֶה חֶלְקִי גַם אָנִי. לְעוֹרֵר לִבִּי אַהֲבַת צוּר עָשָׂנִי וְכוֹנְנָנִי. וּלְעָבְדוֹ תָּמִיד בְּחֶדְוָה. רֹב חַסְדּוֹ אֲשֶׁר זִכָּנִי. לְהַלֵּל בְּפִי וּלְשׁוֹנִי. סוֹד שַׁבָּת זָכוֹר וְשָׁמוֹר. אוֹת בְּרִית בֵּינוֹ וּבֵנִי:

PREPARATION IN WORD

Part of the preparation for Shabbat is preparation in word – our Torah study during the week and on Shabbat eve especially.

---

3. Paraphrasing Job 32:17. Translation from *The Living Nach*, trans. by M.H. Mykoff, Gavriel Rubin and Moses Schapiro (Jerusalem: Moznaim Publishing Corporation, 5758).
4. "The Rock Who made me": See Tractate Megilla 14a, Ps. 28:1.
5. Paraphrasing Ex. 31:7

The work called *Chok LeIsrael,* based on the course of study recommended by Rabbi Chaim Vital, presents sections of the weekly Torah portion, of the Prophets, Mishna, Talmud, Zohar, ethical teachings and halakha for every single weekday, so that every day, right after morning prayers, we may read the corresponding portions.[6]

The major part of our spiritual preparations for Shabbat takes place on Friday, the sixth weekday; but there is an aspect of Shabbat preparation in word that begins on Thursday night, which we will discuss first.

Our Shabbat preparations on the sixth weekday reflect the verse in which we were told about the double portion of *manna* falling on Friday: "and it shall be (*vehaya*) on the sixth day when they prepare (*vehechinu*) what they bring."[7] However, that is only according to the literal understanding of this verse. The word *vehaya* – וְהָיָה – is made up of the four letters of The Name spelled with four letters, whose numerical value is 26. If we see the word *vehaya* as a permutation of this Name and focus on its numeric value, we may read the beginning of this verse as "26 on the sixth day." Then the word *vehechinu* (and they will prepare) alludes to the aspect of Shabbat preparation that we do verbally, beginning on Thursday night. The verse is thus hinting to us to start the preparation verbally by reading twenty-six verses of the weekly *parasha* on Thursday night, starting with the verse following the last verse we read in the Thursday morning selection of *Chok LeIsrael*. Ideally, we should engage in this reading after *chatzot* (midnight), but we can even do it earlier if we know we will not be able to rise for the midnight prayer.

---

6. *Chok LeIsrael Hameforash: Lilmod Bekhol Yom Keseder Parshiyot HaTorah, Mikraot min Torah, Neviim UKetuvim* (Jerusalem: Bloom Sefarim, 5760). It is important to know that there is a computer program presenting the texts of *Chok LeIsrael* with corresponding English annotated translations on the facing page as well as annotated explanations in easy-to-understand-Hebrew (eChok.com; tel. 718 – 377 – 0047). Readers will benefit from purchasing the newly published edition of *Chok LeIsrael* with clear vocalized texts, in which the Zohar selections appear with the Hebrew interpretations based on the teachings of Rabbi Daniel Frisch side by side; it may be purchased by sending a fax to the publisher in Jerusalem, Israel: 972 - 2 - 523 24 85 or writing to Rechov Yoel 30, Jerusalem.
7. Ex. 16:5.

Key to the Locked Garden

Reading the twenty-six verses that follow what we read on Thursday morning is among the first of the Friday preparations. On Friday morning we read the entire weekly Torah portion, verse by verse, twice in Hebrew and once in Aramaic translation. This helps us be ready to receive the additional Shabbat soul.

One whose Hebrew skills are not adequate this study, but who still wants to receive the full strength of the Shabbat additional soul, can ask any Jew who does this study every day to have him/her in mind. Alternatively, s/he can read the first portion of the weekly *parasha* on Sunday, twice in Hebrew and once in Aramaic; then the second portion on Monday, the third on Tuesday, etc., saving the sixth and seventh portions for Friday, when s/he has finished the physical Shabbat preparations. Upon starting to read the *parasha* on Friday, one should try to set aside enough time in order to be able to finish it without any interruptions. It is important not to interrupt the reading in any way, not even for Torah teachings.

It is important to read the Aramaic translation, for it is part of what helps us to distance ourselves from the other side. And we must really learn the Rashi as well although not necessarily at this time, because we want to understand the *parasha*.

In addition, we must read the *Haftara* (prophetic section corresponding to the *parasha*), for this reading is the *chitzoniut* (external) aspect of what we have just accomplished in the *penimiut* (inner aspect) by reading the Torah portion, and it is what will help us internalize its light.

When we finish this reading on Friday morning, we should read Psalms 92 and 93, as our indication that we have completed this aspect of the Preparation in Word and are ready to receive the corresponding soul level.

PREPARATION IN THOUGHT

In addition to the preparation in word, we have a preparation in thought and a preparation in deed.

The preparation in thought essentially involves yearning for the Shabbat holiness to come and attempting to be ready to receive it. Hence, after finishing this reading, it is advisable to take some time to examine what we have done throughout the past week with a critical eye, having

On the Sixth Day

in mind to do *teshuva* for anything unworthy.[8] Although it is not easy to feel regret, at this time we have help from on High; for after we read each verse of the *parasha* twice in Hebrew and once in Aramaic, the "other side" has distanced itself from holiness due to the power of our reading. This is our chance to arouse ourselves to feel thoughts of repentance and cleanse ourselves from wrongdoing, so that we may merit "to behold the sweetness of Hashem and to abide in His Sanctuary."[9]

After this time of introspection, we may say a prayer written by Rabbenu Yona of Gerona that is included in our Appendix III among the "Mystical Readings for Shabbat." At the beginning of this prayer, we may add our confession of all the wrongs committed during the past week.

Cleansing our soul from the impurity of sin at the time that there is an energy from Heaven helping us do it will enable us to attain the Shabbat *menucha* which is to become a dwelling place for the Holy One. As the verse says, "This is My sole resting place forever; here I will dwell, for I have desired her."[10]

After we have done this reading, we have the spiritual ability to receive the additional soul by going to the *mikve* and immersing, even if this is before the fifth hour of Friday. All the collective souls of Israel are at this point like the bride purifying herself to be with her bridegroom after the *kiddushin*.

Rabbi Masud sings:

| By sanctifying that which is already holy you will find grace.[11] Read the *parasha*, twice in Hebrew with holiness and once in Aramaic with reverential awe. You must then immerse in a *mikve* in order to cleanse yourself. Then, you will be established through righteousness.[12] | וּלְקַדֵּשׁ נֹגַהּ חֵן תִּמְצָא. פָּרָשַׁת שָׁבוּעַ תִּקְרָא. שְׁנַיִם מִקְרָא בִּקְדֻשָּׁה. וְאֶחָד תַּרְגּוּם בְּמוֹרָא. טְבִילַת מִצְוָה לְרָחְצָה. תִּטָּבֵל בְּמִקְוֵה טָהֳרָה. אָז בִּצְדָקָה תִּכּוֹנָנִי: |

---

8. The teaching that follows is adapted from the work *Chemdat Yamim* (Jerusalem: Yerid Hasefarim, 2003), 81-124. The author of this work wanted to remain anonymous.
9. Ps. 27:4.
10. Ps. 132:14.
11. The word *chen* (grace) may allude to the Torah's inner dimension.
12. Paraphrasing Is. 54:14.

Men should first have a shower at home and then go to the *mikve*. The intention of the first immersion may be to shed the impurity of the weekdays. That of the second immersion may be order to shed our soul's weekday garments, and that of a third may be in honor of Shabbat, to receive the aspect of the additional Shabbat soul coming at this time. We must have in mind that the level of additional soul coming to surround us as we complete our immersion in the *mikve* is our real Shabbat garment.

Friday immersion in a *mikve* is not an option for most women. However, a woman who is not in her time of ritual impurity and who has access to a women's *mikve* in which she will be allowed to immerse for spiritual reasons may do these immersions on Thursday evening.

If possible, men should immerse again on Shabbat morning, for the holy light available at this time is loftier than that extended to us at the beginning of Shabbat, and allow the purifying water of the *mikve* to dry on their skin rather than drying it off with a towel. Only one immersion is needed at this time, for we no longer have to shed weekday garments, but rather receive a higher level of spiritual garment. Moreover, according to the Shabbat laws, it is preferable to wait a moment before drying oneself, in order to allow some of the bodily water to drain on its own.

PREPARATION IN DEED

The preparation in deed first includes preparing all the dishes that we will serve at the Shabbat meals. As we have seen, in order to have time for spiritual preparation on Friday it is advisable to have the cooking done on Thursday night. However, the Sages have advised us to do the preparations on Friday. One way of complying with the Sages' advice while leaving time for spiritual preparation is to have everything almost ready by Thursday night, but to leave one or two details that we may do on Friday so that technically the dishes will only be ready on Friday.

We try to do the cooking on our own, aware of the honor of preparing the King's *seudot*, and only allow helpers to prepare the ingredients of a dish and clean up after the work is complete. Indeed, the Sages teach that when we strive to prepare the Shabbat needs by ourselves with joy even if we could ask another to do it for us, this helps to expiate our sins on High.

As Rabbi Masud states in his *piyyut*:

| The eve of Shabbat is on Friday. Buy all the needs for your Shabbat. Prepare – do it by yourself, and not by means of another, for the King sitting on the Throne – a guest coming toward you – What will you say and what will you answer? | עֶרֶב הַשַּׁבָּת יוֹם שִׁשִּׁי. תִּקְנֶה כָּל צֹרֶךְ שַׁבַּתְּךָ. תָּכִין בְּעַצְמְךָ תַּעֲשֶׂה. וְלֹא עַל יְדֵי זוּלָתְךָ. אֶל מֶלֶךְ יוֹשֵׁב עַל כִּסֵּא. אוֹרֵחַ הַבָּא לִקְרָאתְךָ. מַה תֹּאמַר וּמַה תַּעֲנֶה: |

The last element we may leave undone may be the adding of spices, or even the correction of the spices. It is important to taste all the delicacies prepared for all the Shabbat meals in order to project the image of one who is preparing the King's reception and is checking to see if all the dishes are tasty and worthy, so that if they are not, we can add the correct spices. However, the Zohar recommends that we leave one or, better, two dishes from the second and third meals that we do not taste. With all of this, we are showing eagerness to receive the royal guest.

The optimum time to do this tasting is on Friday afternoon as we are warming the dishes of the first Shabbat meal. When the dishes are warm, before putting them on the hotplate, we go systematically from dish to dish so that we will not forget anything, tasting only a spoonful, making sure to say a blessing after we finish tasting everything.

Even if we do our main Shabbat shopping on the weekdays, still, we should leave certain items to be purchased on Friday morning, for the Friday shopping in honor of Shabbat is part of the elements of the spiritual Shabbat preparation. And while we are purchasing what we need, we say, "This is in honor of Shabbat."[13]

After the *mikve*, one should go to a synagogue in which they pray Mincha early and join them. As mentioned earlier, the Ari z"l revealed

---

13. It is written in the *Sefer Divrei Shalom* that on the way to buy the Shabbat needs, one should say: "I am on my way to buy the Shabbat needs in honor of Shabbat in order to fulfill the *mitzva* alluded to in the verse: "and it shall be on the sixth day when they prepare what they bring," with the intention of rectifying the heavenly root of this *mitzva* הריני הולך לקנות לכבוד שבת כדי לקיים מצות והיה ביום הששי והכינו את אשר יביאו לתקן את שורש מצוה זו במקום עליון." One should then recite the verse *vihi noam*… (Ps. 90:17).

Key to the Locked Garden

to us that there are spiritual dimensions above our physical world. With each of our prayers we elevate the spiritual dimensions above us, linking one within the other. This process begins on Friday at midday, at the time of Mincha. That is why it is important to go to Mincha at the earliest opportunity.

Rabbi Masud says about the Mincha prayer:

> At the Mincha prayer in the afternoon begins the ascent of souls. Unify the letters of The Name one with the other, with the Names emerging from them. Within your thoughts they should be engraved. He calms my soul; He leads me.[14]
>
> בִּתְפִלַּת מִנְחָה בָּעֶרֶב. מַתְחִיל עֲלוּי הַנְּשָׁמוֹת. אוֹתִיוֹת הַשֵּׁם לְקָרֵב. אַחַת בְּאַחַת עִם שֵׁמוֹת הַיּוֹצְאִים מֵהֶם בְּקֶרֶב מַחְשְׁבֹתֶיךָ יִהְיוּ נֶרְשָׁמוֹת. נַפְשִׁי יְשׁוֹבֵב יַנְחֵנִי.

Before going to the *mikve*, we must trim our nails in honor of Shabbat. As the Zohar explains, even women must be stringent with themselves about the trimming of nails. It is not worthwhile for women to have long nails, for they have a *zuhama* (spiritual impurity) which brings about *dinim kashim* (a severe measure of strict justice), and the outside forces find nourishment from the part of the nail protruding past the fingertip.[15] This allows the *klippot* to absorb a great concentration of holiness and permits them to dominate the world. The longer your nails are, the more the *dinim*, Hashem's forces of severe strict justice, gain power over you. You should thus take care to trim your nails every Friday in honor of Shabbat.

Giving charity is another element of Shabbat preparations. Ideally, one should inform oneself about soup kitchens who donate cooked food before Shabbat and Yom Tov and give some money periodically to one of this organizations, maybe specifying that it is given for Shabbat food. I will be glad to supply a few choices to one who inquires by email.[16]

---

14. Paraphrasing Ps. 23:3
15. Zohar, *Vayakhel* 208b.
16. simchahbenyosef@yahoo.com

All week long, the outside forces have the ability to attach themselves to the side of holiness and derive their sustenance from all the holy particles that we lose when we do not fulfill divine will.[17] As Shabbat approaches we have a respite, and they are soon going to have to let go. Consequently, Friday afternoon can indeed be a challenge, particularly for one who is unaware of the *avoda ruchanit* (spiritual service) which the Ari z"l transmitted to us to separate ourselves from them. It may happen that a child or even a close relative may do something that may irritate us. If the person falls into anger there goes the Shabbat…and much more. I will be glad to send advice on how to avoid anger to anyone who requests it by email. Alternatively, something can go wrong at home just when everything seems to be ready. We have to remember what is at stake and deal with what happened while trying to distance ourselves from the emotions that we want to avoid.

The Ari z"l reveals that as Shabbat approaches there is a certain *klippa* which is aware of the great concentration of spiritual light that will be soon flowing down to us, and so it tries to ascend and seize some for itself.[18] A spiritual flame of fire is then emitted on High from the forces of divine restraint, pushing this *klippa* back down to the lower world. It is at this time that we trim our nails and go to the *mikve*. After going to the *mikve*, we wash our face, hands and feet in hot water, thus expressing our awareness of the divine flame's action and our willingness to participate in the process by means of hot water, which emulates the cleansing flame.

The ritual is as follows: in the room adjoining the bathroom, we prepare a basin, a small towel and a *kli* (vessel) for the ritual washing of hands. We fill the *kli* with hot water from the kitchen – as hot as we can stand without burning ourselves – and bring it out into the adjoining room; alternatively, we may engage in this practice in the kitchen. We then use the hot water to wash our face, thinking of that beautiful verse at the end of Shir Hashirim that speaks of "a flame from the Divine." (We should think of this verse in the original

---

17. The teachings that follow are adapted from "Shalhuva de esha beErev Shabbat," in *Sefer Pitchei Tefilla*, vol. 3, 64.
18. *Siddur Rechovot haNahar* (Jerusalem: Yeshivat Nahar Shalom, 5765), 29.

Hebrew).[19] We have in mind that at this time a *shalhevet* (divine flame) emerges from the divine name spelled *Yud* and *Heh*, mentioned at the end of this verse, in order to get rid of the outside forces in our midst. Then we dry our face and repeat the process with our hands and then with our feet.

After this ritual of washing with hot water, we should recite this verse:

| Of every remnant that will be in Zion and every remaining one in Jerusalem, holy will be said of him.[20] | וְהָיָה הַנִּשְׁאָר בְּצִיּוֹן וְהַנּוֹתָר בִּירוּשָׁלִַם קָדוֹשׁ יֵאָמֶר לוֹ: |

Rabbi Masud refers to the washing with hot water in his *piyyut*:

| You will now fulfill the injunction of hot water [by pouring hot water on] face hands and feet – speaking the mystery of the divine flame [by saying] the verse "inscribed for life."[21] You will then subdue the outside forces from within Jerusalem. Speedily may it be established and rebuilt! | דִין מַיִם חַמִּים תַּדִּיחַ. פָּנִים יָדַיִם רַגְלַיִם. סוֹד שַׁלְהֶבֶת יָ"ה תָּשִׂיחַ. פָּסוּק הַכָּתוּב לְחַיִּים. אָז הַקְּלִיפוֹת תַּזְנִיחַ. מִקֶּרֶב יְרוּשָׁלַיִם. מַהֵר תְּכוֹנֵן וְתִבָּנֶה: |

To this teaching of the Ari z"l Rabbi Luria adds from the teachings of Chasidut a whole level of meaning, which, he says, may help to explain the inner meaning behind this ritual. Upon telling us to keep Shabbat, Hashem asks us "to know *(ladaat)* that I am Hashem Who makes you

---

19. Song 8:6.
20. Is. 4:3. Cited from Rabbi Akiva Yosef Eisenbach (compiler), *Or HaShabbat: Yalkut Maamarim BeInyanei Shabbat Kodesh* (Jerusalem: privately published, שנת יגדל כח השבת), 109.
21. Paraphrasing the verse we have to say upon washing the face, hands and feet with hot water in preparation of Shabbat (Is. 4:3).

holy." [22] The Hebrew word *Daat* (intimate knowledge) refers to a higher state of consciousness in which we are imbued with *devekut* to Hashem. *Daat* is the biblical term for marital union, which is the metaphor used in Shir Hashirim to describe Hashem's love for Israel – a love which is exclusive and demands exclusivity in return.

However, warns Rabbi Luria,[23] the word *daat* has two different meanings which contradict one another. On the one hand, *daat* indicates closeness and *devekut*; on the other, it has connotations of destruction and distance, as in the verse: "He punished *(vayeda)* the people of Sukkot,"[24] and also: "He destroyed *(vayeda)* their palaces."[25]

Rabbi Luria explains that when the light of *daat* shines down, it is permeated with such an intense attachment that it requires *hasachat hadaat* (diverting one's attention from the surroundings) in order to zero in on one issue exclusively, thus becoming oblivious to everything else. Now, as Shabbat approaches, we are asked to focus on our love for Hashem, to the exclusion of everything else in our lives. This results in a *shevira* (breaking) of the outside forces.

By washing with hot water and having in mind the "flame of the Divine," we are, as it were, arousing *devekut* on High. The light of *daat* is then ignited and this causes a breakage and weakening in the outside forces, preventing them from ascending on High.

To go over the order of events again: we first trim our nails and shower. Then we go to the *mikve* and go to synagogue to say Mincha. Upon coming home, whenever we are ready to finish getting dressed for Shabbat, we first do the ritual of washing face hands and feet in hot water. Then we get dressed, donning our Shabbat clothes. Rabbi Chaim Vital notes that his teacher the Ari z"l was careful about this and recommended that every single Shabbat garment, whether inner or outer, be designated for wearing only on Shabbat and never on the weekdays. Furthermore, if possible we should try to wear white garments on Shabbat.

---

22. Ex. 31:13.
23. *Sefer Pitchei Tefilla*, vol. 3, 65.
24. Judges 8:16.
25. Ezek. 19:7.

As Rabbi Masud sings:

Four white garments. [The work] *Minchat Chasidim* is taught. We are invited to honor the Shabbat – to serve with clean garments, alluding to heavenly lights – the four letters of the *Shem Havaya*. Clothe me in garments of salvation.[26]	אַרְבַּע בְּגָדִים לְבָנִים. מִשְׁנַת חֲסִידִים שְׁנוּיָה. לִכְבוֹד שַׁבַּת מְזֻמָּנִים. לְשָׁרֵת בִּכְסוּת נְקִיָּה. רֶמֶז לְאוֹרוֹת עֶלְיוֹנִים. אַרְבַּע אוֹתִיוֹת הֲוָי"ה. בִּגְדֵי יֶשַׁע תַּלְבִּישֵׁנִי:

Even though the housewife is entrusted with the task of making the home ready for Shabbat, the husband must personally make sure that this is done fittingly and must contribute as much as he can. He must prepare the lights that his wife will ignite in honor of Shabbat, using pure olive oil rather than candles.[27]

One should change the bed with fresh sheets and set the table in a way that it will be fit for the King. It is also important to sharpen the knife in honor of Shabbat. This is part of the process of driving away the outside forces. We may trim the knife that will be used for the last-minute Shabbat preparations. Again, our intention is to drive away the forces of impurity. As with any of these preparations, we must make sure we say verbally that we are doing this in order to fulfill the *mitzva* alluded to in the verse: "and it shall be on the sixth day when they prepare what they bring."

Upon sharpening his Shabbat knife, Rabbi Alexander Ziskind would say, "My Maker and Creator, I am now sharpening my knife in honor of Shabbat as hinted to in our holy Torah, 'they prepare what they bring.' My main intention is to bring You pleasure."[28]

---

26. Paraphrasing Is. 61:10.
27. The practice of putting the wicks in a little glass in which some water has been poured and then is filled with olive oil is discouraged by some *poskim* (halachic authorities) because the wick is extinguished by the water when the olive oil ends. A good solution is to purchase small tubes to contain the wicks, with several holes to let in the oil. With these wicks, there is no need to add water. These wicks are sold in Israel under the name *Tzinorot Lapetil*. The telephone number of the manufacturer in Israel is 03-6183042.
28. *Yesod Veshoresh Haavoda*; cited from *Or HaShabbat, Yalkut Maamarim Be'inyanei Shabbat Kodesh*, 39.

On the Sixth Day

All these elements of the spiritual preparation contribute to make our Shabbat a profound experience – an experience that can grow on every succeeding week. It is well, then, to do our utmost to carry out every one of them. Alas, the effect of our sins is that our human mind tends to forget, even what is essential. It is therefore advisable to make a bullet list of the main elements of this preparation, including all the verses we are to say and even the intentions we would like to have. We could have the list laminated and keep it the room where we plan to do the hot water ritual. We may then look at it briefly on Thursdays as well as after the hot water ritual.

Women point out that in earlier generations there was no refrigerator and women were unable to prepare for Shabbat until Friday morning. Why should the women of our generation act differently?

Rabbi Israel Avichai answers that in Tractate Shabbat in the Talmud the question when to prepare Shabbat is dealt with in a debate between Beit Shammai and Beit Hillel. The school of Shammai claims that one should prepare all week long, whereas the school of Hillel recommended that one begin preparing on Thursday. Consequently, a couple who yearn for spiritual elevation will follow the way of Beit Shammai in their way of preparing the Shabbat needs. However, while in exile in the past generations, the life of the Jews was fraught with difficulties and people could not devote themselves to spiritual elevation. In our times, *Hakadosh Barukh Hu* has perfected the world in order to enable us to become more spiritual.[29]

I also asked Rabbi Avichai about some women's claim that the *Chok LeIsrael* and the reading of the *parasha* on Fridays are a divine service incumbent on men (according to this Kabbalisic tradition) but not on women. Rabbi Avichai answered: "For a man it is an obligation; for a woman it is a merit." Indeed, all the elements of the *Tosefet Shabbat*

---

29. "In Tractate Shabbat there is a dispute between the disciples of Shammai and the disciples of Hillel. According to Shammai one prepares for Shabbat all week, according to Hillel only before Shabbat from Thursday on. Therefore, in order that man and woman may arrive at Shabbat with spiritual might, they prepare like Shammai. Unfortunately, in the exile the circumstances were difficult and so they did not devote themselves to spirituality; but now the Holy One, blessed be He, has improved the world so that we can be more spiritual." (Personal communication with Rabbi Israel Avichai.)

form part of man's divine service that the woman was not asked to take upon herself. However, it is not like the wearing of tallit and tefillin, which women may not do. On the contrary, when the woman is able to involve herself in the elements of *Tosefet Shabbat* in such a way that her household is not affected, it is considered a merit.

    The Ari z"l emphasizes that the period of time from midday Friday till the end of Shabbat is a time of compassion. That is the time in which the People of Israel begin to anticipate the closeness to the Holy One that Shabbat produces, and when the *Shekhina* begins to return to her rightful place. We must have in mind that all this *avoda ruchanit* that we do on Friday is not only for our sake, but rather for the ultimate purpose of contributing to the return Home of the *Shekhina*.

Chapter 16

I Came into My Garden

We have seen how the love between *Hakadosh Barukh Hu* and *Knesset Yisrael* resembles the marital bond and evokes the closeness of soul companions. However, human soul mates are traditionally understood as one single soul with a masculine half and a feminine half who were separated in order to be born into this world as male and female. Then, if they merit meeting when they grow up, they will get married and have a perfect relationship. Given this explanation, we can only wonder: How can the concept of soul mates apply to our relationship with *Hakadosh Barukh Hu*?

The creation of the Torah and *Knesset Yisrael* preceded *Hakadosh Barukh Hu*'s creation of this world, as we know it. The loftiest expression of *Knesset Yisrael*'s relationship with Hashem is portrayed in the words of Shir Hashirim with the expression *achoti kalla* (My sister, My bride). As Rabbi Luria explains: Our Sages have said that the Torah, *Hakadosh Barukh Hu* and Israel are One, for the Torah connects Israel with *Hakadosh Barukh Hu*, making them One in the way of *achoti*.[1]

We may ask: How can the closeness of soul companions be represented by the image of fraternal love? If the intensity of parental

---
1. "Achoti Rayati Yonati Tamati," *Sefer Beit Genazai: Shir Hashirim*, 145a.

Key to the Locked Garden

love is like sleeping waters in comparison to that of soul companions, fraternal love may not even be compared to parental love, let alone to the passion between man and woman!

However, the idea of fraternal love, in the verses as well as in the Zohar, does not focus on the intensity of love between siblings but rather on the degree of relationship between them. In the bond of *achoti kalla*, the love between bride and groom acquires the permanent quality of the attachment between siblings. The bond between siblings exists from birth and can never be broken. In contrast, a man and woman who want to get married have to undergo the marriage ceremony of *kiddushin* and *nissuin*. After the marriage ceremony, the bride will form part of her groom's essence and they will become one flesh. Yet their bond could be broken apart, for divorce cancels the bond created by *kiddushin* and *nissuin*. But a bond that is present from before Creation is impossible to break.

The first manifestation of the relationship between *Hakadosh Barukh Hu* and *Knesset Yisrael* with the unique togetherness of soul companions happened as a result of the Egyptian exile.[2] Hashem promised them:[3]

Anochi ered imkha mitzrayima	אָנֹכִי אֵרֵד עִמְּךָ מִצְרַיְמָה
vanochi aalkha gam alo	וְאָנֹכִי אַעַלְךָ גַם עָלֹה

This verse is translated "I will go down to Egypt with you and I will also bring you up again." However, some verses seem to ask us to probe further than the published translations, and examine what the simple meaning of the words is telling us. This is where the Torah's inner dimension comes in – to teach us about the meaning not only of each word in a verse, but even more, of each letter. If we pay attention to the wording of the verse, we notice that the word for 'ascent' appears twice, repeated in different grammatical forms. *A'alkha* is future tense (I will cause you

---

2. "Maamar Anochi Hashem Elokecha Asher Hotzetikha Me'eretz Mitzrayim," *Sefer Geulat Mitzraim*, 187-208.
3. Gen. 46:4.

I Came into My Garden

to ascend) and *gam alo* is an intensification of the preceding statement, meaning "I will make you ascend again."

Moreover, on the day of the Exodus, the verse says: "All of Hashem's armies left Egypt."[4] This verse implies that when the People of Israel went down to their Egyptian exile, *Hakadosh Barukh Hu*'s "armies" – if it can be said – went down together with them and at the end of their bondage left Egypt together with them. Our Sages have thus expounded that when Moses was shown the burning bush he was perceiving the revelation of the *Shekhina*, implying what is alluded to in the verse "I am with him in [the midst of] his distress."[5]

The Sages stress that this means not only that Hashem shared their distress, but rather, literally, to the extent that we can express it, that He inflicted the Egyptian exile on Himself as well. The Egyptian exile is thus seen as a period of *ibur* (gestation) in a spiritual womb. By sharing their gestation and emerging together with them, Hashem was creating the unique bond in which *Knesset Yisrael* became *etzem meatzamav* (part of His very essence). Hence the concept of soul companions in relation to our bond with Hashem.

In his work on Shir Hashirim, Rabbi Luria relates that Rabbi Akiva had a unique connection with King Solomon's masterpiece. The great Sage was drawn to the Song, for he was evidently able to understand all the allusions it contains. Reading the Song thus triggered his perception of our unique togetherness with Hashem. The Zohar gives a glimpse into a scene in which Rabbi Akiva is reading Shir Hashirim on Shabbat and his tears start flowing beyond his control. When his students express surprise at their great Torah master crying on Shabbat, Rabbi Akiva tells them that it was not sorrow that caused his tears, but on the contrary, the thought that all their suffering in the Egyptian bondage had an awesome purpose – that of enabling them to become part of His essence. As the Ari z"l teaches, just like gold is initially covered with layers of dirt and must be refined by burning away the outside layers until the gold shines through, similarly suffering refines our vessels until we make more space to receive the light Hashem wants to

---

4. Ex. 12:41.
5. Ps. 91:15.

give us. As the *Tikkunei Zohar* expresses it, when suffering is accepted with love, strict justice becomes lovingkindness.[6]

The great sage could not contain his tears of delight as he dwelt on the *devekut* that resulted from this bond. Rabbi Akiva understood that all the commandments are essentially instructions telling us what to do and what to avoid in order to attain and maintain the ultimate goal of the Torah: being in a constant state of *devekut* with the Source of life.

"The world was not worthwhile until the appearance of Shir Hashirim: all songs are holy but Shir Hashirim is the Holy of Holies," said Rabbi Akiva.[7] In order to explain Rabbi Akiva's statement, Rabbi Luria discusses the three levels of holiness in the Temple, pointing out that the divine service done in these corresponded to the three levels of closeness between *Hakadosh Barukh Hu* and *Knesset Yisrael*: There was the *Azara* (Court), the *Heikhal* (Sanctuary), and the *Kodesh Kodashim* (Holy of Holies). The Court is where they used to present the offerings and thus corresponds to the closeness of a servant with his Master. In the *Heikhal*, referred to as *Kodesh* (holy) were the table, the show-bread and the candelabra, all of which are evocative of children at their father's table. The innermost room – in which were placed the *Aron* (Ark) and the *Keruvim* (cherubs) – was referred to as *Kodesh Kodashim*.

The light of the Torah was in both the *Kodesh* and the *Kodesh Kodashim*, but these were two different types of light. In the *Heikhal* was the *menora* whose light represents the light of the Torah. The *menora* symbolized the togetherness that was prevalent *before* the Egyptian bondage and ensuing Exodus. It had seven branches, one separate from the others, and its middle branch was never extinguished as a miraculous sign of the *Shekhina*'s dwelling space with the People of Israel.[8] The *menora* was thus a token of the *Shekhina*'s togetherness with the People of Israel. In the *Kodesh Kodashim* was the Ark containing the Tablets of the Torah, and on top of the Ark were the cherubs, which represented the unification between *Hakadosh Barukh Hu* and *Knesset Yisrael*. The

---

6. *Tikkunei Zohar*, p. 95a.
7. Midrash Tanchuma on *Parshat Tetzave*; cited from Rabbi Luria, "Shir Hashirim Kodesh Hakodashim," in *Sefer Geulat Mitzrayim*, 268-269.
8. Tractate Shabbat 21; cited by Rabbi Luria in *Sefer Geulat Mitzrayim*, 269.

I Came into My Garden

Talmud teaches that on the festivals, the *Kohanim* would draw the curtain, revealing the golden cherubs who were miraculously embracing one another, and say to the people, "See how Hashem loves you!"[9] Rabbi Luria explains that Holy of Holies represents the unification of *Hakadosh Barukh Hu* and *Knesset Yisrael* His soul companion after leaving Egypt, when Israel had become *etzem meatzamav* (essence of His essence). They emerged, as it were, in the manner of twin souls, soul companions.

The Egyptian bondage may be seen as a time of *ibur* (gestation); on the other hand, it was also the *nesira* (separation) in which this One Soul had to be split into two so that the two could come together as One. This is because during gestation there is no consciousness. During their bondage the bond they would eventually have with Hashem as *etzem meatzamav* was coming into being, but they had no consciousness of it. Just as one does not have consciousness while in the womb, the People of Israel lost the sense of closeness to their Maker during their hard bondage.

After the *nesira* of the Egyptian bondage came the unification at the Giving of the Torah. The Ark and the Tablets of the Torah it contained represented the heavenly bond at the Giving of the Torah. As the Zohar teaches,[10] "*Hakadosh Barukh Hu*, the Torah and Israel are One," for the Torah is Hashem's wisdom and essence that He is extending to us so that our *devekut* to Him may reflect that we are part of His essence.[11]

Again, the comparison of Hashem's bond with Israel with fraternal love, as portrayed in Shir Hashirim and in the Zohar, is not based on intensity of feeling but rather on the fact of their being blood relatives! The idea of "sister" appearing in Shir Hashirim alludes to a very lofty concept, and Rabbi Luria reveals that Rabbi Akiva's deep emotion upon reading the Song on Shabbat was due to the great Sage's perception of the extraordinary nature of our relationship with Hashem.

The Sages have said that one of the things that distinguished Rabbi Akiva is his understanding that the love between *Hakadosh Barukh Hu* and *Knesset Yisrael* would never diminish, not even in the presence of

---

9. Tractate Yoma 54b.
10. Zohar, *Vayikra* 15 a-b.
11. "Shir Hashirim Kodesh Hakodashim," in *Sefer Geulat Mitzrayim*.

exile and affliction, because to the extent that we can express it, they are part of His very essence. Therefore, even though the spiritual entity of *Knesset Yisrael* was there before Creation, her unique relationship with Hashem only manifested in this world after the Exodus from Egypt, and it is impossible to cancel such a bond.

Rabbi Akiva's special contribution was thus to help us understand the mystery of Hashem's love for *Knesset Yisrael*. As the Isaiah expressed it, "Which is the bill of divorce (*sefer keritut*) with which I sent your mother away?"[12] Although the Hebrew expression is translated as "divorce," if we consider the literal meaning of the words, *keritut* means "cutting," and such a severance does not apply to a bond in which the essence of one is attached to that of the other.

It was Rabbi Akiva who taught: "Praiseworthy are you, O Israel! Before Whom do you cleanse yourselves? Who cleanses you? Your Father in Heaven. […] And it is also written: 'Hashem is Israel's *mikve*.'[13] Just as a *mikve* purifies those who are impure, so does *Hakadosh Barukh Hu* purify Israel."[14] The two types of closeness represented in the ideas of *Kodesh* versus *Kodesh haKodashim* are both reflected in these citations about purity. There is one type of purity stemming from "your Father in Heaven," and the very wording of the Mishna tells us that it evokes the closeness of children to their parents. Then there is a loftier type captured by the words of the Mishna: "*Hakadosh Barukh Hu* purifies Israel," for they are *etzem meatzamav*. Since He is the very Source of purity, it follows that in consequence they are pure as well.

The great Sage understood that the *tahara* (purification) of the People of Israel does not come from an external source, as in the case of those who need to immerse in a *mikve* in order to attain purity. When the People of Israel become Torah observant and cleave to their Source, they automatically shed all former impurity. In the prophecy of Isaiah Hashem says, "For My sake, for My sake I will do."[15] Hashem is saying

---

12. Is. 50:1.
13. Jeremiah 17:13. The usual interpretive translation of this verse is "God is Israel's hope (*mikve*)." I am citing the verse with the literal understanding of the word *mikve*.
14. Tractate Yoma 8:9.
15. Is. 48:11.

that He is doing the great kindness of helping us get rid of our mistakes by getting close to Him – for His sake. The expression *lemaani* (for My sake) implies that it is for the sake of His *Shekhina* who had to undergo the separation from the Beloved, for we are an integral part of her – we are the basis of her crown, and there cannot be a King without subjects.

At the Giving of the Torah there was a unification on High, as a result of which the People of Israel cleaved to their Source and shed all traces of impurity. Rabbi Avika thus understood that since in their essence, the People of Israel are *etzem meatzamav,* the heavenly unification at this time in which they received His Torah was, as Rabbi Luria puts it, *kechad,* like One complete entity – a bond of that same quality and intensity.

Rabbi Luria explains that right after the Golden Calf, we lost the ability to re-experience such a bond and in order to comfort us, Hashem made us build the *Mishkan* (portable Sanctuary) while in the desert, rather than waiting until we reached the Land, as it was originally planned. Rabbi Luria points out that this is why the Song starts with a wish: "O that He could kiss me…," expressing the people's desire to regain the bond of the Giving of the Torah!

This yearning could not be fulfilled until they purified all the levels of their soul from the terrible mistake committed. Hashem thus allowed them to build a portable Temple so that they would have some way of recapturing was they had tasted – even if only partially – until they earned to regain what they had lost. The *Mishkan* would only reveal the bond of two separate entities coming together like that of the embracing cherubs, but not the loftier bond in which – to the extent that we can express it – their spiritual stature could be said to resemble the Holy One.

This higher bond would only be revealed in the Land of Israel for only after coming into the King's home, His *dira batachtonim* (dwelling space below) which was the inner purpose of Creation, could there be the spiritual counterpart of *biah* (culmination of the marital bond) that seals the *nissuin,* making the bride and groom into one single entity. Hence, in the case of the built Temple in Jerusalem,

> [Rabbi Akiva] was the one who grasped the message of the Song. The sage understood the idea of the Holy of Holies transmitted by the embraced cherubs, namely that not only [did it evoke a

unification] in the way of *kiddushin* and *nissuin* but [more than that, it was an extension of] the bond in which they were part of His essence.[16]

And yet the revelation of the *Shekhina* in the Holy Temple was for all the People of Israel who came, and not everyone merited a total revelation of such caliber. In contrast, when it came to the *eitanei olam* – the elite souls such as those of the patriarchs who had attained the level of perfection required, the righteous who had led hard lives, struggling, yearning to attain that level, prodded on by their love of Hashem – the unification was complete. However, elsewhere, Rabbi Luria teaches:

> On the day selected for the Giving of the Torah the unification was with each and every soul of Israel, as the verse indicates, "face to face." […] The meaning of these teachings is that on this day the People of Israel ascended to the lofty spiritual level in which the unification was able to be with Israel Themselves and did not need to come about by means of their soul roots on High.[17]

Rabbi Moses Alshikh,[18] who was the teacher of Rabbi Chaim Vital before the holy Ari, poses the question: What was the purpose of the Holy Temple? Rabbi Alshikh begins by citing the verse in which Hashem is asking us to build it:[19] "They shall make a Sanctuary for Me so that I may dwell among them *(betocham)*." Rabbi Alshikh asks: Why does it say *betocham*, which literally means "within them," instead of saying *betocho* (within it) – namely within the Temple? This would have made sense, for the Temple was to provide a pure place in which the *Shekhina* would be able to dwell. Rabbi Alshikh's answer is that the main function of the Temple was served on the weekdays, during which the *Shekhina* indeed dwelt in the Sanctuary, "within it." With the Temple standing, the Children of Israel were

---

16. "Shir Hashirim; Kodesh Hakodashim," *Sefer Geulat Mitzraim*, 11b.
17. "Dodi yarad legano," *Sefer Beit Genazai: Shir Hashirim*, 172.
18. The completion of this chapter is adapted from the essay "Bati Legani," *Sefer Bet Genazai: Shir Hashirim*, 141.
19. Ex. 25:8.

able to repent from any transgression committed on the weekdays and attain expiation by bringing an offering to the Sanctuary. Thus they were cleansed of impurity and could be part of the Shabbat ascent.[20]

On Shabbat, however, when all the elements of Creation attain spiritual completion and no offerings of expiation were required, the Divine Presence would literally dwell within each soul of Israel, as it is written: "*veshakhanti betokham*," meaning I will dwell within each and every one."[21] On Shabbat each and every person was a Sanctuary for the Divine Presence; the unification was not limited to our heavenly soul roots at the level of the *Shekhina on High* as it was on weekdays. Although in the Temple days the unification was not as lofty as the *yichud* of Mount Sinai, still, it included us here below – namely *Knesset Yisrael Themselves*. Once again, the expression *Knesset Yisrael Themselves* refers to our inner souls in a state of togetherness, as opposed to *Knesset Yisrael* on High alluding to the aspect of our souls on High of which we have no perception.

As mentioned, the different levels of closeness of these two kinds of unification – the unification of two independent entities and the unification in the way of the bond of One – manifest in prayer. Rabbi Luria links these two types of unification to a moving verse from the Prophet Hoshea:[22]

It is stated in the prophets: "At that time, you will call me *Ishi* and no longer will you call me *Baali*."[23] The word *baali* alludes to a unification between two *nifradim* (separate entities) with the goal of transmitting *shefa* from the Giver [*Hakadosh Barukh Hu*] to the Receiver *Shekhina* who will receive it and transmit it to us].	כמו שמבואר בנביאים ביום ההוא תקראי לי אישי ולא תקראי לי בעלי, כי בעלי הוא יחוד של שני נפרדים שיש בזה תכלית של השפעה מהמשפיע למקבל, אבל בחינת אישי הוא שיש ביניהם קרבה שנעשה כחד עם היחוד, וכמו שהוא נקרא איש כך היא נקראת אשה. וזה מעלתו של שבת שהיחוד בו על ידי שנעשו כחד, וזה משום שהוא יום שבו העולמות עולים למעלה מיד עם תחילת

---

20. *Sefer Bet Genazai: Shir Hashirim*, 141.
21. Ibid.
22. The teachings that follow are adapted from Rabbi Moshe Luria, "Shinuy Tefilot Chol VeShabbat [Beit]" in *Sefer Pitchei Tefilla*, vol. 3, 134ff.
23. Hosea 2:18.

> In contrast, the aspect of *Ishi* connotes a degree of kinship which became *kechad* (a bond of One) by means of the *yichud* [...]. And this the unique quality of Shabbat: the *yichud* is of the kind of *kechad* (the bond of One), for at this time the heavenly words ascend from the very beginning of the day, and the higher they ascend, the more is revealed the kinship – namely that all [the souls of *Knesset Yisrael*] are emanated from One same Source. [This revelation] is concealed on the weekdays, and therefore the *yichud* of the weekly prayers is that of two separate entities. [...]
>
> היום, וכל מה שהם עולים למעלה מתגלה יותר הקשר של הנאצלים שהם באים משורש אחד ודבר זה נעלם בחול ולכן זה נשאר יחוד של נפרדים [...]

It is important to be aware of these teachings, for what happens on High at the time of the *Amida* prayer affects us directly, depending on our level of understanding as well as of readiness or merit.

Therefore, if we may restate the preceding: on Shabbat each and every person has the potential to become a Sanctuary for the Divine Presence. As Rabbi Luria writes:

> Therefore, there was no pilgrimage to the Holy Temple on Shabbat, because each [Jewish soul has the potential to become] an actual Sanctuary – *Knesset Yisrael*, His soul companion.[24]
>
> ולכן, אין עלי' לרגל בשבת משום שכל אחד יש בו אותה בחינה של מקדש כנסת ישראל בת זוגו [...]

---

24. "Maamar hayichud beShabbat uMoadim baMikdash veEretz Israel," in *Sefer Beit Genazai: Eretz Israel*, vol 2, 548ff.

I Came into My Garden

On Shabbat the people did not have to go to the Temple as they did on the festivals, because all the People ascended on High and merged with the Source.

In the days leading up to the festivals in Temple times, when the people were not fulfilling divine will, the cherubs turned their faces toward the Temple itself, away from each other. In such cases, the *kohanim* would not draw aside the *parokhet* (curtain). In contrast, on Shabbat the cherubs were always looking at each other with love, thus suggesting the *yichud* with *Knesset Yisrael Themselves*.

When the enemy overcame Israel and burst into the Holy Temple, upon entering the Holy of Holies they found the cherubs locked in their holy embrace. How could this be the case? If it was permitted on High that the enemy should have the upper hand, it surely meant that the People were not fulfilling divine will! How then, could the cherubs be intertwined when the enemy came in? Rabbi Luria answers that the enemy came in on Shabbat, when the cherubs were always intertwined, regardless of the people's behavior.

Consequently, in the Temple days and after its destruction the unification with *Knesset Yisrael Themselves* continues to be. We thus sing in the *zemirot* (holy songs): "Those who love Hashem and anticipate the rebuilding of the Ariel [holy Temple], celebrate and rejoice on the Shabbat day as at the Giving of the Torah."²⁵ This may be likened to the Generation of the Desert who themselves acted as the divine bride ever since the Giving of the Torah. Such a unification may only take place in the Land of Israel, however, the appropriate place for unification. Outside of Israel, such a unification may not take place because the outside forces are rampant.	נמצא שבשבתות בזמן המקדש ואחר החורבן הם באותה בחינה יחוד עם כנ״י עצמם, ולכן אומרים בזמירות אוהבי ה׳ המחכים בבנין אריאל ביום השבת שישו ושמחו כמקבלי מתן נחליאל כמו דור המדבר שהאיר אצלם בחינה זו של הם עצמם כלה לז״א מעת מתן תורה. והאומנם נראה שיחודזה אינו יכול להיות אלא בארץ ישראל ששם הוא המקום של היחוד אבל בחו״ל אין מקום ששם יכול להיות היחוד שהרי כוחות הטומאה שולטים שם.

---

25. "Kol Mekadesh Shevii" Sefer Zemirot In Honor of Shabbos, from the Jerusalem Siddur, trans. Rabbi Avraham Sutton (New York: Targum Press, 1996), 27-29.

Rabbi Luria writes that Rabbi Akiva was thus particularly moved because he was reading the Song at the time of *Tosefet Shabbat*, "for at this time it is revealed that *Knesset Yisrael* is His soul companion without being hindered by [errors committed in] the weekdays. Consequently, there was no [need to bring a] sin offering on Shabbat."[26] We have what it takes to leave behind all our mistakes and merit attaining the level of *Knesset Yisrael*, His soul companion. When we read Shir Hashirim close to the beginning of Shabbat, we are reminded that even now, at this time all is forgiven and we may all attain an experiential perception of the bond.

There is no greater delight than reading the beautiful verses of the Song when we understand how much love and longing is concealed in every verse. One of these verses says,[27] "*Bati legani achoti kalla* (I have come to My garden, My sister, My bride!)"

As Rabbi Luria explains, *Knesset Yisrael Themselves* – that is, all of us – *we* are Hashem's "garden." That is why Shabbat is called *yom simchatchem* (your day of joy), for the unification is also with Israel Themselves.

And as Rabbi Aryeh Kaplan writes: "The Additional Soul enters man on the Sabbath, and […] [to the extent that we can express it] God dwells within man. It is thus written: *Come into My garden*."[28]

---

26. *Sefer Beit Genazai: Shir Hashirim*, 11b.
27. Song 5:1.
28. The Mezricher Magid, *Magid Devarav Le Yaakov* 39; cited from Rabbi Aryeh Kaplan *The Light Beyond: Adventures in Hassidic Thought* (New York: Moznaim Publishing Corp., 1981), 271.

Appendix I

Soul Levels

It is important to have in mind that we are receiving the different levels of the Additional Shabbat soul at the time they come down Heaven.

- We receive the first level of the additional Shabbat soul at the fifth hour on Friday morning.
- We receive another level at *chatzot yom* (midday).
- We receive other levels as we say *Vaychulu* before the Shabbat evening *Amida*, during the *Amida*, and during the Kiddush.
- We receive the additional level of *nefesh* associated with the evening time as we say *boi kalla* (come O Bride) at the end of the song *Lekha Dodi* during *Kabbalat Shabbat*.
- We receive the additional *ruach* as the congregants in synagogue say *Barekhu*.
- One who is unable to go to synagogue may receive the *ruach* by reading a Zohar text, designed for such a purpose, which is included in many siddurim for laymen.[1]

---

1. See *Kegavna* in *The Complete ArtScroll Siddur, Nusach Sephard,* 356-357.

Key to the Locked Garden

- We receive the additional level of *neshama* associated with the evening time as we say *ufros aleinu sukkat shelomekha* (extend upon us Your canopy of peace) before saying the *Amida*.
- On Shabbat morning we receive the loftier daytime aspects of the additional level of *nefesh* after saying *Nishmat col chai*, when the congregants in synagogue say *Barekhu*.
- We receive the additional level of *ruach* as we say the words *Hashem sefatai tiftach* (Hashem, open my lips" at the beginning of the *Amida*.
- We receive the additional level of *neshama* at the *kedusha* section of *Mussaf*, as the congregants say *Ayeh mekom kevodo* (where is the place of His glory).
- We receive another level of Additional soul throughout the second Shabbat *seuda*.
- We receive another daytime aspect of the additional level of soul at the end of the Mincha *Amida* on Shabbat afternoon, before the repetition of the *Amida*.
- We receive the last aspect of the additional level of soul as we say *tzidkatecha* after the *Amida* of Mincha.

Appendix II
Birkat HaLevana
Insights into the inner teachings of a mysterious ritual

RABBI MOSHE LURIA ON BIRKAT HALEVANA

Once a month, Havdala is followed by *Birkat HaLevana* (the Blessing of the Moon). Both Shabbat and the new month are especially favorable times for closeness between the Holy One, blessed be He, and His *Shekhina*, though the ways in which the closeness is arrived at are very different. Rabbi Luria discusses this in an essay entitled *Birkat HaLevana*,[1] from which the following discussion is adapted.

Rabbi Luria bases his essay on the following passage, which is part of the *Birkat HaLevana* service:

> It was taught in the academy of Rabbi Yishmael: Even if Israel merited no other privilege than to greet their Father in heaven once a month, it would be sufficient for them.[2] Abayye said, "Therefore we must recite it standing."[3]

---
1. In *Sefer Pitchei Tefilla*, vol. 4, 470ff
2. Sanhedrin 42a.
3. Ibid.

Rabbi Luria links the two Talmudic statements in this passage to a verse from Shir Hashirim:

> Who is this coming up from the wilderness, leaning on her Beloved?[4]

Rabbi Luria's essay brings out the connections among these three things, which appear unrelated at first glance.

The verse from the Song of Songs, in its original context, is followed by a verse that is literally translated "Under the apple tree I aroused your love for me." However, quoting from the work *Avodat Panim*, Rabbi Luria gives a homiletic interpretation of these two verses:

> How worthy she is ascending from the wilderness bearing Torah and His Presence, clinging to her Beloved? Under Sinai suspended above me, there I roused Your love…

This interpretation is based first of all on Rashi's interpretation of the words "Who is she?":

> *Hakadosh Barukh Hu* and His court of law say about the Community of Israel. "How worthy she is ascending from the wilderness … at the Giving of the Torah and shows her love to all while she is still in exile!

Thus with "under the apple tree I aroused your love for me," the Community of Israel is saying to her Beloved, "Remember how, when I was under Mount Sinai suspended over my head like an apple, I aroused Your love for me?" This, says Rashi, is like an intimate conversation during the night with the wife of one's youth.

Night, Rabbi Luria continues, is the time of concealment of the Divine Presence in which the unification on High between *Hakadosh Barukh Hu* and the Community of Israel is not complete. And yet, there is still a relationship like to that with the wife of one's youth, in which

---

4. Song 8:5.

the Community of Israel arouses her Beloved in order to awaken a desire Above for passionate attachment with the Community of Israel below.

Thus even in times in which divine flow is restrained (just as man's attention is diminished while sleeping), still, through our initiative from below (when Israel is longing for closeness to *Hakadosh Barukh Hu*), there comes about a complete unification similar to that in the times of spiritual completion such as Shabbat or Yom Tov. This, Rabbi Luria relates to Rabbi Yishmael's statement: "Had Israel not been privileged to greet the countenance of their Father in Heaven except for once a month, it would have sufficed them."[5] That is, by means of their longing for closeness to *Hakadosh Barukh Hu*, they draw downward a time of spiritual completion and unification which is not the product of an orderly ascent from level to level. As a result, they are spared all *dinim* (acts of strict justice).

Basing himself on *Meor Enayim*[6], Rabbi Luria writes that the time of *Birkat HaLevana* is a great time of divine favor, when we are able to arouse within us the desire for divine closeness. This in turn brings about the desire Above to be "face to face" with the People of Israel. Hence Abaye's statement, in the passage quoted above, that *Birkat HaLevana* must be recited while standing.

"Standing" recalls the *Amida* prayer whose main goal is to initiate the heavenly unification that will take place at the last blessing, *Sim Shalom* (grant peace). In the case of the *Amida* prayer, however, this unification comes about at the apex of the building we erect through the order of prayer, as one ascends the steps of a building, going in orderly way from level to level. But at the time of *Birkat HaLevana* we can attain this spontaneously by means of the yearning we show as in the verse "leaning upon her Beloved."

Thus there are two times of "face-to-face" unification. One is the product of the completion of the spiritual building of the unification on

---

5. This statement is taken from Sanhedrin 42a.
6. A major Chassidic work written by the Maggid of Chernobyol (1739-1797) and edited by his disciple Rabbi Eliyahu, created and edited in Chernobyol and first published in Slovita in 1798. It is considered one of the most treasured Chassidic works. Publication data not available.

High by mean of our divine service, while the second one comes about at the time when the People of Israel inspire divine desire to be close to them. The completion of the spiritual building comes about on Shabbat, as is known, for the heavenly worlds are adjusted to completion on Shabbat according to the order of ascent initiated by our divine service in the three parts of Shabbat.[7] The second unification takes place on Rosh Chodesh, which begins the renewal of the moon. At that time the Community of Israel is built anew; they can therefore bring about completion on High by means of the desire they show below.

According to Rabbi Luria, the unification on Rosh Chodesh is referred to in a verse from Ezekiel about the eastward-facing gate of the inner Temple courtyard. This gate remained closed on weekdays but would open on Shabbat and on Rosh Chodesh. Rabbi Luria cites a midrashic passage from *Pirkei debei Eliezer,* chapter 51, which builds on the references in Ezekiel:

> Rabbi Yehuda says: On every Shabbat in the Temple days, the Children of Israel would see the gate of the Temple's inner courtyard open on its own: Then they would know that the Shabbat had started and they would begin to sanctify the Shabbat [with their prayers]. And the same would happen on every Rosh Chodesh. The Children of Israel would come to the Temple and when they saw the gates open on their own, they knew that the new moon had just come to be and they would then say the prayers to sanctify the month, whose inception is announced to the Children of Israel by the sight of the new moon. When, upon being there, they would see the gates miraculously open as if by their own volition, they would be conscious of the Divine Presence of the Holy One, blessed is He – the *Shekhina* – about whom it is said [Psalms 89:9] "Hashem, God of Legions, who is like You, O Strong One, God?" And also, [Ezekiel 44:2], Hashem said to me: "This gate shall be closed; it shall not be opened; no man may come through it, because Hashem, the God of Israel, has come through it; it shall be closed." [The people] would then immediately bow and prostrate

---

7. I.e. the Shabbat evening *tefilla* and ensuing *seuda*, the morning *tefilla* and following *seuda*, and the afternoon Mincha prayer followed by the third *seuda*.

themselves before their Maker, as the verse says [Ezekiel 46:3] "The People of the land prostrated themselves at the entrance of that gate *(vehishtachavu am haaretz patach hashaar hahu)*."

The word "gate" is made up of the letters *peh* (פ), *tav* (ת), and *chet* (ח). Written without the vowels, as on a Torah scroll, these letters could be read as either *petach* (entrance) or *patach* (opened). The standard translation of the verse, based on the first reading, is "The People of the land prostrated themselves at the entrance *(petach)* of the gate [on Shabbat and Rosh Chodesh]. The midrash, however, adopts the second reading and understands the verse as saying, "When the People of the land prostrated themselves, that gate opened *(patach)*."

The message of this midrash is that no matter what our suffering in exile, if just once a month, when the moon is renewed, we could succeed in greeting the countenance of our Father in Heaven, in attaining "face to face" closeness – it would be, as Rabbi Ishmael Yishmael says, enough. The face-to-face unification is a type of closeness with Hashem we otherwise have only on Shabbat and on the festivals; the rest of the time we are struggling against life challenges. The awareness that a similar time of closeness is available at the beginning of every month enables us to illuminate our inner darkness as we cause joy on High. One who reads *Birkat HaLevana* with joy at the thought that his service and bond to the Creator is being renewed at this moment is permeated with the divine favor flowing down at this time.

Similarly, the Talmud teaches that on the festivals, the *kohanim* would unroll the curtain before the Holy of Holies so that the People of Israel could see the cherubs, one of whom represented Hashem and the other one the Community of Israel.[8] On the festivals the cherubs were in a state of embrace, and the *kohanim* would tell the people, "See how the Holy One loves you!" On festivals they would have to unroll the curtain – they had to perform an action below to bring about this union Above. But on Shabbat and Rosh Chodesh it happened on its own. On Shabbat the union was set up from Above and completed by our service below, whereas on Rosh Chodesh it was inspired by our yearning below.

---

8. Tractate Yoma 54b.

Key to the Locked Garden

We may now examine another statement from the text of *Birkat HaLevana*:

> Who with His utterance created the heavens, and with the breath of His mouth all their legion. A decree and a schedule did He give them that they did not alter their assigned task.

These words allude to the unification on High parallel to the action of the heavens and all their legion. In contrast, the words that follow, "They are joyous and glad to perform the will of their Owner," allude to what we, the People of Israel, do below with our divine service, and as we say in the *brakha*, who are destined to renew themselves just like the moon which is a code word alluding for the Community of Israel.

We thus read the sequence of Rabbi Yishmael's statement, followed by the verse from the Song to indicate that by emulating the action of "leaning upon her Beloved," we can draw down from Heaven the same type of unification, even at this moment in which it is not initiated on High. Hence in *Birkat HaLevana* we also say the verse: "He comes, leaping upon the mountains, skipping upon the hills."[9]

May we merit experiencing this yearned moment, drawing down our awaited *Geula* before its time, as we did at the time in the Exodus from Egypt.

THE BEN ISH CHAI ON BIRKAT HALEVANA

I have reproduced below the halakhot as well as advice regarding *Birkat HaLevana* from the compilation of the Ben Ish Chai (Rabbi Yosef Chayim),[10] the eminent Torah sage of Bagdad, known for his responsa as well as for his Kabbalistic writings, with their translation.

> [22] You should recite *Birkat HaLevana* with joy and careful enunciation, for it is a way of greeting the *Shekhina*. Pious men and Torah scholars have the custom to immerse in a *mikve* on the day prior

---

9. Song 2:8-9.
10. *Sefer Ben Ish Chai: Chelek Halakhot. Hotzaat Sefarim Mercaz haSefer,* Jerusalem, 1954, 134-135.

to *Birkat HaLevana* and this is a good custom, in particular if one has marital relations. If you were fasting during the daytime you should taste something before reciting *Birkat HaLevana*. Do not recite the blessing until it is totally nightfall and the light of the moon may be clearly discerned on the ground.

[23] Seven full days must elapse after the *molad* before reciting *Birkat HaLevana*; these are counterpart of the *sefirot* (divine emanations) *keter* (crown), *chochma* (wisdom), *bina* (understanding), *daat* (knowledge, *chesed* (lovingkindness), *gevura* (restraint), *tiferet* (harmony). If a cloud – even thin – is covering the moon, do not recite the blessing. You may recite the blessing all night long, even after *chatzot* (midnight). Keep your feet together, as when reciting the *Amida* prayer, and when saying *ki er'eh shamecha* [Psalms 8:4, *when I see Your heaven...*] raise your eyes and look at the moon. However, from the moment that you start saying the *brakha* you must not look at it again.

[24] A blind person should abstain from reciting the *brakha*, for there is halakhic debate on the subject which is not conclusive, and whenever there is a doubt as to the obligation to recite a *brakha* it is preferable to abstain. A blind man should stand near the chazzan who is to recite the *brakha*, asking the chazzan to have in mind that he is including him; he will thus fulfill his obligation to say the *brakha* by hearing it. One who can only see with the help of glasses may say the *brakha* even though he is unable to see [the moon] without glasses.

It is necessary to say the *brakha* under the open sky and not under a roof. Only if a person is unable to go outdoors, because of illness or any other reason, may he say the *brakha* indoors under a roof. [When saying it outdoors] it is preferable to stand over hollow ground [rather than on cement] if possible.[11]

---

11. The earth represents *Malkhut* (the *Shekhina*, who is the collective Soul of Israel). We are welcoming her as we say *Birkat HaLevana*.

[25] You must say three times the formula *keshem she anachnu merakdim* (just like we dance...) in the text of the *Birkat HaLevana*, and each of these three times make three slight jumps as you are saying this.[12] There a mystery behind this teaching related to the ascent of the *sefirot* on which our intention is now focused. And here in our city, Bagdad, it is the custom to make three small jumps when saying *besiman tov tehi lanu* (may it be a propitious sign for us), and I personally have adopted the local custom.

In addition, upon saying *keshem sheanachnu merakdim*, I make three jumps anew and teach others to follow suit. Moreover, our custom here is to make three other small jumps as we say *David melech Israel chai vekayam* (David, king of Israel, is still living).

[26] In the text of the *brakha*, do not say *sheaf hem*, but rather *shegam hem* (they also [are destined to renew themselves like it]). In the phrase *siman tov tehi lanu*, you must say *tehi lanu* (May this be [[a propitious sign for us]]) and not *tihyeh lanu* (This will be [a propitious sign for us]).[13]

If you are reciting the *Birkat HaLevana* on your own rather than together with the congregation, you should say *keshem sheani meraked* (just like I dance...) instead of *keshem she anachnu merakdim* (just like we dance).

It is taught in several manuscripts that when you say *David, melech Israel*, you should have in mind the word David written in full, visualizing the letter *yud* after the letter *vav* (דויד), and this is also my practice.

The main focus of this ritual requires that we say the words *barukh yotzrikh, barukh osikh, barukh, barukh bor'ikh* (blessed is He who formed you, blessed is He who made you, blessed is He who created you, blessed is your Owner). The words must be said in this order so that the initial letters of the second word in each phrase (*yud, ayin, kuf, beit*) spell out the name Yaakov. Furthermore, according

---

12. Alternatively, the ArtScroll siddur suggests rising yourself on your toes as if dancing.
13. *Tehi lanu* is a request ("may this be..."), whereas *tihieh lanu* is a confirmation ("this will be...").

to the inner wisdom of the Torah, the word *yotzrikh* alludes to the heavenly world of *yetzira* (formation), *osikh*, to that of *asiya* (making), *konikh* to atzilut (closeness), and *bor'ikh* to that of *beriya* (creation).

As I have written with the help of Heaven in the holy book *Mekabbezi'el*, this formula is counterpart of the Name of *Havaya* [whose four letters are combined] in twelve permutations, *counterpart of the twelve months of the year*]. This particular permutation [concealed in the formula we are discussing] is that whose divine flow infuses Tishrei, the first month of the year in which the world was created, and this was the time in which Adam started to appoint cycles of time according to those of the moon. We thus say [at the end of *Birkat HaLevana*] *shalom*, alluding to the verse [Isaiah 32:17] *vehaya maase hatzedaka shalom* (the product of righteousness shall be peace).

There are reasons why we do not say *Birkat HaLevana* on Shabbat or Yom Tov, as mentioned in the work *Pachad Yitzhak* but the one of most relevance is that in order to say *Birkat HaLevana* we must arouse a sense of joy within, and on Shabbat, as on Yom Tov, we are already permeated with an inner joy which would not be related to the special joy we are to feel at the birth of the new moon.

Furthermore, as I wrote in the holy work *Mekabbezi'el*, another reason is that in the formula of *Birkat HaLevana* we are to curse our enemies, as in the verse *tipol aleihem emata…* (may terror fall upon them…), and we may not curse on Shabbat or Yom Tov, just as we may not issue a decree of *cherem* (excommunication) on these days.

[27] After the small jumps, say the verse [Psalms 51:12] *lev tahor…* (a pure heart…), repeating it seven times, counterpart of the seven *sefirot keter, chochma, bina, daat, chesed, gevura, tiferet,* followed by [Psalm 121] *Shir HaMaalot esa 'enai…* (Song of Ascents: I lift my eyes…), as well as [Psalm 150] "*Hallelu-yah, Hallelu El bekodsho…* (Praise *El* (the loving God) in His heavenly sanctuary)," as indicated in the siddur of our master the RaShaSh z"l (Rabbi Shalom Shaarabi).

Furthermore, it is written in the manuscript work *Keter Malchut* that it is now recommended to recite [Isaiah 30:26] *vehaya or halevana...* (and the light of the moon will be...). The author does not give any reason to explain the preceding but I have found an explanation [in the teachings of the Ariz"l] at the end of the work *Mavo Shearim* (125b and 126a) that this verse subsumes the essence of *Birkat HaLevana* [in a concealed form]. [Rabbi Chaim Vital] explains all the kabbalistic allusions concealed within this verse, linking them to the text of *Birkat HaLevana*. Also may be consulted *Pri Etz Chayim* page 108, column 4 as well as the siddur of kabbalistic *kavanot* (intentions) of Rabbenu haRaShaSh. It is thus recommended to recite this verse at this time.

As noted by Rabbi Mordechai Eliyahu zt"l, men who are single and would like to get married should be taught that they when saying *Birkat HaLevana* with intent and together with a congregation they will be drawing down to themselves a special divine favor to fulfill their yearning. They should strive not to miss a single opportunity to participate in the ritual of *Birkat HaLevana*.[14]

---

14. One who would like to receive these teachings about *Birkat HaLevana* from Rabbi Luria as well as from the Ben Ish Chai in Hebrew as well as in English may request it by email: simchahbenyosef@yahoo.com

Appendix III

Mystical Readings for the Shabbat Table

This Appendix should only be used by one who has read and integrated the teachings in this book as it contains readings that are regularly used on Shabbat by those who follow these teachings. I am also including two *piyyutim* that are not part of the liturgy but that summarize the teachings about Shabbat.

Please note that when reading these texts aloud on Shabbat the divine name written as *Elokim* should be pronounced "Elohim."

PRAYER OF RABBENU YONA[1]

This prayer was written by Rabbenu Yona of Gerona and is included in the compendium *Or HaShabbat.* Some read this prayer before eating with the intention that the meal that they are about to have may atone for any

---

1. The prayer stems from *Sefer Yesod HaTeshuva LeRabbenu Yona meGerona*. It is included in *Siddur Rechovot HaNahar, Chelek Ohr Hashabbat* (Jerusalem: Yeshivat Nahar Shalom, 5765), 17.
Rabbenu Yona's classic *Gates of Repentance-Shaarei Teshuva* is available in vocalized Hebrew with side by side English translation (Jerusalem: Torah Classics Library, 2014).

Key to the Locked Garden

sin inadvertently committed. Rabbi Benayahu Yissachar Shemueli, Rosh Yeshiva of Nahar Shalom, who edited this compendium of prayers and intentions for the Shabbat day, adds that before going to the *mikve* on Friday, one should repent of one's past errors and say the following prayer.

Please Hashem, I have detached myself from You in sin; I have acted intentionally and perversely; I have done these things *(kazot vekazot)* from the time I came in to the world until today.[2] And now my heart inspires me and my spirit moves me to return to You in truth, with a good and complete heart, with all my heart, my soul and all my means, to admit, abandon and throw away all sin from myself. [I want] to create for myself a new heart and spirit, to be cautious and zealous in my awe of You. You, Hashem my God, Who opens Your hand to penitents, and helps those who come to be purified, open Your hand and accept my complete repentance before You. Support my attempt to deepen my awe of You and help me against the Satan who is fighting me with deception and who wants to take my soul to kill me, destroying my soul forever. Prevent him from overcoming me. Distance him from my two hundred and forty-eight body parts, and cast him onto

וְאַתָּה יי אֱלֹהַי, הַפּוֹתֵחַ יָד בִּתְשׁוּבָה וּמְסַיֵּיעַ לַבָּאִים לִטָּהֵר, פְּתַח יָדְךָ וְקַבְּלֵנִי בִּתְשׁוּבָה שְׁלֵימָה לְפָנֶיךָ, וְסַיְּיעֵנִי לְהִתְחַזֵּק בְּיִרְאָתֶךָ, וְעָזְרֵנִי נֶגֶד הַשָּׂטָן הַנִּלְחָם בִּי בְּתַחְבּוּלוֹת וּמְבַקֵּשׁ נַפְשִׁי לַהֲמִיתֵנִי לְבִלְתִּי יִמְשׁוֹל בִּי. וְהַרְחִיקֵהוּ מִמָּאתַיִם וְאַרְבָּעִים וּשְׁמוֹנָה אֵבָרִים שֶׁבִּי, וְתַשְׁלִיכֵהוּ בִּמְצוּלוֹת יָם, וְתִגְעַר בּוֹ לְבִלְתִּי יַעֲמוֹד עַל יְמִינִי לְשִׂטְנִי. וְעָשִׂיתָ אֶת אֲשֶׁר אֵלֵךְ בְּחֻקֶּךָ, וַהֲסִירוֹתִ לֵב הָאֶבֶן מִקִּרְבִּי, וְנָתַתָּ לִי לֵב בָּשָׂר.

See the section "Preparation in Thought" in Chapter 15, "On the Sixth Day," for an additional explanation of the time in which this prayer should be read.

2. The Hebrew words *kazot vekazot* allude to the spiritual process caused by transgression and have to read as they appear in the Hebrew text. In addition, one who wants to add his/her own errors committed in that particular week, may do so.

the deep recesses of the sea, so that he can no longer stand on my right side in order to make me sin. And You made it happen that I should walk according to the dictates of Your law, and I will: Remove the stone heart from within me, as You gave me a heart of flesh.

I beseech You, Hashem my God, hear Your servant's prayer and supplication, and accept my repentance. Do not allow any sin or transgression to delay my prayer from being fulfilled in my repentance. Let there be defending angels before Your Throne of Glory to speak on my behalf, and if so great is my sin that I have no defending angel, You Yourself make me a tunnel under Your Throne of Glory and accept my repentance, and Your gesture will not return empty handed for You are He Who listens to prayer.

אָנָּא יי אֱלֹהַי שְׁמַע אֶל תְּפִלַּת עַבְדְּךָ וְאֶל תַּחֲנוּנָיו, וְקַבֵּל תְּשׁוּבָתִי, וְאַל יְעַכֵּב שׁוּם חֵטְא וְעָוֹן אֶת תְּפִלָּתִי וּתְשׁוּבָתִי. וְיִהְיוּ לִפְנֵי כִסֵּא כְבוֹדְךָ מְלִיצֵי יוֹשֶׁר לְהַמְלִיץ בַּעֲדִי לְהִכָּנֵס לְפָנֶיךָ. וְאִם בְּחֶטְאִי הָרַב וְעָצוּם אֵין לִי מֵלִיץ יוֹשֶׁר, חֲתוֹר לִי אַתָּה מִתַּחַת כִּסֵּא כְבוֹדְךָ וְקַבֵּל תְּשׁוּבָתִי וְלֹא אָשׁוּב רֵיקָם מִלְּפָנֶיךָ, כִּי אַתָּה שׁוֹמֵעַ תְּפִלָּה:

After this prayer, the *Chemdat Yamim* recommends that we should read Psalms 92 and 93 in order to receive the beginning influx of the Shabbat additional soul.

FIRST SHABBAT *SEUDA*

The Ari z"l wrote three songs with the intention that they should be sung at each of the three Shabbat *seudot*. *Azamer Bishvachin* is the first, to honor *Malkhut*, who is alluded to as Field of Holy Apples. Facing each stanza is the transliteration of the song. Following the song is Rabbi Moses Luria's interpretation of each stanza.[3]

---

3. "Azamer Bishvachin," *Sefer Pitchei Tefilla*, vol. 3, 280ff. I only refer to Rabbi Luria's interpretations that are within the scope of this book. The terminology I use in these translations is based on explanations that I have written throughout this book.

Key to the Locked Garden

AZAMER BISHVACHIN

אַתְקִינוּ סְעוּדָתָא דִמְהֵמְנוּתָא שְׁלֵימָתָא. חֶדְוָתָה דְמַלְכָּה קַדִישָׁא.
אַתְקִינוּ סְעוּדָתָא דְמַלְכָּה. דָּא הִיא סְעוּדָתָא דַחֲקַל תַּפּוּחִין קַדִישִׁין. וּזְעֵיר אַנְפִּין
וְעַתִּיקָא קַדִישָׁא אַתְיָן לְסַעֲדָה בַּהֲדֵיהּ.

Prepare the meal of perfect faith, the joy of the Holy King.

Prepare the meal of the King. This is the feast of *Chakal Tapuchin Kadishin* (the "Field of Holy Apples"). *Zeir Anpin* and *Atika Kadisha* also come to feast at this meal.

Azamer bishvachin	אֲזַמֵּר בִּשְׁבָחִין.
Leme'al go fitchin	לְמֵיעַל גּוֹ פִתְחִין.
Debachakal tapuchin	דְּבַחֲקַל תַּפּוּחִין.
De inun kadishin.	דְּאִנּוּן קַדִישִׁין:
Nezamin lah hashta	נְזַמִּין לָהּ הַשְׁתָּא.
Biftora chadeta	בִּפְתוֹרָא חַדְתָּא.
Ubimnarta tavta	וּבִמְנַרְתָּא טַבְתָּא.
Denahara al reshin.	דְּנָהֲרָא עַל רֵישִׁין:
Reshimin ustimin	רְשִׁימִין וּסְתִימִין.
Bego kol almin	בְּגוֹ כָּל עָלְמִין.
Beram Atik Yomin	בְּרַם עַתִּיק יוֹמִין.
Hala batish batishin	הֲלָא בָּטִישׁ בַּטִישִׁין:
Yehei raava kameh	יְהֵא רַעֲוָא קַמֵּיהּ.
Detishrei al ameh	דְּתִשְׁרֵי עַל עַמֵּיהּ.
Veyit'aneg lishmeh.	דְּיִתְעַנַּג לִשְׁמֵיהּ.
Bimtikin vedubshin.	בִּמְתִיקִין וְדוּבְשִׁין:
Asader lidroma	אֲסַדֵּר לִדְרוֹמָא.
Menarta disetima	מְנַרְתָּא דִסְתִימָא.
Veshulchan im nahama	וְשֻׁלְחָן עִם נַהֲמָא.
Bitzfona arshin	בִּצְפוֹנָא אַרְשִׁין:

Mystical Readings for the Shabbat Table

Bechamra go khasa	בַּחֲמְרָא גּוֹ כַסָּא.
Umedanei asa	וּמְדָאנֵי אַסָּא.
Learus vaarusa	לְאָרוּס וַאֲרוּסָה.
Lehitakfa chalashin.	לְהִתַּקְפָא חַלָּשִׁין:
Ne'ater lehon kitrin	נְעַטֵּר לְהוֹן כִּתְרִין.
Bemilin yakirin	בְּמִלִּין יַקִּירִין.
Beshav'in iturin	בְּשַׁבְעִין עִטּוּרִין.
De'al gabei chamshin.	דְּעַל גַּבֵּי חַמְשִׁין:
Shechinta tit'atar	שְׁכִינְתָּא תִּתְעַטָּר.
Beshit nahamei listar	בְּשִׁית נַהֲמֵי לִסְטָר.
Bevavin titkatar	בְּוָוִין תִּתְקַטָּר.
Vezinin dechnishin.	וְזִינִין דִּכְנִישִׁין:
(Shevitin ushvikin	(שְׁבִיתִין וּשְׁבִיקִין.
Mesaavin dirchikin	מְסָאֲבִין דִּרְחִיקִין.
Chavilin dime'ikin	חֲבִילִין דִּמְעִיקִין.
Vekhol zinei charshin.)	וְכָל זִינֵי חַרְשִׁין:)

Rabbi Moshe Luria's Commentary

I will sing in His praises in order to enter the holy gates of the Apple Field's higher consciousness. On Leil Shabbat at this time, *Malkhut* receives light from *Zeir Anpin*. We thus express our desire to join in and receive as well light from *Malkhut*. As we sing this song, we ascend together with *Malkhut*, becoming included within her and becoming illuminated with the lights she receives.

Let us now invite her with a newly set table and a good candelabra, emanating light onto the heads of each person, and of every member of the Community of Israel. As the children of the holy *Malkhut*, by inviting her we are asking her to draw upon us some of the light she now receives by means of the Shabbat lights we have ignited.

The right and the left and between them the Bride who comes adorned with jewels and garments. This is an allusion to the Shabbat candles and the heavenly unification the candlelighting brings about, as explained in the teachings of the Ari z"l. The jewels and garments allude to all the fallen holy sparks *Malkhut* gathered while in the world below during the weekdays, that she now elevates to their Source.

Her husband hugs her – that is, arouses her from the stupor of exile, instilling a longing that will grow until the heavenly unification that will occur in *Mussaf*. From the beginning of Shabbat, we join the *Malkhut* and receive together with her the *devekut*, passionate attachment of the spiritual embrace occurring at this time. Our *devekut* will grow until the time of Mincha in which we become Hashem's soul companions. The words *katish katishin* allude to her total *bittul*, giving everything over to Hashem at this time, which is also true regarding Israel Themselves.

Cries and grief are comforted and are no longer. We have new countenances, new spirits and souls. Under the influence of the above-mentioned spiritual hug, *Malkhut* puts aside all the *dinim*, against the Children of Israel. In a similar way, infused by longing for closeness because of the light directed below at this time, all our causes for anguish evaporate as if we had no material bodies, no cause for concern, but only new faces and souls. We only want to get closer and closer; that is why on Shabbat we may not ask for personal prayers, for if we did it would seem that our ability to experience *teshuka* (longing) was damaged. Overcome by the fire of longing, we forget all material concerns.

Much joy will now come – not once but twice as much. Light will be drawn [toward us] and blessings will infuse our souls. The increased closeness to Hashem of the beginning of Shabbat brings a great joy – a double joy, for on Shabbat everything is double (we need two challa breads; we say the *Amida* of *Mussaf* after the morning *Amida*, etc.). This joy brings a spiritual light and blessings to us although the unification is not yet taking place at this time.

Let all those who escort the Bride approach and bring about the tikkunim, rectifications, order to cause an arousal Above and below for the heavenly unification, thus drawing down good fruits, that is, material as well as spiritual blessings, that will become multiplied just like fish.

[The heavenly unification] will create [holy] souls and new spirits with the thirty-two… spreading down to the three branches [*Bina*, *Zeir Anpin* and *Malkhut*, and then to us].

And her seventy heavenly crowns and the King Above – the Holy of Holies – alluding to the unification of *Mussaf*, in which *Zeir Anpin* and *Malkhut* will be with Chochma and Bina, glowing with an illumination from *Keter*.

We learn from the Ari z"l that we should say at the beginning of the first Shabbat meal "*Atkinu Seudata Dimehemnuta* (Prepare the meal of perfect faith)" [...]; this is the feast of the Field of Holy Apples. *Zeir Anpin* and *Atika Kadisha* also come to feast at this meal. We derive from this statement that the unification of *Zeir Anpin* and *Malkhut* brings about a heavenly unification of the loftier manifestations of divine revelation. That is why, even though this is the *seuda* honoring the *Malkhut*, the statement tells us that the other levels are present as well, "feasting" with her, that is, receiving an illumination from the unification of *Zeir Anpin* and *Malkhut*. The far-ranging outcome of our spiritual arousal at the beginning of Shabbat, our reading of Shir Hashirim and our candle-lighting, affects the unification on High of not only of *Zeir Anpin* and *Malkhut*, but also of all the levels of divine revelation.

May it be Hashem's will to dwell on His people [and that we will] delight for the sake of His Name through sweets and honey. After explaining above the effect on High of all the expressions of our arousal at the beginning of Shabbat, we emit the prayer that the honey sweetness of the heavenly unification in *Mussaf* be extended to the unification at the time of Mincha with Israel Themselves. We are asking that the People of Israel below should also experience the delight of the unification with Hashem just as it occurred on High. Most importantly, we are asking that the sweetness of His closeness should give us the strength to distance ourselves from temptations during the coming week and focus instead on our longing for closeness.

I set up on the south side the Menora, the mysterious candelabra, and a table with bread shall I place on the north side. Each one of us should arrange at home that the Menora be on the south side and the table on the north side, just as it was in the Holy Temple. Since we are asking for the same quality of unification with us below, we should arrange our homes as it was in the Temple when the Holy King would come to dwell with *Knesset Yisrael*.

With wine in the glass and two branches of myrtle to honor the Groom and Bride to imbue with spiritual strength those who are weaker

Key to the Locked Garden

in faith – with the help of the wine which fills the heart with joy, and the fragrance which imbues the soul with delight.

Let us now crown the precious words with seventy crowns that supersede the fifty. Through the words of our Kiddush, *Malkhut* will become illuminated with the *Keter* of *Zeir Anpin*. These are seventy crowns that transcend the level of Bina who is associated with the Fifty Gates of Understanding. These supernal crowns are extended as well to *Knesset Yisrael Themselves*, who receive directly from the heavenly *Malkhut*.

The *Shekhina* will crown herself with the six loaves of bread on each side. We are now asking that at the time of Mincha, *Knesset Yisrael Themselves* rise to be soul companions, just like the *Shekhina*. May the six challot on each side of the bread tray act in the way of the letter *vav*, whose numeric value is six. Just like the letter *vav* means "and," thus joining words together, may we join the heavenly unification, and become crowned by the *vavin*, thus receiving all the lights still concealed on High.

(May the forces of destruction and all that afflicts us be distanced and destroyed.) The divine revelation we receive on Shabbat evening distances the forces of impurity who attach themselves to the People of Israel during the weekdays, for they cannot stand the loftiness of the light now illuminating *Knesset Yisrael*.

VIHEI RAAVA

When we say the Aramaic prayer *vihei raava* (may it be Your will) just before all three *seudot*, we are asking for the divine *shefa* to come from *Atika Kadisha* to *Zeir Anpin*, who will transmit it to the heavenly *Malkhut* and then to *Knesset Yisrael Below*. Then we will be able to receive the good gift of Shabbat from the Hidden House of Treasures at the top of the *koma elyona* (divine structure)

Vihei raava min kodam Atika	וִיהֵא רַעֲוָא מִן קֳדָם עַתִּיקָא
Kadisha dekhol kadishin. Temira	קַדִּישָׁא דְּכָל קַדִּישִׁין. טְמִירָא
Dekhol temirin setima dekhola	דְּכָל טְמִירִין סְתִימָא דְּכֹלָא
Deyitmashekh tala ilaa mineh	דְּיִתְמְשֵׁךְ טַלָּא עִלָּאָה מִנֵּהּ
Lemalia resheh diZeer Anpin	לְמַלְיָא רֵישֵׁיהּ דִּזְעֵיר אַנְפִּין
Ulehatil lechakal tapuchin kadishin	וּלְהַטִּיל לַחֲקַל תַּפּוּחִין
Binehiru deanpin beraava	קַדִּישִׁין בִּנְהִירוּ דְאַנְפִּין בְּרַעֲוָא

Mystical Readings for the Shabbat Table

Ubechedvata dekhola veyitmashekh min	וּבְחֶדְוָתָא דְכֹלָּא וְיִתְמַשֵׁךְ מִן
kodam Atika Kadisha dekhol	קֳדָם עַתִּיקָא קַדִּישָׁא דְכָל
Kadishin temira dekhol temirin	קַדִּישִׁין טְמִירָא דְכָל טְמִירִין
Setima dekola reuta verachamei	סְתִימָא דְכֹלָּא רְעוּתָא וְרַחֲמֵי
China vechisda binehiru ilaa	חִנָּא וְחִסְדָּא בִּנְהִירוּ עִלָּאָה
Bir'uta vechedvata alai veal kol	בִּרְעוּתָא וְחֶדְוָתָא עָלַי וְעַל כָּל
Benei beti vekol hanilvim elai	בְּנֵי בֵיתִי וְעַל כָּל הַנִּלְוִים אֵלַי
Veal kol benei Israel ameh	וְעַל כָּל בְּנֵי יִשְׂרָאֵל עַמֵּיהּ
Vayifrekinan mikol atkin bishin	וְיִפְרְקִינָן מִכָּל עַקְתִּין בִּישִׁין
Deyeitun lealma. Veyeitei lana ulekhol	דְיֵיתוּן לְעָלְמָא. וְיֵיתֵי לָנָא וּלְכָל
Nafshatana china vechisda vechayei	נַפְשָׁתָנָא חִנָּא וְחִסְדָּא וְחַיֵּי
Arikhei umezonei revichei	אֲרִיכֵי וּמְזוֹנֵי רְוִיחֵי וְרַחֲמֵי מִן
verachamei min kadameh,	קֳדָמֵיהּ אָמֵן כֵּן יְהִי רָצוֹן אָמֵן
amen ken yehi ratzon, amen veamen.	וְאָמֵן:

May it be the will of *Atika Kadisha*, holiest of all holy, most hidden of all hidden, who is concealed from all, that the heavenly dew flow from Him to *Zeir Anpin* and to the "Field of Holy Apples" with the light of His countenance, with desire and joy for all. May there be drawn from *Atika Kadisha*, holiest of all holy, most hidden of all hidden, who is concealed from all, desire and compassion, grace and loving kindness, with a radiant light, with desire and joy, [directing them] upon me and the members of my household, upon all those who are dependent on me, and upon all the Children of Israel, His people. May He redeem us from all the evil troubles which befall the world. May He bring us and all our souls grace and kindness, long life, ample nourishment, and compassion from Himself, Amen, may such be His will. Amen and Amen.

ZOHAR READING BEFORE EVENING KIDDUSH[4]

As taught in the work *Chemdat Yamim*, the Zohar describes and explains what the early Sages used to say before Kiddush at the onset of Shabbat, for this beautiful text cited below contains the entire mystery of the Kiddush

---

4. Zohar, *Vayak'hel* 207b. It is with gratitude to *Hakadosh Barukh Hu* that I present the annotated translation of the Zohar texts we may read in the Shabbat *seudot*. The

Key to the Locked Garden

we say at this time. When those who not know how to focus their intent on the Kabbalistic mysteries read this text, it will be considered on High as if they had directed their intention on all the mysteries in the Kiddush.[5]

Rabbi Shimon bar Yochai helps us internalize the Infinite Light of the Holy *Ein Sof* directed toward us at this time as we read the special texts about each of the three *seudot*. These readings are not obligatory, unlike the prayers instituted by our Sages for the Shabbat; rather they constitute our personal offering to contribute to the divine joy at these times. A practical suggestion is to read the Zohar texts before the Grace after Meals in order to avoid disturbing other participants in the *seudot*, even though at this time one may be too tired to concentrate in Zohar reading. Alternatively, those who accept the Shabbat upon themselves early may have the time to read the Zohar texts before the *seuda* begins.[6] It is important to realize, however, that Shalom is one the Names of *Hakadosh Barukh Hu*; we must not jeopardize peace and harmony in our homes for the sake of reading these holy texts, if there a chance that it will cause frustration to any of the meal participants. The Zohar texts below appear with a facing transliteration and are followed by their translation into English based on the teachings of the above mentioned *Matok Midevash*. I have rendered the Zohar as literally as possible, sometimes at the expense of English expression, in order to best transmit the meaning of the text; it important to understand, however, that in order to appreciate the message of the Zohar one needs to study it with a master.

Yoma da mitatera beshivin itrin	יוֹמָא דָּא, מִתְעַטְּרָא בְּשִׁבְעִין עִטְרִין
Ushema ilaah kadisha ishtelim bekhol sitrin,	וּשְׁמָא עִלָּאָה קַדִּישָׁא, אִשְׁתְּלִים בְּכָל סִטְרִין,

---

annotations within all the Zohar translations in this Appendix stem from *Matok MiDevash*, the Zohar commentary of Rabbi Daniel Frish (zt"l).

5. *Chemdat Yamim*, 7.
6. It is the kabbalistic tradition to read an additional Zohar text at this time, found in Zohar, *Vayakhel* 203b. I have omitted it because it is beyond the scope of this book. This text is included in Rabbi Mordechai Eliahu's siddur.

Mystical Readings for the Shabbat Table

Veitnehiru kulehu dargin	וְאִתְנְהִירוּ כֻּלְּהוּ דַּרְגִּין,
Vekola bechedva debirkan,	וְכֹלָּא בְּחֶדְוָה דְּבִרְכָאן,
Ubikedusha al kedusha, vetosefet dikedusha,	וּבִקְדוּשָׁה עַל קְדוּשָׁה, וְתוֹסֶפֶת דִּקְדוּשָׁה:
Kidusha demaalei Shabta, da ihi kedusha deShabbat Bereshit.	קְדוּשָׁה דְּמַעֲלֵי שַׁבְּתָא, דָּא אִיהִי קְדוּשָׁה דְּשַׁבָּת בְּרֵאשִׁית.
Deha itkadash mitlatin utren shevilin, utlat dargin detapuchin kadishin.	דְּהָא אִתְקַדָּשׁ מִתְּלָתִין וּתְרֵין שְׁבִילִין, וּתְלַת דַּרְגִּין דְּתַפּוּחִין קַדִּישִׁין.
Uba'enan leadkara al hai kidusha kelala deovada dibereshit, venaicha beraza detlatin utren shevilin, utlat dargin deitkelilan behu	וּבָעֵינָן לְאַדְכָּרָא עַל הַאי קְדוּשָׁה, כְּלָלָא דְּעוֹבָדָא דִּבְרֵאשִׁית, וְנַיְיחָא בְּרָזָא דִּתְלָתִין וּתְרֵין שְׁבִילִין, וּתְלַת דַּרְגִּין דְּאִתְכְּלִילָן בְּהוּ
Raza desahaduta deovada dibereshit, dehainu "vaikhulu hashamayim vehaaretz vekhol tzevaam,"	רָזָא דְּסַהֲדוּתָא דְּעוֹבָדָא דְּבְרֵאשִׁית, דְּהַיְינוּ "וַיְכֻלּוּ הַשָּׁמַיִם וְהָאָרֶץ וְכָל צְבָאָם וְגוֹ'.
Vaikhal Elokim, de it besahaduta da tlatin vechamesh teivin. Tlatin utren shevilin, utlat dargin detapuchin kadishin:	וַיְכַל אֱלֹהִים, דְּאִית בְּסַהֲדוּתָא דָּא, תְּלָתִין וַחֲמֵשׁ תֵּיבִין. תְּלָתִין וּתְרֵין שְׁבִילִין, וּתְלַת דַּרְגִּין דְּתַפּוּחִין קַדִּישִׁין:
Tlat Dargin, deinun: shevii, shevii, shevii.	תְּלַת דַּרְגִּין, דְּאִינּוּן: שְׁבִיעִי. שְׁבִיעִי. שְׁבִיעִי.
Ve it beh raza de'alma ilaa, ve raza de'alma tataah, veraza de khol mehemnuta.	וְאִית בֵּיהּ רָזָא דְּעָלְמָא עִלָּאָה, וְרָזָא דְּעָלְמָא תַּתָּאָה, וְרָזָא דְּכֹל מְהֵימְנוּתָא.

Key to the Locked Garden

Tlat zimnin Elokim, chad alma tataah, ve chad pachad Itzchak, ve chad, alma ilaah kadisha, kodesh kudshin.	תְּלַת זִמְנִין אֱלֹהִים, חַד, עָלְמָא תַּתָּאָה. וְחַד, פַּחַד יִצְחָק. וְחַד, עָלְמָא עִלָּאָה קַדִּישָׁא, קֹדֶשׁ קוּדְשִׁין.
Ba'ei bar nash lemis'had sahaduta da vechedva, bire'uta de liba, le as'hada kamei marei demehemnuta.	בָּעֵי בַּר נָשׁ לְמִסְהַד סַהֲדוּתָא דָא, בְּחֶדְוָה, בִּרְעוּתָא דְלִבָּא, לְאַסְהֲדָא קַמֵּי מָארֵיהּ דִּמְהֵימְנוּתָא.
Vekhol man deyas'hid da, veyishvei libeh ure'uteh leda, mekhaper al kol chovoi.	וְכָל מַאן דְּיַסְהִיד דָּא, וִישַׁוֵּי לִבֵּיהּ וּרְעוּתֵיהּ לְדָא, מְכַפֵּר עַל כָּל חוֹבוֹי:
Barukh Ata Hashem Elokeinu Melekh haolam, asher kideshanu bemitzvotav veratza banu, vekhulei...	בָּרוּךְ אַתָּה ה' אֱלֹקֵינוּ מֶלֶךְ הָעוֹלָם אֲשֶׁר קִדְּשָׁנוּ בְּמִצְוֹתָיו וְרָצָה בָנוּ וְכוּ'
Hai kidusha ihu bechad matkela, lakobel sahaduta dimehemnuta,	הַאי קִידּוּשָׁא אִיהוּ בְּחַד מַתְקְלָא, לָקֳבֵל סַהֲדוּתָא דִּמְהֵימְנוּתָא,
Veinun tlatin vachamesh teivin acharanin, kema de it bevaykhulu	וְאִינּוּן תְּלָתִין וַחֲמֵשׁ תֵּיבִין אַחֲרָנִין, כְּמָה דְּאִית בְּוַיְכֻלוּ
Kola salkin leshiv'in teivin, leit'atera behu Shabbat, dema'alei shabta.	כֹּלָּא סַלְקִין לְשִׁבְעִין תֵּיבִין, לְאִתְעַטְּרָא בְּהוּ שַׁבָּת, דְּמַעֲלֵי שַׁבְּתָא.
Zakaah chulakeh debar nash, dikhaven re'uteh lemilim ilen, likara demareh.	זַכָּאָה חוּלָקֵיהּ דְּבַר נָשׁ, דִּיכַוֵּון רְעוּתֵיהּ לְמִלִּין אִלֵּין, לִיקָרָא דְמָארֵיהּ:
Baruch Adonai leolam Amen veAmen.	בָּרוּךְ ה' לְעוֹלָם. אָמֵן וְאָמֵן:

This day is crowned with seventy crowns. And the holy supernal Name is completed in all ways, and all the levels are illuminated, and everything is permeated with the joy from the blessings and with holiness at the added outpouring of holiness. The holiness of the onset of Shabbat is permeated with the same holiness of the Shabbat of Creation, for it is sanctified by means of thirty-two paths and three levels of "holy apples." We have to mention the work of Creation according to its rules that resulted from it, in the secret of the thirty-two paths and the three levels which are included in it. The secret of our testimony to the divine work of Creation is reciting *Vaychulu* ("On the seventh day *Elokim*, God completed His work which He had done, and He abstained on the seventh day from all His work which He had done. *Elokim* blessed the seventh day and hallowed it, because on it He abstained from all His work which *Elokim* created to make"),[7] for this testimony contains thirty-five words – thirty-two paths and three levels of holy apples.[8]

The three levels are alluded to in the three occurrences of the word "seventh."[9] We have here a secret from the heavenly world, a secret from the lower world, and a secret of all consciousness.[10] The Name *Elokim* is mentioned three times. One stands for the lower world; one for *Pachad Yitzchak* (Isaac's Fear), and one for the upper world, which is holy – the Holy of Holies. One must state this testimony with joy and desire of the heart, in order to present their testimony before the Master of Faith.[11] And all those who state this testimony while focusing their hearts' desire have expiated all their transgressions.

---

7. Gen. 2:1-2.
8. By stating the testimony of the Kiddush, we are adding levels of holiness to *Malkhut*, for of the 35 words of this Kiddush the initial 32 words allude to the 32 paths of wisdom, and the last 3 words allude to *Zeir Anpin's* three upper sefirot, *Chesed, Gevura*, and *Tiferet*, referred to as "holy apples."
9. As we say the word "seventh" three times we are alluding to the "holy apples," i.e. *Chesed, Gevura*, and *Tiferet*.
10. The first "seventh" alludes to *Bina*, or Divine Presence (*Shekhina*) in the World to Come; the second "seventh" is the heavenly *Malkhut*, or Divine Presence ruling over us in the lower world; the third "seventh" alludes to the lower *Malkhut*, the *Shekhina* – for the faith of Israel is in Hashem's Kingship over us. Our faith in Hashem's Presence with us on earth must have a strength bordering on consciousness, for one who merits such faith is helping His Presence be clearly revealed to all.
11. The Master of Faith is *Malkhut* – the *Shekhina* – in whom is the faith of Israel.

"Blessed are You, Hashem, our God, King of the universe, Who sanctified us With His commandments and took pleasure in us, etc..." This *Kiddush* (sanctification) is the exact testimony of this faith.[12] [The section of the Kiddush after the blessing on wine] contains another set of thirty-five words, just like in the paragraph *Vaykhulu*. Altogether this amounts to seventy words with which to crown the Shabbat at the beginning of Shabbat. Great is the reward of the person who directs his heart's attention on these words, for the sake of honoring his Maker.[13]

ZOHAR ON THE FIRST SEUDA[14]

As the *Shela haKadosh* taught,[15] it was the practice of the early Torah sages to state verbally their intention of fulfilling a mitzva before the action, as indeed we see from the words of Rabbi Abba in the Zohar cited below. The Zohar also tells us how the women involved in the artistic elaboration of the elements in the *Mishkan* would explicitly say:[16] "This is for the altar; this is for the curtain," etc.

Zachor et yom haShabbat lekadesho. Rabbi Isaac amar, ketiv vaybarekh Elokim et yom hashevii, ukhtiv baman: "sheshet yamim tilketuhu ubayom hashevii Shabbat lo yihieh bo.

(שמות כ) זָכוֹר אֶת יוֹם הַשַּׁבָּת לְקַדְּשׁוֹ. רַבִּי יִצְחָק אָמַר, כְּתִיב (שמות כ) וַיְבָרֶךְ אֱלֹהִים אֶת יוֹם הַשְּׁבִיעִי, וּכְתִיב בַּמָּן (שמות טז) שֵׁשֶׁת יָמִים תִּלְקְטֻהוּ וּבַיּוֹם הַשְּׁבִיעִי שַׁבָּת לֹא יִהְיֶה בּוֹ.

Keivan dela mishtechach beh mezonei, mah birketa ishtekhach beh.

כֵּיוָן דְּלָא מִשְׁתְּכַח בֵּיהּ מְזוֹנֵי, מַה בִּרְכְתָא אִשְׁתְּכַח בֵּיהּ:

---

12. This refers to what we stated in the first part of this Kiddush.
13. By means of this testimony, you are rectifying all that was done in the work of Creation and binding all of Hashem's forces together within your mind, thus causing heavenly light to illuminate the world below.
14. Zohar, *Yitro* 88a.
15. Shela haKadosh, Shaar Haotiot, 17: Ot Alef, Emet Veemuna.
16. Zohar, *Tazria* 50a. As taught in Simcha H. Benyosef, *The Beginning of Wisdom: Unabridged of THE GATE OF LOVE from Rabbi Eliyahu de Vidas' RESHIT CHOCHMAH*, Chapter Nine, section "State your intention," 284.

Mystical Readings for the Shabbat Table

Ela hakhi tana, kol birkan dile'ela vetata, beyoma shevi'ata talian. Vetana, amai la ishtekhach mana beyoma sheviaah.	אֶלָּא הָכִי תָּאנָא, כָּל בִּרְכָאן דִּלְעֵילָא וְתַתָּא, בְּיוֹמָא שְׁבִיעָאָה תַּלְיָין. וְתָאנָא, אֲמַאי לָא אִשְׁתְּכַח מָנָא בְּיוֹמָא שְׁבִיעָאָה.
Mishum dehahu yoma, mitbarkhan kol shita yomin ilain, vekhol chad vechad yahiv mezoneh letata, kol chad beyomoi, mehahi berakha demitbarkhan beyoma sheviaah.	מִשּׁוּם דְּהַהוּא יוֹמָא, מִתְבָּרְכָאן מִינֵיהּ כָּל שִׁיתָא יוֹמִין עִלָּאִין, וְכָל חַד וְחַד יָהִיב מְזוֹנֵיהּ לְתַתָּא, כָּל חַד בְּיוֹמוֹי, מֵהַהִיא בְּרָכָה דְּמִתְבָּרְכָאן בְּיוֹמָא שְׁבִיעָאָה:
Beginei kakh, man deihu bedarga dimehemnuta,	וּבְגִינֵי כַּךְ, מַאן דְּאִיהוּ בְּדַרְגָּא דִּמְהֵימָנוּתָא,
Ba'ei lesadra patora, uleatkena seudata belelia deShabta, begin deyitbarekh patoreh, kol inun shita yomin,	בָּעֵי לְסַדְּרָא פָּתוֹרָא, וּלְאַתְקְנָא סְעוּדָתָא בְּלֵילְיָא דְשַׁבְּתָא, בְּגִין דְּיִתְבָּרֵךְ פָּתוֹרֵיהּ, כָּל אִינּוּן שִׁיתָא יוֹמִין,
Deha behahu zimna, izdeman berakha, leitbarekha kol shita yomin deShabta, ubirkhata la ishtekhach befatora rekania. Ve al kakh, ba'ei lesadra patoreh belelia deShabta, benahamei ubimezonei.	דְּהָא בְּהַהוּא זִמְנָא, אִזְדְּמַן בְּרָכָה, לְאִתְבָּרְכָא כָּל שִׁיתָא יוֹמִין דְּשַׁבְּתָא, וּבִרְכְּתָא לָא אִשְׁתְּכַח בְּפָתוֹרָא רֵיקַנְיָא. וְעַל כַּךְ, בָּעֵי לְסַדְּרָא פָּתוֹרֵיהּ בְּלֵילְיָא דְשַׁבְּתָא, בְּנַהֲמֵי וּבִמְזוֹנֵי:
Rabbi Isaac amar, afilu beyoma deShabta namei.	רַבִּי יִצְחָק אָמַר, אֲפִילוּ בְּיוֹמָא דְשַׁבְּתָא נָמֵי.
Rabbi Yehuda amar, ba'ei lehit'anega behai yoma, ulemeikhal telat seudadtei beshabeta, begin deyishtechach sav'a ve'inuga behai yoma be'alma.	רַבִּי יְהוּדָה אָמַר, בָּעֵי לְאִתְעַנְּגָא בְּהַאי יוֹמָא, וּלְמֵיכַל תְּלַת סְעוּדָתֵי בְּשַׁבְּתָא, בְּגִין דְּיִשְׁתְּכַח שָׂבְעָא וְעִנּוּגָא בְּהַאי יוֹמָא בְּעָלְמָא:

Rabbi Abba amar, leizdamna birkheta beinun yomin dileela, demitbarekhan mehai yoma.

רִבִּי אַבָּא אָמַר, לְאִזְדַּמְּנָא בִּרְכְתָא בְּאִינּוּן יוֹמִין דִּלְעֵילָּא, דְּמִתְבָּרְכָאן מֵהַאי יוֹמָא.

Behai yoma, malia resheh deZeir Anpin, mitala denachit me'Atika Kadisha setima dekhola,

וְהַאי יוֹמָא, מַלְיָא רֵישֵׁיהּ דִּזְעֵיר אַנְפִּין, מִטַּלָּא דְּנָחִית מֵעַתִּיקָא קַדִּישָׁא סְתִימָא דְּכֹלָּא,

Veatil lechakla detapuchin kadishin, telat zimnei makad ayil Shabta, deyitbarekhun kulehu kachada.

וְאָטִיל לְחַקְלָא דְּתַפּוּחִין קַדִּישִׁין, תְּלַת זִמְנֵי, מִכַּד עָיֵיל שַׁבְּתָא, דְּיִתְבָּרְכוּן כֻּלְּהוּ כַּחֲדָא:

Ve al da ba'ei bar nash leit'anega telat zimnin ilen, deha beha talia mehemnuta dile'ela, beAtika Kadisha, ubi Zeir Anpin, ubeChakla detapuchin.

וְעַל דָּא בָּעֵי בַּר נָשׁ, לְאִתְעַנְּגָא תְּלַת זִמְנִין אִלֵּין, דְּהָא בְּהָא תַּלְיָא מְהֵימְנוּתָא דִּלְעֵילָּא, בְּעַתִּיקָא קַדִּישָׁא, וּבִזְעֵיר אַפִּין, וּבְחַקְלָא דְּתַפּוּחִין.

Uba'ei bar nash leit'anga behu, ulemeichdei behu. Uman degara' seudata minaihu, achzei pegimuta leela ve'onesheh dehahu bar nash sagi.

וּבָעֵי בַּר נָשׁ לְאִתְעַנְּגָא בְּהוּ, וּלְמֶחֱדֵי בְּהוּ. וּמַאן דְּגָרַע סְעוּדָתָא מִנַּיְיהוּ, אַחֲזֵי פְּגִימוּתָא לְעֵילָּא, וְעוֹנְשֵׁיהּ דְּהַהוּא בַּר נָשׁ סַגִּי:

Beginei kakh, ba'ei lesadera patoreh, telat zimnei, mikad 'ayel Shabta, vela yishtekach patoreh rekania, vetishrei birkheta 'aleh, kol shear yomei deShabta.

בְּגִינֵי כָּךְ, בָּעֵי לְסַדְּרָא פָּתוֹרֵיהּ, תְּלַת זִמְנֵי, מִכַּד עָיֵיל שַׁבְּתָא, וְלָא יִשְׁתְּכַח פָּתוֹרֵיהּ רֵיקַנְיָא, וְתִשְׁרֵי בִּרְכְתָא עֲלֵיהּ, כָּל שְׁאָר יוֹמֵי דְּשַׁבְּתָא.

Ubehai mila, achzei, vetalei mehemnuta leela.

וּבְהַאי מִלָּה, אַחֲזֵי, וְתָלֵי מְהֵימְנוּתָא לְעֵילָּא:

Mystical Readings for the Shabbat Table

Rabbi Shimon amar, hai man deashlim telat seudatei beShabata kala nafik umakhreza aleh, az tit'anag al Adonai, da seudata chada, lakobel Atika Kadisha dekhol kadishin.

רַבִּי שִׁמְעוֹן אָמַר, הַאי מַאן דְּאַשְׁלִים תְּלַת סְעוּדָתֵי בְּשַׁבַּתָּא, קָלָא נָפִיק וּמַכְרְזָא עָלֵיהּ, (ישעיה נח) אָז תִּתְעַנַּג עַל יְיָ, דָּא סְעוּדָתָא חֲדָא, לָקֳבֵל עַתִּיקָא קַדִּישָׁא דְּכָל קַדִּישִׁין.

Vehirkavtikha al bamotei aretz, da seudata tiniana, lakobel chakla detapuchin kadishin. Vehaakhaltikha nachalat Yaakov avikha, da hu shelimu deishtelim beZeir Anpin.

וְהִרְכַּבְתִּיךָ עַל בָּמֳתֵי אָרֶץ, דָּא סְעוּדָתָא תִּנְיָינָא, לָקֳבֵל חַקְלָא דְּתַפּוּחִין קַדִּישִׁין. וְהַאֲכַלְתִּיךָ נַחֲלַת יַעֲקֹב אָבִיךָ, דָּא הוּא שְׁלִימוּ דְּאִשְׁתְּלִים בִּזְעֵיר אַפִּין:

Ulekoblaihu ba'ei leashlema seudatei, uba'ei leit'anega bekhulehu seudatei, ulemechedei bekhol chad vechad minaihu, mishum deihu mehemnuta shelemata.

וּלְקָבְלַיְיהוּ בָּעֵי לְאַשְׁלְמָא סְעוּדָתֵיהּ, וּבָעֵי לְאִתְעַנְּגָא בְּכֻלְּהוּ סְעוּדָתֵי, וּלְמֶחֱדֵי בְּכָל חַד וְחַד מִנַּיְיהוּ, מִשּׁוּם דְּאִיהוּ מְהֵימָנוּתָא שְׁלֵימָתָא.

Uvegin kakh, Shabta ityekar mikol shear zimnin vechagin, mishum dekola beh ishtekhach, vela ishtekhach hakhi bekhulehu zimnei vechagei.

וּבְגִין כַּךְ, שַׁבְּתָא אִתְיַקַּר מִכָּל שְׁאָר זִמְנִין וְחַגִּין, מִשּׁוּם דְּכֹלָּא בֵּיהּ אִשְׁתְּכַח, וְלָא אִשְׁתְּכַח הָכִי בְּכֻלְּהוּ זִמְנֵי וְחַגֵּי.

Amar Rabbi Chiya, begin kakh, mishum deishtekhach kola beh, idkar telat zimnin. Dikhtiv, vaykhal Elokim bayom hashevii. Vayishbot bayom hashevii. Vaybarekh Elokim et yom hashevii.

אָמַר רַבִּי חִיָּיא, בְּגִין כַּךְ, מִשּׁוּם דְּאִשְׁתְּכַח כֹּלָּא בֵּיהּ, אִדְכַּר תְּלַת זִמְנִין. דִּכְתִיב, (בראשית ב) וַיְכַל אֱלֹהִים בַּיּוֹם הַשְּׁבִיעִי. וַיִּשְׁבּוֹת בַּיּוֹם הַשְּׁבִיעִי. וַיְבָרֶךְ אֱלֹהִים אֶת יוֹם הַשְּׁבִיעִי:

Rabbi Abba, kad hava yativ biseudata deShabta, havei chadei, bekhol chad vechad, vahava amar, da hi seudata kadisha de Atika Kadisha setima dekhola. Biseudata achara hava amar, da hi seudata deKudsha Brikh Hu. Vekhen bekhulehu seudateh, vahava chadei bekhol chad vechad. Kad hava ashlim seudatei, amar ashlimu seudatei dimehemnuta.	רַבִּי אַבָּא, (נ״א רב המנונא סבא) כַּד הֲוָה יָתִיב בִּסְעוּדָתָא דְּשַׁבְּתָא, הֲוֵי חַדֵּי, בְּכָל חַד וְחַד, וַהֲוָה אָמַר, דָּא הִיא סְעוּדָתָא קַדִּישָׁא, דְּעַתִּיקָא קַדִּישָׁא סְתִימָא דְּכֹלָּא. בִּסְעוּדָתָא אָחֳרָא הֲוָה אָמַר, דָּא הִיא סְעוּדָתָא דְּקוּדְשָׁא בְּרִיךְ הוּא. וְכֵן בְּכֻלְּהוּ סְעוּדָתֵי, וַהֲוָה חַדֵּי בְּכָל חַד וְחַד. כַּד הֲוָה אַשְׁלִים סְעוּדָתֵי, אָמַר אַשְׁלִימוּ סְעוּדָתֵי דִּמְהֵימְנוּתָא:
Rabbi Shimon, kad hava atei liseudaa, hava amar hakhi, atkinu seudata dimehemnuta ilaa, atkinu seudata demalka, vahava yativ vechadei. Kad ashlim seudata telitaa, havo makhrizei aleh, az tit'anag al Adonai, vehirkavitkha al bamotei aretz vehaakhaltikha nachalat Jacob avikha.	רַבִּי שִׁמְעוֹן, כַּד הֲוָה אָתֵי לִסְעוּדָתָא, הֲוָה אָמַר הָכִי, אַתְקִינוּ סְעוּדָתָא דִּמְהֵימְנוּתָא עִלָּאָה, אַתְקִינוּ סְעוּדָתָא דְּמַלְכָּא, וַהֲוָה יָתִיב וְחַדֵּי. כַּד אַשְׁלִים סְעוּדָתָא תְּלִיתָאָה, הֲווֹ מַכְרְזֵי עֲלֵיהּ, אָז תִּתְעַנַּג עַל יְיָ וְהִרְכַּבְתִּיךָ עַל בָּמֳתֵי אָרֶץ וְהַאֲכַלְתִּיךָ נַחֲלַת יַעֲקֹב אָבִיךָ:
Amar Rabbi Elazar liavui, ilen seudatei hekh mittaknin.	אָמַר רַבִּי אֶלְעָזָר לְאָבוּי, אִלֵּין סְעוּדָתֵי הֵיךְ מִתְתַּקְּנִין.
Amar leh, lelia deShabta, ketiv, vehirkavtikha al bamotei aretz. Beh belelia, mitbarekha Matronita, vekhulehu chakal tapuchin, umitbarekha patoreh debar nash, venishmeta itosfat, vehahu lelia, chedva deMatronita havei. Uba'ei bar nash lemechdei bechedvata ulemeikhal seudata deMatronita. Barukh Adonai leolam Amen veAmen.	אָמַר לֵיהּ, לֵילְיָא דְּשַׁבְּתָא, כְּתִיב, וְהִרְכַּבְתִּיךָ עַל בָּמֳתֵי אָרֶץ. בֵּיהּ בְּלֵילְיָא, מִתְבָּרְכָא מַטְרוֹנִיתָא, וְכֻלְּהוּ חֲקַל תַּפּוּחִין, וּמִתְבָּרְכָא פָּתוֹרֵיהּ דְּבַר נָשׁ, וְנִשְׁמְתָא אִתּוֹסְפַת, וְהַהוּא לֵילְיָא, חֶדְוָה דְּמַטְרוֹנִיתָא הֲוֵי. וּבָעֵי בַּר נָשׁ לְמֶחֱדֵי בְּחֶדְוָותָא, וּלְמֵיכַל סְעוּדָתָא דְּמַטְרוֹנִיתָא: בָּרוּךְ ה׳ לְעוֹלָם. אָמֵן וְאָמֵן:

[The verse says:] "Remember the Shabbat day to sanctify it" [Ex. 20:8]. Rabbi Isaac said: As it is written, "And God blessed the seventh day," [Gen. 2:3] and it is written about the manna: "Six days shall you gather it, but the seventh day is a Shabbat; on it there will be none" [Ex. 16:26]. Since there is no sustenance on this day, what kind of blessing is found in it?[17] Conversely, it is taught: All the blessings Above and below are dependent on the seventh day. And it is also taught: Why isn't there any manna found on the seventh day? Because all six lofty days [namely, the six *sefirot* of Creation] derive their blessings from that day, and each one of them gives sustenance below, each according to its own day, depending on the blessing that it itself derives from the seventh day.[18]

Because of this, one who has reached level of faith[19] needs to set the table and prepare the *seuda* for the Shabbat eve [even if his

---

17. We derive from the absence of manna on Shabbat that the nature of the divine blessing flowing down on Shabbat is not physical sustenance. What is then, this special Shabbat blessing?
18. For instance, *Chesed* exercises its dominion on Sunday, the first day of the week, and directs divine bounty onto *Malkhut*, the seventh *sefira* who has no light of its own other than what it receives from the *sefirot* above her. *Malkhut* is thus blessed with a lovingkindness stemming from that which the first day receives on Shabbat from *Bina*. The same happens with *Gevura* on Monday, the second day of the week, and the same is true of *Yesod*, who exercises its effect upon the sixth weekday – Friday – for it also directs onto *Malkhut* the bounty it receives on the Shabbat from *Bina*. *Malkhut* then distributes the bounty it receives to mankind below.

The six sefirot are conduits of divine *shefa* for the world below. On Shabbat these six conduits return to the Source of all blessings in order to absorb a renewed *shefa*. Consequently, on Shabbat the six conduits do not direct any divine bounty below, for at the time that they are themselves receiving it and thus do not give. This is what we learned from the words "God blessed the seventh day," namely, that all blessings for Above and below are dependent on the seventh day, since the seventh day, which corresponds to *Bina*, is the Source of all blessings. On Shabbat we thus able to receive spiritual bounty directly from *Malkhut*, whereas on the weekdays the bounty goes through the channels of lower spiritual worlds and becomes materialized in the process, to serve as physical nourishment for humans.
19. One who has reached the level of faith because his/her soul is part of the Community of Israel, whose souls stem from the world of *Atzilut*, referred to as emuna (faith). Our faith is imbued with the consciousness that our divine service is directed to the *Ein Sof*, Infinite Being, Who is revealed to us below by means of what may be represented as a spiritual structure consisting of levels interconnected like the rungs

situation is such that he has little or nothing to eat], so that his table will be blessed throughout all the six days, for at this time is directed below the blessing to infuse all six weekdays, and no blessing dwells on a breadless table. Consequently, it is necessary to set the table on the Shabbat eve with bread and food.[20] Rabbi Isaac said: In the daytime on Shabbat, one must do this as well.[21] Rabbi Abba said: [We must actually eat] in order to cause [literally: invite] the divine blessing to come upon those six lofty days – alluding to the six *sefirot* of Creation – for they derive their blessing from this day. On this day the upper facet of *Zeir Anpin* becomes filled with dew flowing from *Atika Kadisha*, the most concealed of all; and it [this dew] is given to the Field of Holy Apples [*Malkhut*] at three [different] times from the onset of Shabbat, so that all will receive the heavenly blessing as one.[22] And because of this Man is thus required to experience delight at these three times, for on this depends the consciousness on High[23] of *Atika Kadisha, Zeir Anpin*, and the Field of Holy Apples [*Malkhut*]. It is thus necessary that man delights and rejoices together with them.[24] When one misses one of these *seudot* [it is as if s/he] shows a flaw on High,[25] and the punishment s/he brings upon him/herself is grave. Because of this, man needs to prepare

---

of a chain, and the light flows constantly from the Source of all blessings till the end of the structure.

20. We learn from this teaching that we should always leave one challa bread [no more than one] under the bread cloth on the table at all times throughout the Shabbat day.
21. The table alludes to *Malkhut*, that is, the aspect of divine revelation from which sustenance flows to man below, just man receives his physical nourishment from the table. We thus begin to receive the Shabbat blessing from divine revelation at the level of *Malkhut* in the first *seuda*. In addition, however, we will receive a higher Source of blessings in the Shabbat morning *seuda*.
22. Hence the importance of delighting in the three *seudot*, for as one feels delight below s/he arouses delight on High and as a result draws downward the Shabbat *shefa* (bounty) from the holy *Ein Sof*, by means of *Atika Kadisha, Zeir Anpin* and *Malkhut*.
23. For only to the extent to which man derives spiritual delight from these three Shabbat *seudot* is *shefa* drawn down from the holy *Ein Sof* onto the different divine revelations whose names are going to be mentioned in the Zohar text above.
24. Namely, with the three different revelations of the Divine that correspond to the three *seudot*.
25. For s/he is preventing one of these divine revelations of *Atzilut* from receiving *shefa* from the holy *Ein Sof*.

his table three times from the onset of Shabbat, so his table should never happen to be empty, and the blessing will dwell on him during all the ensuing weekdays.[26] On this word [on the above-mentioned blessing] depends the consciousness [i.e. the *shefa* drawn from the holy *Ein Sof*] pervading the heavenly worlds.[27] Rabbi Shimon said: When one partakes of all three *seudot* on Shabbat, a Voice proclaims about him/her:[28] "Then you will delight *over* Hashem's Name," in the *seuda* which is counterpart of *Atika Kadisha*, holiest of all.[29] "And I will mount you astride the heights of the world" refers to [our preparations for] the second Shabbat meal to receive a share from the *Chakal deTapuchin Kadishin*, "the Field of Holy Apples."[30] "And I will provide you the heritage of your forefather Jacob" alludes to [the Shabbat afternoon prayer and ensuing third meal, in which] fulfillment comes upon *Zeir Anpin*. And how do you receive it [namely, that blessing]? – By [saying aloud to Hashem that you are] fulfilling these three *seudot*. We must experience delight at all these meals and rejoice in each and every one of them, because in this consists the full measure of consciousness.[31] Consequently, Shabbat is more precious than all other special times and festivals, because all [the levels of divine revelation] are [in direct contact with us] on Shabbat, and [the phrase *lehit'anag al Hashem*, to delight *over* the Name] is not mentioned at all times and festivals. Rabbi Chiya said: Because of

---

26. After the evening *seuda* the Arizal would leave a wrapped fragment of challa in the bread tray set on the tablecloth. The Shabbat wine cup remained on the table as well, with a few drops of wine left from the Kiddush recited on it. The wine cup was washed prior to the morning *seuda*. The fragment of challa bread is to be left on the tray after the second and third Shabbat *seudot* as well.
27. I.e. if man does not receive this blessing in the world below, all the heavenly entities will not receive it either.
28. Is. 58:14; literal translation my own.
29. This Zohar teaches that one who participates in this *seuda* is permeated with an *oneg* (delight) stemming from *Atika Kadisha*, whose space on high is at the top of the structure of divine revelation.
30. One who partakes of this meal will ascend with the *Malkhut* to receive *shefa* from *Zeir Anpin* together with her.
31. On Shabbat all the levels of divine revelation from the heavenly world of *Atzilut* are present before us and cast their illumination upon us in their corresponding *seudot*. In contrast, in each of the festivals, only one of these divine manifestations is revealed to us.

this, because all is revealed on Shabbat, it is repeated three times: "By the seventh day God completed His work…; and He abstained on the seventh day…; God blessed the seventh day…" [Gen. 2: 2-3] [Namely, each time "the seventh day" is mentioned it alludes to one of the three *seudot*, and we only receive the blessing upon participating in all three.] When Rabbi Abba [other extant versions say Rabbi Hamnuna Saba] sat down to partake of a Shabbat *seuda*, he rejoiced in each one of them, and he would say: This is the holy *seuda* of *Atika Kadisha*, most concealed of all. At another *seuda*, he would say: This is the *seuda* of the Holy One, Blessed is He. In this way, he would rejoice as he participated in each of the *seudot*. When he completed the *seudot* he would say: The *seudot* of *emuna* (consciousness) are now fulfilled.[32] [Namely, one who does not actually state that the *seuda* he is participating in is for Hashem, as in the statements written by the Ari z"l beginning with the word *Atkinu*, will not receive the blessing mentioned here.] When Rabbi Shimon came to partake of the *seuda*, he would say this in a loud voice: Let us prepare the *seuda* of the higher consciousness; let us prepare the King's *seuda*. He would sit and rejoice. When he would finish the third *seuda*, there was a heavenly proclamation about him: *Then you will delight over* Hashem's *Name* [that is, above divine revelation to man]; *and I will mount you astride the heights of the world; I will provide you the heritage of your forefather Jacob*. Said Rabbi Elazar to his father: These *seudot*, how are they fulfilled? Rabbi Shimon said to him:[33] About the Shabbat eve, it is written, "And I will mount you astride the heights of the world." In the middle of this night, the Queen is blessed, and all the Shabbat becomes one. Man's table is then blessed and an additional *neshama* (higher soul) comes upon him. That night brings about the

---

32. The reason why he would verbally announce the nature of each of the *seudot* rather than merely having it in mind is that in this way he would be involved in the *seuda* with his mind, speech and deed. By means of his *kavana* (intention) he would draw onto himself the power of *Chokhma*, thus involving the divine thought processes. Through his use of speech, he would draw onto himself the force of *Tiferet*, and by the actual eating he would draw onto himself the power of *Malkhut*.

33. The proper order of the *seudot* is clearly not as it appears in the Isaiah 58:14, according to which it is seems that the first *seuda* is that of *Atika Kadisha*, but rather as Rabbi Shimon explains to Rabbi Elazar in the lines that follow.

Queen's joy, [for *Malkhut* is finally together with *Zeir Anpin* in a *yichud*]. Man therefore has to rejoice as well, [thus sharing in *Malkhut*'s joy] and eat of the Queen's *seuda*.

SONG OF THE SHABBAT DAY

This *piyyut* was authored by Rabbi Masud Abuchatsira, and the first word of every stanza form the acrostic of his name. Rabbi Masud was the father of the famed kabbalist and miracle worker Rabbi Israel Abuchatsira, known as *Baba Sali*.

A psalm: song for the Shabbat day.	מִזְמוֹר שִׁיר לְיוֹם הַשַּׁבָּת.
I too will state my piece.[34]	אֶעֱנֶה חֶלְקִי גַם אָנִי.
To arouse my heart to love the Rock[35]	לְעוֹרֵר לִבִּי אַהֲבַת צוּר
Who made me and established me.[36]	עֹשֵׂנִי וַכוֹנְנָנִי.
To serve Him always with passion.	וּלְעָבְדוֹ תָּמִיד בְּחִבַּת.
[To express my awareness of] the infinite kindness He bestowed upon me. To praise Him with my mouth and tongue. The mystery of Shabbat is *zachor* (remember) and *shamor* (guard).	רֹב חַסְדּוֹ אֲשֶׁר זִכַּנִי. לְהַלֵּל בְּפִי וּלְשׁוֹנִי. סוֹד שַׁבָּת זָכוֹר וְשָׁמוֹר. אוֹת בְּרִית בֵּינוֹ וּבֵנִי:
It is a sign of the covenant between Him and me.[37]	

The Shabbat has precious properties, influencing us throughout the six days.	סְגֻלַּת שַׁבָּת יְקָרָה. מַשְׁפַּעַת בְּיָמִים שִׁשָּׁה.
Three from the preceding Shabbat and from the next one another three.	שָׁלֹשׁ מִשַּׁבָּת שֶׁעָבְרָה. וּמִן הַבָּאָה שְׁלֹשָׁה.
Every person needs to remember to draw holiness upon himself – the poor person, the wealthy one as the impoverished one.	צָרִיךְ כָּל אָדָם זְכִירָה. לְהַמְשִׁיךְ עָלָיו קְדֻשָּׁה. כַּדַּל כֶּעָשִׁיר כָּעָנִי:

---

34. Paraphrasing Job 32:17. *The Living Nach*.
35. A name of Hashem.
36. The Rock Who made me: See Tractate Megilla 14a and Ps. 28:1
37. Paraphrasing Ex. 31:7.

Key to the Locked Garden

On Shabbat eve – Friday –	עֶרֶב הַשַׁבָּת יוֹם שִׁשִׁי.
Buy all you need for your Shabbat.	תִּקְנֶה כָּל צֹרֶךְ שַׁבָּתְךָ.
Prepare it yourself,	תָּכִין בְּעַצְמְךָ תַּעֲשֶׂה.
and not by means of someone else,	וְלֹא עַל יְדֵי זוּלָתְךָ.
for the King sitting on the Throne –	אֵל מֶלֶךְ יוֹשֵׁב עַל כִּסֵּא.
a guest coming toward you –	אוֹרֵחַ הַבָּא לִקְרָאתְךָ.
What will you say and what will you answer?	מַה תֹּאמַר וּמַה תַּעֲנֶה:

By sanctifying that which is already holy you will find grace.[38]	וּלְקַדֵּשׁ נֹגַהּ חֵן תִּמְצָא.
Read the Torah portion,	פָּרָשַׁת שָׁבוּעַ תִּקְרָא.
twice in Hebrew with holiness	שְׁנַיִם מִקְרָא בִּקְדֻשָּׁה.
and once in Aramaic with reverential awe.	וְאֶחָד תַּרְגּוּם בְּמוֹרָא.
You must wash yourself and then immerse	טְבִילַת מִצְוָה לִרְחִצָּה.
in a mikve in order to purify yourself.	תִּטָּבֵל בְּמִקְוֵה טָהֳרָה.
Then, you will be established through righteousness.[39]	אָז בִּצְדָקָה תִּכּוֹנָנִי:

You will now fulfill the injunction of hot water [by pouring hot water on] face hands and feet – speaking	דִּין מַיִם חַמִּים תָּדִיחַ.
	פָּנִים יָדַיִם רַגְלַיִם.
the mystery of the divine flame [by saying] the verse "inscribed for life."[40]	סוֹד שַׁלְהֶבֶת יָ"הּ תָּשִׂיחַ.
	פָּסוּק הַכָּתוּב לַחַיִּים.
You will then withdraw the outside forces from within Jerusalem.	אָז הַקְּלִיפּוֹת תַּזְנִיחַ.
	מִקֶּרֶב יְרוּשָׁלַיִם.
Speedily, may it be established and rebuilt.	מַהֵר תִּכּוֹנֵן וְתִבָּנֶה:

---

38. The word *chen*-grace may allude to the Torah's Inner Dimension.
39. Paraphrasing Is. 54:14.

Mystical Readings for the Shabbat Table

Four white garments.	אַרְבַּע בְּגָדִים לְבָנִים.
[The work] *Minchat Chasidim*	מִשְׁנַת חֲסִידִים שְׁנוּיָה.
is taught.	לִכְבוֹד שַׁבָּת מְזֻמָּנִים.
We are invited to honor the Shabbat –	לְשָׁרֵת בִּכְסוּת נְקִיָּה.
to minister with clean garments,	רֶמֶז לְאוֹרוֹת עֶלְיוֹנִים.
alluding to heavenly lights –	אַרְבַּע אוֹתִיּוֹת הֲוָיָ"ה.
the four letters of the *Shem Havaya*.	בִּגְדֵי יֶשַׁע תַּלְבִּישֵׁנִי:
Clothe me in garments of salvation.[41]	

At the Mincha prayer in the afternoon	בִּתְפִלַּת מִנְחָה בָּעֶרֶב.
begins the ascent of souls.	מַתְחִיל עֲלוּי הַנְּשָׁמוֹת.
Bring closer the letters of the Name	אוֹתִיּוֹת הַשֵּׁם לְקָרֵב.
one with the other, with the Names	אַחַת בְּאַחַת עִם שֵׁמוֹת
emerging from them: Within your thoughts they should be engraved.	הַיּוֹצְאִים מֵהֶם בְּקֶרֶב
He calms my soul; He leads me.[42]	מַחְשְׁבֹתֶיךָ יִהְיוּ נִרְשָׁמוֹת.
	נַפְשִׁי יְשׁוֹבֵב יַנְחֵנִי.

Going out to the field, to receive the Shabbat Queen.	יְצִיאַת שָׂדֶה לְהַקְבִּיל.
Sparks of Cain and Abel	אֶת פְּנֵי שַׁבָּת מַלְכְּתָא.
we must elevate from the depths,	נִיצוֹצוֹת קַיִן וְהֶבֶל
causing them to find the hereditary portion.[43]	לַעֲלוֹת מִנֵּי עֲמִיקְתָּא.
My soul yearns, even pines.[44]	יִמְצְאוּ נַחֲלַת חֶבֶל.
She will then declare: Here I am.	נַפְשִׁי נִכְסְפָה גַּם כָּלְתָה.
	תְּשַׁוַּע תֹּאמַר הִנֵּנִי:

---

40. Paraphrasing the verse we have to say upon washing the face, hands and feet with hot water in preparation for Shabbat (Is. 4:3):
41. Paraphrasing Is. 61:10.
42. Paraphrasing Ps. 23:3.

Key to the Locked Garden

It is our duty to ignite two lights – always.
The light we are commanded to ignite will reveal
two radiant lights:
The *Shem* Adnut in its simple form and the *Shem* El, each letter spelled out in full.
Three unifications cast their light.[45]
The joint numerical value of all their letters adds up to that of the word *ner*-light: There will encamp the inner letters of the *Shem Shakai* [when spelled in full].

Conduits of blessed divine flow will stream down as we answer *Barekhu*[46] – a holy divine inspiration will be drawn
onto every person, each according to his/her level,
to the extent that s/he is Hashem's true servant appointed by order of his King.
Let a generous spirit sustain me.[47]

חוֹבָה שְׁתֵּי נֵרוֹת תַּדְרִים.
נֵר מִצְוָה יְגַלֶּה
שְׁנֵי מְאֹרוֹת מַזְהִירִים.
אדנו״ת פָּשׁוּט וא״ל מָלֵא.
שָׁלֹשׁ יִחוּדִים מְאִירִים.
מִסְפָּרָם לְנֵר יַעֲלֶה.
מִלּוּי שד״י שָׁם יַחֲנֶה:

צִנּוֹרֵי שֶׁפַע בְּרָכָה
יָרִיקוּ בַּעֲנִיַּת בָּרְכוּ.
רוּחַ הַקֹּדֶשׁ נִמְשָׁכָה.
עַל כָּל אָדָם לְפִי עֶרְכּוֹ.
עֶבֶד נֶאֱמָן עַל כָּכָה.
הָפְקַד בְּמַאֲמַר מַלְכּוֹ.
רוּחַ נְדִיבָה תִסְמְכֵנִי:

---

43. Paraphrasing Zech. 2:16.
44. Paraphrasing Ps. 84:3.
45. Alluding to the unifications involving the holy names *Havaya Ekieh; Havaya Elokim; Havaya Adnut*.
46. See Chapter Twelve, "Ascending with the *Tosefet Shabbat*."
47. Paraphrasing Ps. 51:14.

Pray *Arvit* with awe, with a loud voice and good reasoning.[48] Say the blessings of the Shema with pleasantness, with focused intention and good taste.[49]
 [As we say *ufros alenu*,] extend [upon us] the additional soul level.[50] Focus your intention in the midst of a congregation of people. Enlighten me by granting me the essence of the *Shem Shaddai*.

יִתְפַּלֵּל עַרְבִית בְּאֵימָה.
בְּקוֹל גָּדוֹל בְּסוֹד טַעַם.
בְּרָכוֹת שְׁמַע בִּנְעִימָה.
בְּכַוָּנָה וּבְטוּב טַעַם.
וּפְרוֹשׁ תּוֹסֶפֶת נְשָׁמָה.
תְּכַוֵּן בְּתוֹךְ קְהַל עָם.
נִשְׁמַת שַׁדַּ"י תְּבִינֵנִי:

Lofty praises *of El (the loving God)*[51] high and lofty.[52]
Before Him, pleasing as *Tirzah*[53]
His *Malkhut* reigns over all.[54]
She ascended on High and became enclothed
in all twenty-four bridal ornaments.[55]
He brought me to His chambers.[56]

רוֹמְמוֹת אֵל רָם וְנִשָּׂא.
בִּמְקוֹם כְּבוֹדוֹ הַלַּיְלָה.
לְפָנָיו נָאוָה כְּתִרְצָה.
מַלְכוּתוֹ בַּכֹּל מָשָׁלָה.
עָלְתָה לְמַעְלָה וְלָבְשָׁה.

כָּל כ"ד קִשּׁוּטֵי הַכַּלָּה.
אֶל חֲדָרָיו הֱבִיאַנִי:

---

48. Paraphrasing Ps. 119:66.
49. Alluding to Ps. 34:9: טַעֲמוּ וּרְאוּ כִּי טוֹב ה' אַשְׁרֵי הַגֶּבֶר יֶחֱסֶה בּוֹ. "Contemplate (literally: taste) and see that Hashem is good." The mystery of Shabbat as an experiential perception of divine closeness is embedded in this verse.
50. See Chapter 12, "Ascending with the *Tosefet Shabbat*."
51. Paraphrasing Ps. 149:6.
52. Paraphrasing Is. 6:1.
53. Paraphrasing Shir Hashirim 6:4.
54. Paraphrasing Ps. 103:19.
55. Alluding to the twenty-four Mishnah Tractates on Shabbat that we are to read throughout each Shabbat.
56. Paraphrasing Shir HaShirim 1:4.

Then must be said the testimony of kidushin, established in the three times [we say] *vaykhulu*.[57]
The *Malkhut* is first [namely, the first time we say *vaykhulu*, just before the Shabbat evening *Amida*,] referred to as Chakal.
As we say the Kiddush, she is referred to as Chakal Tapuchin.
Then, at the completion of the evening *seuda*, she is referred to as *Chakal Tapuchin Kadishin*.
Allot to me my daily bread.[58]
The mystery of Shabbat is *zachor* and *shamor*.
It is a sign (a covenant) between Him and Me.[59]

אָז תֹּאמַר עֵדוּת קִדּוּשִׁין.
בְּשָׁלֹשׁ וַיְכֻלּוּ נוֹסָדָה.
רִאשׁוֹנָה חֲקַל נֶגֶד שי״ן.
חֲקַל תַּפּוּחִין אֶחָד עֲמִידָה.
חֲקַל תַּפּוּחִין קַדִּישִׁין.
נִקְרֵאת בְּקִדּוּשׁ סְעֻדָּה.
לֶחֶם חֻקִּי הַטְרִיפֵנִי.
סוֹד שַׁבָּת זָכוֹר וְשָׁמוֹר.
אוֹת בְּרִית בֵּינוֹ וּבֵינִי:

SECOND SHABBAT SEUDA

אַתְקִינוּ סְעוּדָתָא דִמְהֵימְנוּתָא שְׁלֵימָתָא. חֶדְוָתָה דְמַלְכָּה קַדִּישָׁא אַתְקִינוּ סְעוּדָתָא דְמַלְכָּה. דָּא הִיא סְעוּדָתָא דְעַתִּיקָא קַדִּישָׁא. וַחֲקַל תַּפּוּחִין קַדִּישִׁין וּזְעֵיר אַנְפִּין אָתְיָן לְסַעֲדָה בַּהֲדֵיהּ.

Prepare the meal of perfect faith, the joy of the Holy King.
Prepare the meal of the King. This is the meal of *Atika Kadisha*. And the Field of Holy Apples as well as *Zeir Anpin* also come to feast at this meal.

Asader Liseudata[60]

Asader liseudata
betzafra deShabta
veazmin bah hashta
Atika Kadisha.

אֲסַדֵּר לִסְעוּדָתָא.
בְּצַפְרָא דְשַׁבַּתָּא.
וְאַזְמִין בָּהּ הַשְׁתָּא
עַתִּיקָא קַדִּישָׁא:

---

57. See chapter 12, "Ascending with the *Tosefet Shabbat*."
58. Paraphrasing Prov. 30:8.
59. I did not translate this stanza completely because it is based on concepts beyond the scope of this book.
60. Commentary by Rabbi Moses Luria, *Sefer Beit Genazai: Pitchei Tefilla* vol. 3, 358ff.

Mystical Readings for the Shabbat Table

Nehoreh yishrei bah.	נְהוֹרֵיהּ יִשְׁרֵי בָהּ.
Bekidusha rabba.	בְּקִידוּשָׁא רַבָּא.
Ubechamra tava.	וּבְחַמְרָא טָבָא.
Debeh techedei nafsha.	דְּבֵהּ תֶּחֱדֵי נַפְשָׁא:
Yeshader lan shufreh.	יְשַׁדֵּר לָן שׁוּפְרֵיהּ.
Venechezei bikareh.	וְנֶחֱזֵי בִיקָרֵיהּ.
Veyachazei lan sitreh.	וְיַחֲזֵי לָן סִתְרֵהּ.
Deit'amar bilchisha.	דְּאִתְאֲמַר בִּלְחִישָׁא:
Yegaleh lan taamei.	יְגַלֶּה לָן טַעֲמֵי.
Debitreisar nahamei.	דְּבִתְרֵיסַר נַהֲמֵי.
Deinun at bishmeh.	דְּאִינוּן אָת בִּשְׁמֵיהּ.
Kefila uklisha.	כְּפִילָא וּקְלִישָׁא:
Tzerora dileela.	צְרוֹרָא דִלְעֵילָא.
Debeh chayei kola.	דְּבֵיהּ חַיֵּי כֹלָּא.
Deyitrabei cheila.	וְיִתְרַבֵּי חֵילָא.
Vetisak ad resha.	וְתִיסַק עַד רֵישָׁא:
Chadu chatzdei chakla.	חֲדוּ חַצְדֵי חַקְלָא.
Bedibbur ubekala.	בְּדִבּוּר וּבְקָלָא.
Umalilu milah.	וּמַלִּילוּ מִלָּה.
Metika kedubsha.	מְתִיקָא כְּדוּבְשָׁא:
Kodam Ribon Almin.	קֳדָם רִבּוֹן עָלְמִין.
Bemilin setimin.	בְּמִלִּין סְתִימִין.
Tegalun pitgamin.	תְּגַלּוּן פִּתְגָמִין.
Vetemrun chidusha.	וְתֵימְרוּן חִדּוּשָׁא:
Leater patora.	לְעַטֵּר פָּתוֹרָא.
Beraza yakira.	בְּרָזָא יַקִּירָא.
Amika utemira.	עֲמִיקָא וּטְמִירָא.
Velan milta avsha.	וְלָאו מִלְּתָא אֻוְשָׁא:

Key to the Locked Garden

Veilen milaya.	וְאִלֵּין מִלַּיָּא.
Yehon lirkiaya.	יְהוֹן לִרְקִיעָיָא.
Vetaman man sharia.	וְתַמָּן מָאן שָׁרְיָא.
Hala hahu shimsha.	הֲלָא הַהוּא שִׁמְשָׁא:
Revu yatir yisgei.	רְבוּ יַתִּיר יִסְגֵּי.
Le'ela min dargeh.	לְעֵילָא מִן דַּרְגֵּהּ.
Veyisav bat zugeh	וְיִסַּב בַּת זוּגֵהּ.
Dahavat perisha.	דַּהֲוַת פְּרִישָׁא:

Rabbi Moshe Luria's Commentary

I will prepare for the meal on Shabbat morning. I will now invite *Atika Kadisha*. We want to invite the lights of *Keter*, counterpart of the aspect of divine revelation of the Giving of the Torah, referred to as *Atika Kadisha*. The light flowing down at this time is that of Torah mysteries and stems from the *tagin* (crowns) that evoke the light of *Keter* and are related to the heavenly root of the letters.

May the radiance rest upon her, through the Great Kiddush and the good wine, in which the soul rejoices; "her" refers to the Shabbat and by extension, the *Shekhina*. We are asking that the radiance of *Atika Kadisha*, which is too lofty to be enclosed into letters, dwell upon the *Shekhina*. "The good wine" alludes to the Torah mysteries stemming from the light of the above-mentioned *ketarim* (crowns) that shine down on us in this *seuda*.

May He direct upon us His splendor and may we gaze upon His radiance through the perception of the intellect. May He cause us to perceive His mysteries that are transmitted in a whisper. The Aramaic expression *shufreh* stems from the word *shofar* and conveys beauty – albeit a beauty that may not be transmitted by means of letters – it has to be seen. The brain's perception, says Rabbi Luria, is called "sight," as in the expression, "I see what you mean," to convey understanding. May He reveal to us Torah mysteries that are said in a whisper, that is, teachings whose awesome nature may not be confined to letters. Consequently, these teachings are said to be "transmitted" rather than taught, just like Moses transmitted them to Joshua. As the verse says, "Invest him with some of your *hod* (splendor)."[61] The Hebrew expression *mehodecha* (from your splendor) has the same numeric value as *hasod* (the mystery). We learn from this that such mysteries may only be transmitted "in a whisper" and not openly revealed.

May He show us the reasons behind the twelve loaves, which reveal His multi-faceted Name, the double and the weaker one. The Ari z"l explains that the inner meaning of this Shabbat meal is conveyed by the twelve loaves of challa that we must place on the Shabbat tray, representing twelve flows of pure lovingkindness from the Source of all blessings. These flows reflect as well the white spaces between the letters in a Torah scroll, alluding to concepts that have to be perceived in order to be internalized. We are thus asking in the song, "may He reveal to us His mysteries" from the highest of sources, referred to as *Atika* (Ancient). The twelve Shabbat loaves allude to the *vav* (*vavin* in plural) of the *Havaya* Name written in full, for six loaves are on one side of the tray and six on the other side.[62] The name of the letter *vav*, written out, consists of two *vavin*; the first *vav* is counterpart of what is revealed, and the second, the "smaller one," points to what is concealed; and by means of both, one may draw down divine lovingkindness from Above to below. The song is thus asking that the inner meaning of the twelve challa loaves and all the life force linked with each one of them be revealed and directed onto us.

May we be bound up with the heavenly root who infuses life into all living beings; and may her forces be magnified, so that it reaches the head. The word *tzeror* (she who is bound on High) alludes to *Malkhut* who infuses life into all living beings. In the desire to receive the light of Torah shining down at this time, we thus ask that a great light first infuse *Malkhut* so that her forces are magnified and are directed to us below as well. Alternatively, the verse may also allude to the source of the Torah, that is, *Atika Kadisha*, for at that lofty level of holiness are bound up all the divine flows directed to us below. At that level is the life essence of the entire Torah, much like the root of a tree which exudes life force for

---

61. Num. 27:18.
62. *Sefer Siakh Sarfei Kodesh, Parshat Shelach.* Cited from Rabbi Moses Luria, *Sefer Pitchei Tefilla*, vol. 3, 358ff.

the entire tree. Our prayer is thus that the divine flows of this wellspring coming to us from *Hakadosh Barukh Hu*, who gives us the Torah every single day, be increased to the point that they flow downward until they reach our own heads, permeating us with the light of Torah.

Rejoice, O tillers of the field, by means of speech and of voice [by singing beautiful songs] and expressing His word, sweet as honey. Torah Sages dwelling on the inner dimension of the Torah are referred to as "tillers of the field," in the sense that they uproot the sparks of light which fell to the lower worlds and elevate them. However, it is only on the weekdays that we may work to elevate fallen sparks; now, on Shabbat, these Sages express His word at the time of the *seuda* by speaking of the Torah mysteries, thus igniting divine sparks in our souls with their *dibbur* (speech) as well as with their *kol* (voice) by singing. Although the lights pouring down at this time are too lofty to be captured by speech, still they may be expressed by joyful voices singing songs which are sweeter than honey.

Before the Master of the universe, with secret words you can reveal concealed mysteries and say novel Torah insights. The nature of these lofty lights shining down at this time is higher than that of the letters forming our speech; however, this is only true regarding those who study these mysteries, and are unable to express with their words what they received in the form of perception only. However, before the Master of the world, *Hakadosh Barukh Hu*, each member of the Community of Israel is a soul bound to Him on High, whose radiance dwells on man's brain. The message given to us here is thus: you are now able to express secret words made up with the letters of thought to reveal concealed mysteries – novel Torah insights casting light onto what was earlier restricted to perception at the level of thought.

May our Shabbat table be crowned with precious mysteries whose profound and hidden essence human words are unable to capture. You may crown the Shabbat table with the power of thought with precious, hidden mysteries that may not be constricted into words. A voice singing beautiful songs can arouse within you lofty thoughts enabling you to internalize what was before only a perception.

From these words will emerge a new firmament in which will dwell none other than that "supernal sun." The new Torah insights will bring about a new firmament in which will dwell a renewed divine providence whose overflowing radiance will be shine down to illuminate people below, brighter than the brightest sunlight.

It will shine brighter than in the former level, surrounding His soul companion who was separated. Through these new heaven and earth that emerged through the revelation of Torah mysteries on Shabbat, the heavenly unification will be constant, on the weekdays as well, as it was on the Temple days. Rabbi Shimon bar Yochai is thus referred to as "Shabbat" for in his time, the unification was permanent as it is on the Shabbat day.

VIHEI RAAVA

When we say the Aramaic prayer *vihei raava* (may it be Your will) just before all three *seudot*, we are asking for the divine *shefa* to come from *Atika Kadisha* to *Zeir Anpin*, who will transmit it to the heavenly *Malkhut* and then to *Knesset Yisrael Below*. Then we will be able to receive the good gift of Shabbat from the Hidden House of Treasures at the top of the *koma elyona* (divine structure).

Vihei raava min kodam Atika Kadisha dekhol kadishin. Temira Dekhol temirin setima dekhola Deyitmashekh tala ilaa mineh lemalia resheh diZeer Anpin ulehatil lechakal tapuchin kadishin binehiru deanpin beraava ubechedvata dekhola veyitmashekh min kodam Atika Kadisha dekhol kadishin temira dekhol temirin setima dekola reuta verachamei china vechisda binehiru ilaa bir'uta vechedvata alai veal kol benei beti vekol hanilvim elai veal kol benei Israel ameh vayifrekinan mikol atkin bishin deyeitun lealma. Veyeitei lana ulekhol nafshatana china vechisda vechayei arikhei umezonei revichei verachamei min kadameh, amen ken yehi ratzon, amen veamen.	וִיהֵא רַעֲוָא מִן קֳדָם עַתִּיקָא קַדִּישָׁא דְּכָל קַדִּישִׁין. טְמִירָא דְּכָל טְמִירִין סְתִימָא דְּכֹלָּא דְיִתְמַשֵּׁךְ טַלָּא עִלָּאָה מִינֵהּ לְמַלְיָא רֵישֵׁיהּ דִּזְעֵיר אַנְפִּין וּלְהַטִּיל לַחֲקַל תַּפּוּחִין קַדִּישִׁין בִּנְהִירוּ דְּאַנְפִּין בְּרַעֲוָא וּבְחֶדְוָתָא דְכֹלָּא וְיִתְמְשֵׁךְ מִן קֳדָם עַתִּיקָא קַדִּישָׁא דְּכָל קַדִּישִׁין טְמִירָא דְּכָל טְמִירִין סְתִימָא דְּכֹלָּא רְעוּתָא וְרַחֲמֵי חִנָּא וְחִסְדָּא בִּנְהִירוּ עִלָּאָה בִּרְעוּתָא וְחֶדְוָתָא עֲלַי וְעַל כָּל בְּנֵי בֵיתִי וְעַל כָּל הַנִּלְוִים אֵלַי וְעַל כָּל בְּנֵי יִשְׂרָאֵל עַמֵּיהּ וִיפַרְקִינָן מִכָּל עָקְתִין בִּישִׁין דְּיֵיתוּן לְעָלְמָא. וְיֵיתֵי לָנָא וּלְכָל נַפְשָׁתָנָא חִנָּא וְחִסְדָּא וְחַיֵּי אֲרִיכֵי אָמֵן וְאָמֵן וּמְזוֹנֵי רְוִיחֵי וְרַחֲמֵי מִן קֳדָמֵיהּ אָמֵן כֵּן יְהִי רָצוֹן אָמֵן וְאָמֵן׃

Key to the Locked Garden

Zohar Reading before Kiddush on Shabbat Morning[63]

Kidusha deyoma, ha ukmuha bore peri hagefen, vela yatir.	קִידוּשָׁא דְּיוֹמָא, הָא אוּקְמוּהָ בּוֹרֵא פְּרִי הַגֶּפֶן, וְלָא יַתִּיר.
Deha yoma kaim lekadesha leh, ma dilet hakhi belelya, deanan tzrikhin lekadesha leh, behani milin, kema deokimna.	דְּהָא יוֹמָא קָאִים לְקַדְּשָׁא לֵיהּ, מַה דְּלֵית הָכִי בְּלֵילְיָא, דַּאֲנָן צְרִיכִין לְקַדְּשָׁא לֵיהּ, בְּהָנֵי מִלִּין, כְּמָה דְּאוֹקִימְנָא.
Vela itkadash hai lelia, ela be ama kadisha letata, kad sharia alaihu hahu rucha ilaah. Va anan ba'enan lekadesha leh bire'uta deliba, lekhavena da'ta lehai.	וְלָא אִתְקַדַּשׁ הַאי לֵילְיָא, אֶלָּא בְּעַמָּא קַדִּישָׁא לְתַתָּא, כַּד שַׁרְיָא עֲלַיְיהוּ הַהוּא רוּחָא עִלָּאָה. וַאֲנָן בָּעֵינָן לְקַדְּשָׁא לֵיהּ בִּרְעוּתָא דְּלִבָּא, לְכַוְּונָא דַעְתָּא לְהַאי:
Veyoma ihu ka mekadesha leh. VeIsrael mekadshei bitzlotin uba'utin, umitkadeshin bikdushateh, behai yoma. Zakain Israel, ama kadisha, deachasinu yoma da, achasanat yeruta lealmin. Barukh Adonai leolam Amen veAmen	וְיוֹמָא אִיהוּ קָא מְקַדְּשָׁא לֵיהּ. וְיִשְׂרָאֵל מְקַדְּשֵׁי בִּצְלוֹתִין וּבָעוּתִין, וּמִתְקַדְּשִׁין בִּקְדוּשָׁתֵיהּ, בְּהַאי יוֹמָא. זַכָּאִין יִשְׂרָאֵל, עַמָּא קַדִּישָׁא, דְּאַחֲסִינוּ יוֹמָא דָּא, אַחֲסָנַת יְרוּתָא לְעָלְמִין: בָּרוּךְ ה' לְעוֹלָם. אָמֵן וְאָמֵן

It was established that the Kiddush said in the daytime only requires a simple blessing over the fruit of the vine and no more. In the daytime, He sanctifies her. This is not the case in the evening, for we need to consecrate her with the words, as it was established.[64] The Shabbat evening only receives sanctification through the intervention of the holy People of Israel below. When the heavenly spirit dwells on them, we have to direct holiness onto her by means of desire of the heart and a focused

---

63. Zohar, *Vayak'hel* 207b.
64. On Shabbat eve, *Malkhut* only receives divine flow from the higher levels of divine revelation through the intervention of Israel below – according to the ability of the People of Israel to draw levels of holiness from Above.

intention. In the daytime, it was consecrated and we only have to recite the sanctification of the day. Israel draw holiness upon her with our prayers and requests, and we are infused with her holiness on this day. Israel are worthy as the holy nation who inherited the Shabbat day – an eternal inheritance.

ZOHAR ON THE SECOND SEUDA[65]

Beyoma deShabta, beseudata tiniana, ketiv: Az tit'anag al Hashem. Al Hashem vaddai. Dehahi sha'ata itgalia Atika Kadisha, vekulehu almin bechedvata ushelimu vechedvata dileh hu vaddai.

בְּיוֹמָא דְשַׁבְּתָא, בִּסְעוּדָתָא תִנְיָינָא, כְּתִיב (ישעיה נח) אָז תִּתְעַנַּג עַל יְיָ. עַל יְיָ וַדַּאי. דְּהַהִיא שַׁעֲתָא אִתְגַּלְיָא עַתִּיקָא קַדִּישָׁא, וְכֻלְּהוּ עָלְמִין בְּחֶדְוָתָא, וּשְׁלִימוּ וְחֶדְוָותָא דְעַתִּיקָא עֲבַדִּינָן, וּסְעוּדָתָא דִילֵיהּ הוּא וַדַּאי:

Beseudata telitaa deShabta, ketiv veakhaltikha nachalat Jacob avikha. Da hi seudata di Zeir Anpin, de hevei bishlemuta. Vekulehu shita yomin, mehahu shelimu mitbarekhan.

בִּסְעוּדָתָא תְּלִיתָאָה דְשַׁבְּתָא, כְּתִיב "וְהַאֲכַלְתִּיךָ נַחֲלַת יַעֲקֹב אָבִיךָ". דָא הִיא סְעוּדָתָא דִזְעֵיר אַפִּין, דַּהֲוֵי בִּשְׁלֵימוּתָא. וְכֻלְּהוּ שִׁיתָא יוֹמִין, מֵהַהוּא שְׁלִימוּ מִתְבָּרְכָן.

Uba'ei bar nash lemechedei biseudateh, uleashlema ilen seudatei, deinun seudatei mehemnuta shelemata, dezar'a kadisha deIsrael, di mehemnuta ilaah, deha dilehon hi, vela deamim ovdei avoda zara. Ubeginei kakh amar "Beni uben benei Israel."

וּבָעֵי בַּר נָשׁ לְמֶחְדֵּי בִּסְעוּדָתֵיהּ, וּלְאַשְׁלְמָא אִלֵּין סְעוּדָתֵי, דְּאִינּוּן סְעוּדָתֵי מְהֵימָנוּתָא שְׁלֵימָתָא, דְּזַרְעָא קַדִּישָׁא דְיִשְׂרָאֵל, דִּי מְהֵימָנוּתָא עִלָּאָה, דְּהָא דִּילְהוֹן הִיא, וְלָא דְּעַמִּין עוֹבְדֵי עֲבוֹדָה זָרָה. וּבְגִינֵי כַּךְ אָמַר, (שמות לא) בֵּינִי וּבֵין בְּנֵי יִשְׂרָאֵל:

---

65. Zohar, *Yitro* 88b.

Ta chazei, bise'udatei ilen, ishtemode'un Israel, deinun benei malka. De inun meheikhala demalka, de inun benei mehemnuta,

תָּא חֲזֵי, בִּסְעוּדָתֵי אִלֵּין, אִשְׁתְּמוֹדְעוּן יִשְׂרָאֵל, דְּאִינּוּן בְּנֵי מַלְכָּא. דְּאִינּוּן מֵהֵיכָלָא דְּמַלְכָּא, דְּאִינּוּן בְּנֵי מְהֵימָנוּתָא,

Uman defagim chad seudata minaihu, achzei pegimuta leela, veachzei garmeh delav mibnei malka ilaaa hu, velav mibenei hekhala demalka hu delav mizar'a kadisha deIsrael hu.

וּמַאן דְּפָגִים חַד סְעוּדָתָא מִנַּיְיהוּ, אַחֲזֵי פְּגִימוּתָא לְעֵילָּא, וְאַחֲזֵי גַרְמֵיהּ דְּלָאו מִבְּנֵי מַלְכָּא עִלָּאָה הוּא, דְּלָאו מִבְּנֵי הֵיכָלָא דְּמַלְכָּא הוּא וְדְּלָאו מִזַּרְעָא קַדִּישָׁא דְּיִשְׂרָאֵל הוּא.

Veyahavin aleh chumra ditlat milin, dina degehinom vegomer.

וְיָהֲבִין עָלֵיהּ חוּמְרָא דִּתְלַת מִלִּין, דִּינָא דְגֵיהִנָּם וְגוֹ:

Veta chazei, bekulehu shear zimnin vechagim, ba'ei bar nash lechedei, ulemechdei lemiskenei. Ve I hu chadei bilchodoi, vela yahiv lemiskenei, onsheh sagi, veha bilchodoi chadei, vela yahiv chidu leachra.

וְתָא חֲזֵי, בְּכֻלְּהוּ שְׁאָר זִמְנִין וְחַגִּין, בָּעֵי בַּר נָשׁ לְחֶדֵי, וּלְמֶחְדֵי לְמִסְכְּנֵי. וְאִי הוּא חָדֵי בִּלְחוֹדוֹי, וְלָא יָהִיב לְמִסְכְּנֵי, עוֹנְשֵׁיהּ סַגִּי, דְּהָא בִּלְחוֹדוֹי חָדֵי, וְלָא יָהִיב חֵדוּ לְאַחֲרָא.

Aleh ktiv: Vezeriti feresh al peneikhem peresh chageikhem. Ve i ihu beShabata chadei, af al gav dela yahiv leachara, la yahavin alei onsha, kishear zimnin vechagin,

עָלֵיהּ כְּתִיב, (מלאכי ב) וְזֵרִיתִי פֶרֶשׁ עַל פְּנֵיכֶם פֶּרֶשׁ חַגֵּיכֶם. וְאִי אִיהוּ בְּשַׁבְּתָא חָדֵי, אַף עַל גַּב דְּלָא יָהִיב לְאַחֲרָא, לָא יָהֲבִין עָלֵיהּ עוֹנְשָׁא, כִּשְׁאָר זִמְנִין וְחַגִּין,

Dikhtiv peresh chageikhem. Peresh chageichem caamar, velo peresh Shabteikhem. Ukhtiv: chodsheikhem umoadeikhem sanea nafshi. Ve ilu Shabbat la caamar: ubeginei kakh ktiv, "beni uben benei Israel."

דִּכְתִיב פֶּרֶשׁ חַגֵּיכֶם. פֶּרֶשׁ חַגֵּיכֶם קָאָמַר, וְלֹא פֶּרֶשׁ שַׁבַּתְּכֶם. וּכְתִיב (ישעיה א) חָדְשֵׁיכֶם וּמוֹעֲדֵיכֶם שָׂנְאָה נַפְשִׁי. וְאִלּוּ שַׁבָּת לָא קָאָמַר. וּבְגִינֵי כָּךְ כְּתִיב, "בֵּינִי וּבֵין בְּנֵי יִשְׂרָאֵל".

Mystical Readings for the Shabbat Table

Umishum deKhol mehemnuta ishtechach beShabata, yahavin leh lebar nash nishmeta achara, nishmeta ilaa, nishmeta dekhol shelimu bah, kedugma de alma de atei.	וּמִשּׁוּם דְּכָל מְהֵימָנוּתָא אִשְׁתְּכַח בְּשַׁבָּתָא, יָהֲבִין לֵיהּ לְבַר נָשׁ נִשְׁמְתָא אָחֳרָא, נִשְׁמְתָא עִלָּאָה, נִשְׁמְתָא דְּכָל שְׁלִימוּ בָּהּ, כְּדוּגְמָא דְּעָלְמָא דְּאָתֵי.
Ubeginei kakh ikrei Shabbat. Mahu Shabbat. Shema deKudsha Brich Hu. Shema de ihu shelim mikol sitroi.	וּבְגִינֵי כָּךְ אִקְרֵי שַׁבָּת. מַהוּ שַׁבָּת. שְׁמָא דְּקוּדְשָׁא בְּרִיךְ הוּא. שְׁמָא דְּאִיהוּ שְׁלִים מִכָּל סִטְרוֹי.
Amar Rabbi Yossei, vaddai kakh hu. Vai leh lebar nash dela ashlim chedvata de malka kadisha. Uman chedvata dileh. Ilen telat seudatei mehemnuta.	אָמַר רִבִּי יוֹסֵי, וַדַּאי כָּךְ הוּא. וַוי לֵיהּ לְבַר נָשׁ, דְּלָא אַשְׁלִים חֶדְוָותָא דְּמַלְכָּא קַדִּישָׁא. וּמַאן חֶדְוָותָא דִּילֵיהּ. אִלֵּין תְּלַת סְעוּדָתֵי מְהֵימָנוּתָא.
Tana, bahaden yoma mit'ateran avahan, vekhol benin yankin, mah delav hakhi bekhol shear khagin uzmanin. Bahaden yoma, chayabaya degehinam naychin. Bahaden yoma, kol dinin itcafian, vela mit'arin bealma.	תָּאנָא, בַּהֲדֵין יוֹמָא מִתְעַטְּרָן אֲבָהָן, וְכָל בְּנִין יַנְקִין, מַה דְּלָאו הָכִי בְּכָל שְׁאַר חַגִּין וּזְמַנִּין. בַּהֲדֵין יוֹמָא, חַיָּיבַיָּא דְּגֵיהִנָּם נַיְיחִין. בַּהֲדֵין יוֹמָא, כָּל דִּינִין אִתְכַּפְיָין, וְלָא מִתְעָרִין בְּעָלְמָא.
Bahaden yoma oraita mit'atera be'itrin shelemin. Bahaden yoma, chedvata vetafnuka ishtema bematan vechamshin almin. Barukh Adonai leolam Amen veAmen.	בַּהֲדֵין יוֹמָא אוֹרַיְיתָא מִתְעַטְּרָא בְּעִטְרִין שְׁלֵימִין. בַּהֲדֵין יוֹמָא, חֶדְוָותָא וְתַפְנוּקָא אִשְׁתְּמַע, בְּמָאתָן וְחַמְשִׁין עָלְמִין: בָּרוּךְ ה' לְעוֹלָם. אָמֵן וְאָמֵן:

On the Shabbat day, at the second *seuda*, it is written:[66] "Then you will delight *over* the *Havaya* Name" (that is, above divine revelation to man). Above the *Havaya* Name, clearly, for at this time is revealed

---

66. Is. 58:14.

Key to the Locked Garden

Atika Kadisha, and all the worlds are in joy and completeness; and we are bringing about the fulfillment and joy of *Atika Kadisha*:[67] This is clearly His *seuda*.

At the third Shabbat *seuda*, it is written: "I will provide you the heritage of your forefather Jacob"; this is the *seuda* of *Zeir Anpin* now complete.[68] And the six weekdays are blessed from this completion.[69]

Man thus needs to rejoice in his *seuda* in order to complete His *seudot*,[70] as well as to complete all the *seudot* in their wholesome expression, for these *seudot* form the mystery of the divine consciousness of the holy People of Israel, and this lofty consciousness is exclusively their own,[71] and is not for those involved in idolatrous practices. That is why Hashem said, "between Me and the Children of Israel."[72]

---

67. We do this by our participation in this *seuda*.
68. The divine revelation is increased from the weekday level of *Zeir Anpin* to a level above our perception of divine providence.
69. All the good that comes to us throughout the next six days after the Shabbat, whether in the area of finances, success in our enterprises or relationships, etc., is directly connected to the extent to which we derive *oneg* from the Shabbat experience, particularly at the times of the three *seudot*. It is also related to how much we express your awareness of the divine revelations counterpart of each *seuda*. The purpose of the Zohar texts that we read before each of the *seudot* is thus to help us express this awareness.
70. Man has to rejoice in the third *seuda*, which is the counterpart of *Zeir Anpin* or divine revelation to man.
71. The Shabbat *seudot* are directly connected to the mystery of the heavenly sefirot in the world of *Atzilut* and to how these are directed exclusively toward the People of Israel. Their expression of faith in *Hakadosh Barukh Hu* will thus be greatly enhanced by their joyous participation in these *seudot*, so much so that their faith will become a consciousness. Hence my translation of the word *emuna* as "consciousness."
72. Ex. 31:17. "Between Me and the Children of Israel, it [Shabbat] is a sign forever." Shabbat is a covenant between the holy *Ein Sof* and the Children of Israel by means of the sefirot of the world of *Atzilut*; and the nations of the world have no part of this.

Come and see! By means of these *seudot* the People of Israel are showing that they are the King's children,[73] that they stem from the King's palace,[74] and that they have acquired this lofty consciousness.[75]

Thus one who blemishes even one *seuda* of these three is stating that there is a flaw on High,[76] and shows of himself that s/he is not the child of the heavenly King, that s/he does not belong in the King's palace, and that s/he is not part of the holy seed Israel.[77]

Because of this neglect s/he brings upon him/herself a severe consequence made up of three elements in *Gehinom*, etc....[78]

And come and see! In all the other appointed times and festivals man needs to rejoice but also to give joy to the poor. And if he rejoices by himself and does not give to the poor, his punishment is severe, for he is rejoicing on his own without sharing with others.

About such a person, the verse says,[79] "I will scatter filth upon your faces, filth made up of your festival." In contrast, on Shabbat, he may rejoice on his own, even though he does not give food to others. Still, he is not punished as he would have been at appointed times and on festivals.

---

73. In particular when they participate in the third *seuda* thus expressing their implicit awareness that the divine revelation of *Zeir Anpin* is at this time beyond the weekday revelation, they show that they belong in the Palace on High.
74. By participating in the first *seuda* of *Malkhut*, the Shabbat Queen, they show that they are the King's children, for the heavenly root of their soul is in the *Malkhut*.
75. By participating in the second *seuda*, and sharing the joy of *Atika Kadisha* which includes all the world of *Atzilut*, they show that they have acquired the lofty consciousness of the Inner Torah and that their soul stems from *Atzilut*.
76. That is, in the divine revelation that is counterpart of each *seuda*.
77. When one neglects even one of the three *seudot* it is as if s/he had neglected all three, since the three *seudot* form one single entity.
78. Since the three *seudot* correspond to three different revelations of *Hakadosh Barukh Hu*, one cannot show attachment to two of these and ignore the third revelation by failing to participate in the *seuda* celebrating this revelation. When one misses but one of the *seudot* s/he is thus showing that s/he only participated in the other two for personal enjoyment.
79. Mal. 2:3.

The verse thus says, "the filth of your festival meals," but it does not say the filth of your Shabbat.[80] It is also written,[81] "My soul detests your New Moons and your three holidays," and we note that the verse does not mention the Shabbat.[82] It is thus written: "Between Me and the Children of Israel." [83]

Since all the levels of divine revelation are present on Shabbat,[84] man receives an additional soul,[85] a higher soul,[86] a loftier soul which is perfected in every way,[87] comparable to that of the heavenly world.

It is thus called Shabbat. What is Shabbat? Shabbat is the Name of *Hakadosh Barukh Hu*, a Name complete in every aspect.[88]

Said Rabbi Yossei: It is certainly true. Woe to the person who does not fulfill the joy of the Holy King. And what brings about His own joy? It is these three *seudot* of *emuna* (consciousness).[89]

---

80. On Shabbat Hashem is our host, and we are His guests.
81. Is. 1:14.
82. For it is only when we host a festive meal that we have the obligation to share with the poor, not when we ourselves are mere guests.
83. About Shabbat in which Hashem is our Host and we are the guests participating in divine joy.
84. All the levels of divine revelation stemming from *Atzilut*, which is referred to as *emuna* (consciousness), are directed down to us on the Shabbat.
85. On Shabbat eve from *Malkhut*.
86. On Shabbat morning from *Zeir Anpin*.
87. A loftier soul from *Bina*, so that s/he may experience a spiritual delight.
88. A name integrating all the revelations of *Atzilut*. We thus receive soul supplements from all the levels of divine revelation.
89. These *seudot* bring about divine joy for they are instrumental in completing the divine revelation coming through at this time. A revelation from Above is only complete when received below. The Shabbat prayer we recite before each the *seudot* draws the revelation to us at the level of our soul. We only integrate it within us at the level of the body by participating in the *seuda* and we enact our awareness of the revelation by reading the statements of the Zohar associated with each of the *seudot*.

The *seuda* of Abraham,[90] that of Isaac,[91] and that of Jacob,[92] are included in Him and all constitute joy upon joy,[93] helping us attain a total consciousness of the Divine from all sides.[94]

We have learned that on this day the patriarchs are crowned and all the children absorb their essence, which does not occur in all other festivals and special times. On this day those who led their lives in error and are now in Gehinom, can rest. On this day all expressions of strict justice are overcome and do not affect the world.

On this day, the Torah receives a perfect crown. On this day the joy and delight is heard in two hundred and fifty worlds.[95]

THIRD SHABBAT SEUDA

אַתְקִינוּ סְעוּדָתָא דִמְהֵמְנוּתָא שְׁלֵימָתָא. חֶדְוָתָה דְמַלְכָּא קַדִישָׁא אַתְקִינוּ סְעוּדָתָא דְמַלְכָּה. דָא הִיא סְעוּדָתָא דְמַלְכָּה קַדִישָׁא זְעֵיר אַנְפִּין וְעַתִּיקָא קַדִישָׁא וַחֲקַל תַּפּוּחִין קַדִישִׁין אַתְיָן לְסַעֲדָה בַּהֲדֵיה.

Prepare the meal of perfect faith, the joy of the Holy King.

---

90. The second *seuda* counterpart of Atika is the heavenly root of *Chesed* and is thus linked with Abraham.
91. The first *seuda* is counterpart of *Malkhut* and its completion is connected with Isaac's aspect of *Gevura* (restraint).
92. The third *seuda* counterpart of *Zeir Anpin* is connected with Jacob, whose main characteristic trait is linked with *Tiferet* (harmony).
93. The joy of experiential perception of the traits representing the patriarchs, combined with the joy produced by the divine revelations at the levels of *Malkhut*, *Atika Kadisha*, and *Zeir Anpin* that we receive in the three *seudot*.
94. Our involvement the *seudot* allows us to integrate the divine revelation emitted from Above in each of the Shabbat meals.
95. The heavenly joy on Shabbat is caused mainly by the unifications brought about through our prayers preceding the *seudot*. The number two hundred and fifty alludes to the unification of the names *Havaya* with *Ekieh*, *Elokim*, and *Adnut* whose combined numeric value (250) is the same as that of the word *ner* (candle). During the weekdays, we only have an *or penimi* (inner light) of the soul. On Shabbat, we receive our *or makif* (surrounding light), and that is where our additional soul comes from. These *makifim* (surrounding lights) come gradually throughout Shabbat. An aspect of makifim comes to us during the prayer *"Sim shalom"* (the last blessing of the Amida Prayer), and that particular aspect is completed when we go around the Shabbat table prior to the *seuda*, according to the custom of the holy Ari.

Key to the Locked Garden

Prepare the meal of the King. This is the *seuda* meal of the Holy King Zeir Anpin. And *Atika Kadisha* as well as *Chakal Tapuchin Kadishin* also come to feast at this meal.

Benei Heikhala[96]

Benei heikhala dikhsifin.	בְּנֵי הֵיכָלָא דְכְסִיפִין.
Lemechezei ziv diZeir Anpin,	לְמֶחֱזֵי זִיו דִּזְעֵיר אַנְפִּין:
Yehon hakha. Behai taka.	יְהוֹן הָכָא. בְּהַאי תַּכָּא.
Debeh malka begilufin.	דְּבֵיה מַלְכָּא בְּגִלוּפִין:
Zevu lachada. Behai vaada. Bego	צְבוּ לַחֲדָא. בְּהַאי וַעֲדָא.
irin vechol gadfin.	בְּגוֹ עִירִין וְכָל גַּדְפִּין:
Chadu hashta. Behai shaata.	חֲדוּ הַשְׁתָּא. בְּהַאי שַׁעְתָּא.
Debeh raava veleit zaafin.	דְּבֵיה רַעֲוָא וְלֵית זַעֲפִין:
Kerivu li. Chazu cheili.	קְרִיבוּ לִי. חֲזוּ חֵילִי.
Deleit dinin ditkifin.	דְּלֵית דִּינִין דְּתְקִיפִין:
Lebar natlin. Vela alin.	לְבַר נַטְלִין. וְלָא עָאלִין.
Hanei kalbin dechatzifin.	הֲנֵי כַּלְבִּין דַּחֲצִיפִין:
Veha azmin Atik Yomin.	וְהָא אַזְמִין. עַתִּיק יוֹמִין.
Lemitzcha adei yehon chalfin.	לְמִצְחָא עֲדֵי יְהוֹן חַלְפִין:
Re'u dileh. Degalei leh.	רְעוּ דִילֵיה. דְּגָלֵי לֵיה.
Lebatala bekhol kalifin.	לְבַטָּלָא בְּכָל קַלִיפִין:
Yeshavei lon. Benukveihon.	יְשַׁוֵּי לוֹן. בְּנוּקְבֵיהוֹן.
Vitamrun bego khefin.	וְיִטַמְרוּן בְּגוֹ כֵפִין:

---

96. Adapted from "Zemer Benei Heichala," *Sefer Pitchei Tefilla*, vol. 3, 380-381.

242

Arei hashata beminchata.   אֲרֵי הַשְׁתָּא בְּמִנְחָתָא.
Bechedvata diZeir Anpin.   בְּחֶדְוָתָא דִזְעֵיר אַנְפִּין:

Rabbi Moshe Luria's Commentary

Members who yearn to perceive the radiance of *Zeir Anpin*, be here at this *seuda* in which is engraved the King's delight. While *Malkhut* has to remain in the place of *Chokhma* at this time, the members of *Knesset Yisrael* ascend in a state of *yichud* (unification) with *Zeir Anpin*.

This song thus expresses their longing to perceive His radiance at this time, in contrast with the weekdays in which they are in a state of spiritual darkness. The King – that is, *Zeir Anpin* – is in delight, for he is infused with the lights of *Chokhma* and of *Atika Kadisha*. Even in the heavenly unification of *Mussaf Zeir Anpin* was not in such as state of delight as now with *Knesset Yisrael*. *Zeir Anpin* is now in the world of delight and will; and, as it were, *Knesset Yisrael Themselves* are there with Him.

You should long to join this gathering in which many heavenly beings and angels participate. The present lofty situation of *Zeir Anpin* brings about great joy in all the heavenly worlds; the angels rejoice in *Zeir Anpin*'s present light and the People of Israel also rejoice as the light is directed onto them as well.

Rejoice at this time of divine favor in which there is no anger. The intense joy we experience at this moment is due not only to the unification with *Knesset Yisrael*, but also is caused by the revelation of the inner expression of divine will referred to as *raava deraavin* (desire of desires), alluding to the heavenly root of the world of *Atzilut*. In this loftiest of places, it is revealed that there no divine anger toward us, for the flaws caused by our sins do not reach that lofty level.

Come closer to me! Contemplate my strength, for there are no forces of evil of powerful judgments. *Zeir Anpin* himself says to *Knesset Yisrael* to come close to him, for she is usually embarrassed to approach *Hakadosh Barukh Hu* because of the sins of the people that give access to the outside forces. And, how can one come close to the King when dressed in sackcloth?! He thus tells them that in this lofty place these forces do not attach themselves.

They remain outside and do not go up, those brazen dogs. Once one has ascended to the Holy King's palace, no evil can enter this place. Hence, if there are outside forces acting as accusers attached to a person, they are unable to ascend here.

I now invite *Atik Yomin*, so that with this lofty light, they will pass away and go. *Zeir Anpin* is now at this higher level, and from this perspective he invites the lofty illumination mentioned. *Knesset Yisrael* is thus reassured that no outside forces in the lower world will attach to them in this place.

His inner will that is revealed and flagged decimates all the outside forces. It is not only because of the loftiness of this heavenly place that the outside forces are unable to ascend there, but rather because the revelation of the inner will of *Atzilut* nullifies them completely. They only exist at a lower level because the inner will is concealed and this enables them to attach themselves. The revelation of the inner will, however, decimates them so they do not dare ascend to this lofty place.

This causes them to go to their holes in the depths and their rocky caverns. As the verse says, "You make darkness, and it is night."[97] That is when they come out of their nether holes in order to overcome the world, but then, "the sun rises and they are gathered in"[98] – alluding to the "sun" of the inner divine will. About this, the verse says "And [they] will enter caves in the rocks and tunnels in the ground, because of the fear of Hashem and from the glory of His greatness."[99]

I ask this now, at the time of Mincha, at the jubilation of *Zeir Anpin*. This is happening now because of the great light now illuminating *Zeir Anpin*, a time of ultimate joy. This light of joy nullifies the forces of darkness, who attach themselves to sadness. As mentioned in Chapter 11, "A Tunnel under the Throne of Glory," at the time of Mincha on Shabbat we do not say *yismechu* (they will rejoice). On the one hand, the heavenly *Malkhut* does not ascend to the inner divine will at Mincha and is not in a state of joy. On the other hand, however, *Knesset Yisrael Themselves* ascend on High to *Zeir Anpin*, an unparalleled ecstasy.

---

97. Ps. 104:20.
98. Ps. 104:22.
99. Is. 2:19.

Mystical Readings for the Shabbat Table

VIHEI RAAVA

When we say the Aramaic prayer *vihei raava* (may it be Your will) just before all three *seudot*, we are asking for the divine *shefa* to come from *Atika Kadisha* to *Zeir Anpin*, who will transmit it to the heavenly *Malkhut* and then to *Knesset Yisrael Below*. Then we will be able to receive the good gift of Shabbat from the Hidden House of Treasures at the top of the *koma elyona* (divine structure).

Vihei raava min kodam Atika Kadisha dekhol kadishin. Temira Dekhol temirin setima dekhola Deyitmashekh tala ilaa mineh lemalia resheh diZeer Anpin ulehatil lechakal tapuchin kadishin binehiru deanpin beraava ubechedvata dekhola veyitmashekh min kodam Atika Kadisha dekhol kadishin temira dekhol temirin setima dekola reuta verachamei china vechisda binehiru ilaa bir'uta vechedvata alai veal kol benei beti vekol hanilvim elai veal kol benei Israel ameh vayifrekinan mikol atkin bishin deyeitun lealma. Veyeitei lana ulekhol nafshatana china vechisda vechayei arikhei umezonei revichei verachamei min kadameh, amen ken yehi ratzon, amen veamen.

וִיהֵא רַעֲוָא מִן קֳדָם עַתִּיקָא קַדִּישָׁא דְּכָל קַדִּישִׁין. טְמִירָא דְּכָל טְמִירִין סְתִימָא דְּכֹלָּא דְּיִתְמְשַׁךְ טַלָּא עִלָּאָה מִנֵּהּ לְמַלְיָא רֵישֵׁיהּ דִּזְעֵיר אַנְפִּין וּלְהַטִּיל לַחֲקַל תַּפּוּחִין קַדִּישִׁין בִּנְהִירוּ דְאַנְפִּין בְּרַעֲוָא וּבְחֶדְוָתָא דְּכֹלָּא וְיִתְמְשַׁךְ מִן קֳדָם עַתִּיקָא קַדִּישָׁא דְּכָל קַדִּישִׁין טְמִירָא דְּכָל טְמִירִין סְתִימָא דְּכֹלָּא רְעוּתָא וְרַחֲמֵי חִנָּא וְחִסְדָּא בִּנְהִירוּ עִלָּאָה בִּרְעוּתָא וְחֶדְוָתָא עֲלַי וְעַל כָּל בְּנֵי בֵיתִי וְעַל כָּל הַנִּלְוִים אֵלַי וְעַל כָּל בְּנֵי יִשְׂרָאֵל עַמֵּיהּ וְיִפְרְקִינָן מִכָּל עַקְתִין בִּישִׁין דְּיֵיתוּן לְעָלְמָא. וְיֵיתֵי לָנָא וּלְכָל נַפְשָׁתָנָא חִנָּא וְחִסְדָּא וְחַיֵּי אֲרִיכֵי וּמְזוֹנֵי רְוִיחֵי וְרַחֲמֵי מִן קֳדָמֵיהּ אָמֵן כֵּן יְהִי רָצוֹן אָמֵן וְאָמֵן:

May it be the will of *Atika Kadisha*, holiest of all holy, most hidden of all hidden, who is concealed from all, that the heavenly dew flow from Him to *Zeir Anpin* and to the "Field of Holy Apples" with the light of His countenance, with desire and joy for all. May there be drawn from *Atika Kadisha*, holiest of all holy, most hidden of all hidden, who is concealed from all, desire and compassion, grace and loving kindness, with a radiant light, with desire and joy, [directing them] upon me and the members of my household, upon all those who are dependent on me, and upon all the Children of Israel, His people.

Key to the Locked Garden

May He redeem us from all the evil troubles which befall the world. May He bring us and all our souls grace and kindness, long life, ample nourishment, and compassion from Himself, Amen, may such be His will. Amen and Amen.

FIRST ZOHAR FOR THE THIRD SEUDA[100]

Ilen arbaa techot hai chevata kaymin learba sitrei alma, ilen arba kaymei le dalet sitrei alma, veinun memanan leashgacha bekhol inun denatrei yoma deShabta, umeangei Shabta kedeka yaut.

אִלֵּין אַרְבָּעָה תְּחוֹת הַאי חֵיוָתָא קַיְימִין לְאַרְבַּע סִטְרֵי עָלְמָא, אִלֵּין דִּי קַיְימֵי לד' סִטְרֵי עָלְמָא, וְאִינוּן מְמָנָן לְאַשְׁגָּחָא בְּכָל אִינוּן דְּנַטְרֵי יוֹמָא דְּשַׁבְּתָא, וּמְעַנְּגֵי שַׁבְּתָא כְּדְקָא יָאוֹת:

Me ilen arba kad natlei, nafkei shevivin de esha, umeilen shevivin it'abidu shiv'in utren galgelin, melahatan be esha. Mehakha it'abid nehar dinur. Elef alfin yeshameshuneh lehahu nahara, kol inun deme'angei Shabta, ilen deme'angei Shabta, vehai chevata kayema alaihu, venatlei begina techota.

מֵאִלֵּין אַרְבַּע כַּד נַטְלֵי, נָפְקֵי שְׁבִיבִין דְּאֶשָׁא, וּמֵאִלֵּין שְׁבִיבִין אִתְעֲבִידוּ שַׁבְעִין וּתְרֵין גַּלְגַּלִין, מְלַהֲטָן בְּאֶשָׁא. מֵהָכָא אִתְעֲבִיד נְהַר דִּינוּר. אֶלֶף אַלְפִין יְשַׁמְּשׁוּנֵיהּ לְהַהוּא נַהֲרָא, כָּל אִינוּן דִּמְעַנְּגֵי שַׁבְּתָא, אִלֵּין אַרְבַּע מְמָנָן מַשְׁגִּיחָן בְּכָל אִינוּן דִּמְעַנְּגֵי שַׁבְּתָא, וְהַאי חֵיוָתָא קַיְימָא עֲלַיְיהוּ, וְנַטְלֵי בְּגִינָהּ תְּחוֹתָהּ:

Bechol yoma veyoma, nagid hahu nehar dinur, veokid lekhama ruchin, ulekhama shalitin. Ve chad ayil Shabta, karoza nafka, veshakhikh hahu nehar dinur, veza'afin vezikin ushevivin ishtekhakhu.

בְּכָל יוֹמָא וְיוֹמָא, נָגִיד הַהוּא נְהַר דִּינוּר, וְאוֹקִיד לְכַמָּה רוּחִין, וּלְכַמָּה שַׁלִּיטִין. וְכַד עָיֵיל שַׁבְּתָא, כָּרוֹזָא נָפְקָא, וְשָׁכִיךְ הַהוּא נְהַר דִּינוּר, וְזַעֲפִין וְזִיקִין וּשְׁבִיבִין אִשְׁתְּכָכוּ.

---

100. Zohar, *Pekudei* 252b.

Mystical Readings for the Shabbat Table

Vehai chevata azla vesalka al arbaa ilen seraphim dekaamaran. Veal go emtza'ita dehekhala da, vehahu atar deikrei oneg.

וְהַאי חֵיוָתָא אַזְלָא וְסַלְקָא עַל אַרְבָּעָה אִלֵּין שְׂרָפִים דְּקָאָמְרָן. וְעָאל גּוֹ אֶמְצָעִיתָא דְּהֵיכָלָא דָא, בְּהַהוּא אֲתַר דְּאִקְרֵי עֹנֶג:

Hai atar, vad ayel Shabta, mitsadran taman kol patorei dibnei alma, deikru benei hekhala de malka, ve elef alfin, veribo ribevan memanan, kaymei al inun patorei.

הַאי אֲתַר, כַּד עָיֵיל שַׁבְּתָא, מִתְסַדְּרָאן תַּמָּן כָּל פָּתוֹרֵי דִּבְנֵי עָלְמָא, דְּאִקְרוּ בְּנֵי הֵיכָלָא דְּמַלְכָּא, וְאֶלֶף אַלְפִּין, וְרִבּוֹ רִבְוָון מְמַנָּן, קַיְימֵי עַל אִינוּן פָּתוֹרֵי.

Hai chevata ilaa al ilen arbaa serafim, ve al behahu atar, vechama kol inun patorei, veashgach bekhol patora ufatora, vehekh me'angei leh lekhol patora ufatora, vekayma ubarikh leh lehahu patora.

וְהַאי חֵיוָתָא עִלָּאָה עַל אִלֵּין אַרְבָּעָה שְׂרָפִים, וְעָאל בְּהַהוּא אֲתַר, וְחָמָא כָּל אִינוּן פָּתוֹרֵי, (וכל אינון דקיימא עלייהו) וְאַשְׁגַּח בְּכָל פָּתוֹרָא וּפָתוֹרָא, וְהֵיךְ מְעַנְּגֵי לֵיהּ לְכָל פָּתוֹרָא וּפָתוֹרָא, וְקַיְימָא וּבָרִיךְ לֵיהּ לְהַהוּא פָּתוֹרָא.

Vekhol inun elef alfin, veribo ribevan, kulehu patchei veamrei amen.

וְכָל אִינוּן אֶלֶף אַלְפִּין, וְרִבּוֹא רִבְבָן, כֻּלְּהוּ פַּתְחֵי וְאַמְרֵי אָמֵן:

Uma berakha hi debarikh al hai patora demitsadar veit'anega kedeka yaut. Az tit'anag al Adonai, vegomer, ki pi Adonai diber. Vekulehu amrei, az tikra vaAdonai ya'aneh, vegomer.

וּמַה בְּרָכָה הִיא דִּבָרִיךְ עַל הַאי פָּתוֹרָא דְּמִתְסַדָּר וְאִתְעַנְּגָא כְּדְקָא יָאוֹת. (ישעיה נ) אָז תִּתְעַנָּג עַל יְיָ וְגוֹ' כִּי פִי יְיָ דִּבֵּר. וְכֻלְּהוּ אַמְרֵי, (ישעיה נח) אָז תִּקְרָא וַיְיָ יַעֲנֶה וְגוֹ'.

Verucha ilaa deikrei ... kad hahu patora it'anag bekulehu se'udatei, bise'udata batraa telitaa mesayem veamar, al kol inun kadmaei, ve amar, "Az yibaka cashachar orekha ... kevod Adonai yaaspekha."

רוּחָא עִלָּאָה דְּאִקְרֵי [זְכוּ"ת אֵל וְשֵׁם זֶה יְהַרְהֵר בִּלְבַד], כַּד הַהוּא פָּתוֹרָא אִתְעַנַּג בְּכֻלְּהוּ סְעוּדָתֵי, בִּסְעוּדָתָא בַּתְרָאָה תְּלִיתָאָה מְסַיֵּים וְאָמַר, עַל כָּל אִינוּן קַדְמָאֵי, וְאָמַר (ישעיה נח) אָז יִבָּקַע כַּשַּׁחַר אוֹרֶךָ, כְּבוֹד יְיָ וְגוֹ', יְיָ יַאַסְפֶךָ.

Kol inun shiv'im nehorin achranin bekhol sitrin, patchei veamrei, (תהלים קכח) *hineh ki ken yeborakh gaber yerei Adonai." Barukh Adonai leolam Amen veAmen.*

כָּל אִינוּן שִׁבְעִין נְהוֹרִין אַחֲרָנִין בְּכָל סִטְרִין, פַּתְחֵי וְאָמְרֵי, (תהלים קכח) הִנֵּה כִּי כֵן יְבֹרַךְ גָּבֶר יְרֵא יְיָ: בָּרוּךְ ה' לְעוֹלָם. אָמֵן וְאָמֵן:

These four heavenly seraphs stand at the four corners of the world, and they are appointed to supervise all those who observe the Shabbat day, and delight in the Shabbat as is proper.

These four emit sparks of fire as they move and from these sparks come out seventy-two wheels which intensify the fire. The Dinur River is made of this fire.[101] Thousands of thousands give Me their service by using this river. All those who delight the Shabbat are supervised by the four appointed *sefirot* standing over them, and they move under her.

Each day, the Dinur River burns spiritually some spirits and some ruling angels, but when comes Shabbat, a Voice calls and the Dinur River calms down; and then all outside forces are dispelled.

Compassion then rises over the four above-mentioned *sefirot*, and it enters in the middle of the palace, in the place called delight.

In this place, when comes Shabbat, are depicted all the tables of the people called "children belonging in the King's palace," and thousands of thousands appointed angelic entities stand over all those tables.

Then this compassion goes over the four *sefirot* enters this place and observes each Shabbat table [as well as its participants]; it inspects each table, sees as well as how they are experiencing delight at each table, and then stands and blesses that table.

And all the thousands of thousands of angels all respond and say: Amen.[102]

And what kind of blessing does the angel give each table which is [beautifully] set, and on which the Shabbat delight permeates? "Then

---

101. See Rabbi Moses Cordovero, *Tomer Devorah*, Chapter 4.
102. Since all the angels derive delight out of the physical delight of men on Shabbat, they all ratify the blessing of the khaya by answering Amen. We thus derive that the way in which those at the table are experiencing the Shabbat delight determines the shefa that will flow to them from the angel's blessings.

Mystical Readings for the Shabbat Table

you will delight above and beyond divine revelation to man…,[103] for Hashem's mouth has spoken." And they all say, [adding to the above blessing, "Then you will call, and God will answer. You will cry out and He will say, 'Here I am.'"[104]

Then comes a heavenly spirit whose name is…. when the participants at the Shabbat table [under supervision] delight in all the *seudot*, then in the last meal [that is, in the third *seuda*, this heavenly spirit] completes [the first blessing,] and adds, "Then your light will burst forth like the dawn, and God's Glory will flow to you."[105]

All those seven additional lights [will then shine down on you] from each side [that is, for each Shabbat meal] and they will say, "For *ken* (so) is blessed the man who fears Hashem."[106,107]

SECOND ZOHAR FOR THE THIRD SEUDA[108]

Due to the esoteric nature of this Zohar, I have only given an approximate idea of its contents. As above mentioned, when reading Zohar, in particular before a Shabbat *seuda*, it is important to bear in mind that the divine service we are bringing about has the intended effect on High even if we do not understand it.

Mitzcha deigalei beAtika Kadisha, ratzon ikrei, deha resha ilaa da satim leela, dela ityeda pashit chad turna besima yaah, deitkelil bemitzcha. Ubegin deihu raava de khol raavin, ittekan bemitzcha, veitgalia bebusita hai mitzcha ikrei ratzon.	מִצְחָא דְּאִתְגְּלֵי בְּעַתִּיקָא קַדִּישָׁא, רָצוֹן אִקְרֵי, דְּהָא רֵישָׁא עִלָּאָה דָּא סָתִים לְעֵילָא, דְּלָא אִתְיְדַע פָּשִׁיט חַד טוּרְנָא בְּסִימָא, יָאָה, דְּאִתְכְּלִיל בְּמִצְחָא. וּבְגִין דְּאִיהוּ רַעֲוָא דְּכָל רַעֲוִין, אִתְתְּקַן בְּמִצְחָא, וְאִתְגַּלְיָיא בְּבוּסִיטָא, הַאי מִצְחָא אִקְרֵי רָצוֹן:

---

103. Paraphrasing Isaiah 58:14: "and I will mount you astride the heights of the world; and I will provide you the heritage of your forefather Jacob.…"
104. Is. 58:9.
105. Is. 58:8.
106. For the numeric value of the word *ken* (so) is seventy, counterpart of the seventy lights with which the angels bless the head of that table.
107. Ps. 128:4.
108. Interpretative translation of Zohar, *Haazinu: Idra Zuta*, 288b-289a.

Key to the Locked Garden

Vechad ratzon da itgalia, raava deraavin ishtekhach bekulehu almin, vekhol tzelotin diletata mitkablin, umitnaharin anpoi de Zeir Anpin, vekola berachamei ishtekhach, vekhol dinin ittameran veitcafian.

וְכַד רָצוֹן דָּא אִתְגַּלְיָיא, רַעֲוָא דְּרַעֲוִין אִשְׁתְּכַח בְּכֻלְּהוּ עָלְמִין, וְכָל צְלוֹתִין דִּלְתַתָּא מִתְקַבְּלִין, וּמִתְנַהֲרִין אַנְפּוֹי דִּזְעֵיר אַנְפִּין, וְכֹלָּא בְּרַחֲמֵי אִשְׁתְּכַח, וְכָל דִּינִין אִתְטַמְּרָן וְאִתְכַּפְיָין:

BeShabta beshaata detzlota demincha, dehu idan dekhol dinin mit'arin, itgalia hai mitzcha, veitcafian kol dinin, veishtekhachu rachamin bekulehu almin.

בְּשַׁבְּתָא בְּשַׁעֲתָא דִּצְלוֹתָא דְּמִנְחָה, דְּהוּא עִידָן דְּכָל דִּינִין מִתְעָרִין, אִתְגַּלְיָיא הַאי מִצְחָא, וְאִתְכַּפְיָין כָּל דִּינִין, וְאִשְׁתְּכָחוּ רַחֲמִין בְּכֻלְּהוּ עָלְמִין.

Ubegin kakh ishtekhach Shabbat bela dina, la leela vela letata. Va afilu esha de Gehinam ishteka beatreh, venaichin chayavaya. Ve al da itosaf nishmata dechedu beShabta.

וּבְגִין כָּךְ אִשְׁתְּכַח שַׁבָּת בְּלָא דִּינָא, לָא לְעֵילָא וְלָא לְתַתָּא. וַאֲפִילוּ אֶשָּׁא דְּגֵיהִנָּם אִשְׁתְּקַע בְּאַתְרֵיהּ, וְנָיְיחִין חַיָּיבַיָּא. וְעַל דָּא אִתּוֹסַף נִשְׁמָתָא דְּחֵדוּ בְּשַׁבְּתָא:

Uba'ei bar nash lemechedei bitlat se'udatei deShabta, deha kol mehemnuta, vekhol kelala dimehemnuta, beh ishtekhach, uba'ei bar nash lesadra patora ulemekhal tlat se'udatei dimehemnuta, ulemechedei behu.

וּבָעֵי בַּר נָשׁ לְמֶחֱדֵי בִּתְלַת סְעוּדָתֵי דְּשַׁבְּתָא, דְּהָא כָּל מְהֵימְנוּתָא, וְכָל כְּלָלָא דִּמְהֵימְנוּתָא, בֵּיהּ אִשְׁתְּכַח וּבָעֵי בַּר נָשׁ לְסַדְּרָא פָּתוֹרָא, וּלְמֵיכַל תְּלַת סְעוּדָתֵי דִּמְהֵימְנוּתָא, וּלְמֶחֱדֵי בְּהוּ:

Amar Ribi Shimon, ashadna alai lekhol ilen dehakha, deha min yomai la betilna ilen gimmel seudatei, ubegineihon la itzterikhna letaanita beShabta. Vaafilu beyomei acharinei la itzterikhna, kol shekhen beShabta. Deman dezakhei behu, zakhei lemehemnuta shelemata.

אָמַר רִבִּי שִׁמְעוֹן, אַסְהַדְנָא עָלַי לְכָל אִלֵּין דְּהָכָא, דְּהָא מִן יוֹמַאי לָא בְּטִילְנָא אִלֵּין ג' סְעוּדָתֵי, וּבְגִינֵיהוֹן לָא אִצְטְרִיכְנָא לְתַעֲנִיתָא בְּשַׁבְּתָא. וַאֲפִילוּ בְּיוֹמֵי אַחֲרִינֵי לָא אִצְטְרִיכְנָא, כָּל שֶׁכֵּן בְּשַׁבְּתָא. דְּמַאן דְּזָכֵי בְּהוּ, זָכֵי לִמְהֵימְנוּתָא שְׁלֵימָתָא.

Chad, seudata deMatronita. Vechad, seudata deMalka kadisha. Vechad, seudata de Atika Kadisha, setima dekhol setimin. Ubehahu alma yizkei leilen. Hai ratzon kad itgalia, kol dinin itkafian mishulshelehon.	חַד, סְעוּדָתָא דְּמַטְרוֹנִיתָא. וְחַד, סְעוּדָתָא דְּמַלְכָּא קַדִּישָׁא. וְחַד, סְעוּדָתָא דְּעַתִּיקָא קַדִּישָׁא, סְתִימָא דְּכָל סְתִימִין. וּבְהַהוּא עָלְמָא יִזְכֵּי בְּהוּ לְאִלֵּין. הַאי רָצוֹן כַּד אִתְגַּלְיָיא, כָּל דִּינִין אִתְכַּפְיָין מִשׁוּלְשְׁלֵיהוֹן:
Tikuna de Atika Kadisha ittekan betikuna chad, kelala dekhol tikunin. Vehi Chokhma ilaa, setimaa. Kelala dekhol shear, vehai ikrei eden ilaa setima. Vehu mocha de Atika Kadisha. Ve hai mocha itpashat lekhol ibar, mineh itpashat eden achara. Umehai eden itgalaf.	תִּקּוּנָא דְּעַתִּיקָא קַדִּישָׁא אִתְּתַּקַן בְּתִקּוּנָא חַד, כְּלָלָא דְּכָל תִּקּוּנִין. וְהִיא חָכְמָה עִלָּאָה, סְתִימָאָה. כְּלָלָא דְּכָל שְׁאָר, וְהַאי אִקְרֵי עֵדֶן עִלָּאָה סְתִימָא. וְהוּא מוֹחָא דְּעַתִּיקָא קַדִּישָׁא. וְהַאי מוֹחָא אִתְפָּשַׁט לְכָל עִיבָר, מִנֵּיהּ אִתְפָּשַׁט עֵדֶן אַחֲרָא. וּמֵהַאי עֵדֶן אִתְגְּלַף
Vehahu resha setima diberesha deAtika dela ityeda, kad pashit chad turna, dehava mittakan leitnahara, batash behai mocha, veitgelaf, veitnehir bekhama nehirin, veapik vearshim kebosita da, behai mitzcha. Veitreshim beh chad nehora, deikrei ratzon. Vehai ratzon itpeshat letata bedikna, ad hahu atar demityasheva bedikna, veikrei chesed ilaa. Veda ihu notzer chesed.	וְהַהוּא רֵישָׁא סְתִימָא דְּבְרֵישָׁא דְּעַתִּיקָא דְּלָא אִתְיְדַע, כַּד פָּשִׁיט חַד טוּרְנָא, דַּהֲוָה מִתְתַּקַן לְאִתְנַהֲרָא, בָּטַשׁ בְּהַאי מוֹחָא, וְאִתְגְּלַף, וְאִתְנְהִיר בְּכַמָּה נְהִירִין, וְאַפִּיק וְאַרְשִׁים כְּבוֹסִיטָא דָּא, בְּהַאי מִצְחָא. וְאִתְרְשִׁים בֵּיהּ חַד נְהוֹרָא, דְּאִקְרֵי רָצוֹן. וְהַאי רָצוֹן אִתְפָּשַׁט לְתַתָּא בְּדִיקְנָא, עַד הַהוּא אֲתָר דְּמִתְיַשְּׁבָא בְּדִיקְנָא, וְאִקְרֵי חֶסֶד עִלָּאָה. וְדָא אִיהוּ נוֹצֵר חֶסֶד.

The upper facet of *Atika Kadisha* is referred to as *ratzon* (good will). When it comes out of [weekday] concealment, a luminous energy is extended below revealing unparalleled divine good will and desire for the People of Israel.[109]

When this divine favor is revealed, the desire of desires infuses all the worlds, and all prayers from [Israel] below are granted. Then the

---

109. Consequently, Shabbat afternoon is a unique time of favor.

countenance of *Zeir Anpin* becomes radiant [from the light received from *Atika Kadisha*]. Compassion is found [at this time]: All decrees of strict justice are then canceled, for all the lower justice bearers are overcome and concealed.

On Shabbat, at the time of the afternoon prayer, which is the time [in the weekdays] when strict justice begins to exert its action, is revealed this concealed dimension of *Atika Kadisha*; all judgment is then suspended, and compassion permeates all the worlds.

For this reason, on Shabbat there is no din (strict justice) above or below; even the spiritual fire of Gehinom is extinguished at this time, and those expiating past errors can rest. Consequently, we receive an additional soul on Shabbat, [which helps us arouse ourselves to] feel joy.

We must therefore rejoice on the three Shabbat *seudot*,[110] for the entire Torah[111] prevails at this time.[112] Man is thus required to prepare the table [with bread and wine, so that the Shabbat holiness will dwell on it], eat three *seudot* of emuna (consciousness) and show his heightened joy [with Shabbat songs or Torah teachings].

Said Rabbi Shimon bar Yochai, I hereby declare that from the day I reached the age of understanding, I have never missed one of these three *seudot*,[113] and in their merit, I have never needed to fast [after a bad dream] on Shabbat. I did not even have to fast [for a bad dream] on the weekdays, so all the more on Shabbat. For, one who participates [in the three Shabbat meals] merits a perfect emuna.

One of these *seudot* is for the Queen [that is, *Malkhut*, from whom we receive sustenance]. One *seuda* is in honor of the Holy King [that is, the level of divine revelation known as *Zeir Anpin*, from whom we receive sustenance]; and one *seuda* is for *Atika Kadisha*, most concealed of all. One who is careful to participate in the three Shabbat *seudot* will merit,

---

110. And sing Shabbat songs to show our intense inner joy.
111. Referred to as *emuna* (faith), based on the verse (Ps. 19:8) "The Torah of Hashem is perfect – it restores the soul; the testimony of Hashem is *ne'emana* (trustworthy)."
112. For the Shabbat observer is considered as if s/he fulfilled the entire Torah. Furthermore, all the levels of divine revelation are directed upon us at this time.
113. Rabbi Shimon is making a special note that he never missed a Shabbat meal, for he lived in a time before our Sages derived from the Written Torah that we have to eat three meals in Shabbat, and only a select few were aware of it.

in the heavenly world, to receive divine flow [from all the levels of divine revelation]. When the upper facet of *Atika Kadisha* is revealed, then [all outside forces, who are executioners of] strict justice, are overcome.

The rectification of *Atika Kadisha* [whence the light of *Keter* begins to flow] is brought about by one rectification which includes all other rectifications.[114] This, the heavenly concealed wisdom, is the upper facet of *Atika Kadisha*, and it includes all others [wisdoms in the world below]. It is called the higher, concealed Eden, and from here it spreads down to the lower dimensions of Eden.[115]

This concealed upper facet of *Atika Kadisha* directs its radiance below in many divine flows in which is emitted the light of desire. This energy of desire spreads downward [to the Thirteen Attributes of Faith]; it is referred to as heavenly *Chesed* (lovingkindness), [for this is the first emanation of lovingkindness in the world of *Atzilut*,] and is called *notzer chesed* [alluding to the eighth of the Thirteen Attributes, 'He keeps kindness.'][116]

THIRD ZOHAR FOR THE THIRD SEUDA[117]

Ta chazi, bekhol shita yomei deShabta, kad mata shaata ditzlota demincha, dina takifa shalta, vekhol dinin mit'arin. Aval beyoma deShabta, kad mata idan ditzlota demincha, raava de raavin ishtekhach, ve Atika Kadisha galia ratzon dileh, vekhol dinin mitcafian, umishtekhach reuta vechedu bekhola.

תָּא חֲזֵי, בְּכָל שִׁיתָא יוֹמֵי דְשַׁבַּתָּא, כַּד מָטָא שַׁעֲתָא דִצְלוֹתָא דְמִנְחָה, דִּינָא תַקִּיפָא שַׁלְטָא, וְכָל דִּינִין מִתְעָרִין. אֲבָל בְּיוֹמָא דְשַׁבַּתָּא, כַּד מָטָא עִדָּן דִצְלוֹתָא דְמִנְחָה, רַעֲוָא דְרַעֲוִין אִשְׁתְּכַח, וְעַתִּיקָא קַדִּישָׁא גַּלְיָא רָצוֹן דִּילֵיהּ, וְכָל דִּינִין מִתְכַּפְיָין, וּמִשְׁתְּכַח רְעוּתָא וְחֵדוּ בְּכֹלָא:

---

114. It comes down to us as the Thirteen Attributes of Faith.
115. Flowing down to all the successive levels of divine revelation.
116. The Thirteen Attributes are: "1) God, 2) Compassionate, 3) Gracious One, 4) Who is slow 5) to and 6) abounding in kindness 7) And faithfulness – 8) He keeps kindness 9) for thousands [of generations] 10) bears iniquity, 11) sin, 12) and transgression, 13) and absolves [those who repent." *The Orot Sephardic Yom Kippur Machzor*, ed. Rabbi Eliezer Toledano (Lakewood, New Jersey: Orot, Inc., 1962), 550.
117. Zohar, *itro* 89b.

Key to the Locked Garden

Behai ratzon, istalak Moses, nevia mehemna kadisha mealma. Begin leminda, dela bedina istalak, vehahi shaata beratzon de Atika Kadisha nafak mishmateh, veittamar beh.	וּבְהַאי רָצוֹן, אִסְתַּלָּק מֹשֶׁה, נְבִיאָה מְהֵימָנָא קַדִּישָׁא מֵעָלְמָא. בְּגִין לְמִנְדַּע, דְּלָא בְּדִינָא אִסְתַּלָּק, וְהַהִיא שַׁעֲתָא בְּרָצוֹן דְּעַתִּיקָא קַדִּישָׁא נָפַק נִשְׁמָתֵיהּ, וְאִתְטַמַּר בֵּיהּ.
Begin kakh, "velo yada ish et keburato" ketiv. Ma Atika Kadisha, temira mikol temirin, vela yadin ilain vetatain. Uf hakha, hai nishmeta deittamar behai ratzon, deitgalia beshaata ditzlota demincha deShabta, ketiv "velo yada ish et keburato." Vehahu tamir mikol temirin de alma, vedina la shalta beh. Zakaah chulakeh de Moses.	בְּגִין כַּךְ, (דברים לה) וְלֹא יָדַע אִישׁ אֶת קְבֻרָתוֹ כְּתִיב. מַה עַתִּיקָא קַדִּישָׁא, טְמִירָא מִכָּל טְמִירִין, וְלָא יָדְעִין עִלָּאִין וְתַתָּאִין. אוּף הָכָא, הַאי נִשְׁמְתָא דְּאִתְטַמַּר בְּהַאי רָצוֹן, דְּאִתְגַּלְיָא בְּשַׁעֲתָא דִּצְלוֹתָא דְּמִנְחָה דְּשַׁבְּתָא, כְּתִיב וְלֹא יָדַע אִישׁ אֶת קְבֻרָתוֹ וְהוּא טָמִיר מִכָּל טְמִירִין דְּעָלְמָא, וְדִינָא לָא שַׁלְטָא בֵּיהּ. זַכָּאָה חוּלָקֵיהּ דְּמֹשֶׁה:
Tana, behai yoma, deoraita mit'atera beh, mit'atera bekola, bekhol inun pikudin bekhol inun gezerin veonashin, beshiv'in anafin dinehora, denaharin mikol sitra vesitra.	תָּאנָא, בְּהַאי יוֹמָא, דְּאוֹרַיְיתָא מִתְעַטְּרָא בֵּיהּ, מִתְעַטְּרָא בְּכֹלָּא, בְּכָל אִינּוּן פִּקּוּדִין בְּכָל אִינּוּן גְּזֵרִין וְעוֹנָשִׁין, בְּשִׁבְעִין עֲנָפִין דִּנְהוֹרָא, דְּזָהֲרִין מִכָּל סִטְרָא וְסִטְרָא.
Man chamei, anafin denafkin mikol anafa vaanafa, chamisha kaimin bego ilana, kulehu anpin behu achidan. Man chamei, inun tarin demitpatchan bekhol star ustar, kulehu mizdaharin venaharin, behahu nehora denafik vela pasik.	מַאן חָמֵי, עֲנָפִין דְּנָפְקִין מִכָּל עֲנָפָא וַעֲנָפָא, חֲמִשָּׁא קַיְימִין בְּגוֹ אִילָנָא, כֻּלְּהוּ אַנְפִּין בְּהוּ אֲחִידָן. מַאן חָמֵי, אִינּוּן תַּרְעִין דְּמִתְפַּתְּחָן בְּכָל סְטַר וּסְטָר, כֻּלְּהוּ מִזְדַּהֲרִין וְנָהֲרִין, בְּהַהוּא נְהוֹרָא דְּנָפִיק וְלָא פָּסִק.
Kal karoza nafik, itaru kadishei elyonin, it'aru ama kadisha, deitbachar leela vetata. It'aru chedvata lekadmut mareikhon. It'aru bechedvata shelemata.	קָל כָּרוֹזָא נָפִיק, אִתְּעָרוּ קַדִּישֵׁי עֶלְיוֹנִין, אִתְּעָרוּ עַמָּא קַדִּישָׁא, דְּאִתְבְּחַר לְעֵילָּא וְתַתָּא. אִתְּעָרוּ חֶדְוָותָא לְקַדְמוּת מָארֵיכוֹן. אִתְּעָרוּ בְּחֶדְוָותָא שְׁלֵימָתָא.

Mystical Readings for the Shabbat Table

Izdemanu bitlat chedvan, ditlat avahan. Izdemanu lekadmut mehemnuta, dechedva dekhol chedvata. Zakaa chulkekhon, Israel kadishin, bealma den ubealma deatei. Da hu yeruta lekhon, mikol amim ovdei avodat cokhavim umazalot. Ve al da ketiv, "beni uben benei Israel."

אִזְדְּמָנוּ בִּתְלַת חֶדְוָון, דִּתְלַת אֲבָהָן. אִזְדְּמָנוּ לְקַדְמוּת מְהֵימָנוּתָא, דְּחֶדְוָוה דְּכָל חֶדְוָותָא. זַכָּאָה חוּלְקְכוֹן, יִשְׂרָאֵל קַדִּישִׁין, בְּעָלְמָא דֵין וּבְעָלְמָא דְאָתֵי. דָּא הוּא יְרוּתָא לְכוֹן, מִכָּל עַמִּים עוֹבְדֵי עֲבוֹדַת כּוֹכָבִים וּמַזָּלוֹת. וְעַל דָּא כְּתִיב, בֵּינִי וּבֵין בְּנֵי יִשְׂרָאֵל

Amar Ribi Yehuda, hakhi hu vaddai. Veal da ketiv "zakhor et yom haShabat lekadesho," uketiv, "kedoshim tihiu ki kadosh ani Adonai." Ukhtiv, "vekarata laShabbat oneg likdosh Adonai mekhubad.

אָמַר רִבִּי יְהוּדָה, הָכִי הוּא וַדַּאי. וְעַל דָּא כְּתִיב זָכוֹר אֶת יוֹם הַשַּׁבָּת לְקַדְּשׁוֹ וּכְתִיב (ויקרא יט) קְדֹשִׁים תִּהְיוּ כִּי קָדוֹשׁ אֲנִי יְיָ. וּכְתִיב, (ישעיה נח) וְקָרָאתָ לַשַּׁבָּת עֹנֶג לִקְדוֹשׁ יְיָ מְכֻבָּד:

Tana, behai yoma, kol nishmatehon detzaddikaya mit'adnin betafnukei Atika Kadisha, setima dekhol setimin. Verucha chada me'inuga dehahu Atika Kadisha mitpashta bekulehu almin, vesalka venachta, umitpasheta lekulehu benei kadishin, lekulehu neturei oraita,

תָּאנָא, בְּהַאי יוֹמָא, כָּל נִשְׁמָתֵיהוֹן דְּצַדִּיקַיָּא, מִתְעַדְּנִין בְּתַפְנוּקֵי עַתִּיקָא קַדִּישָׁא, סְתִימָא דְּכָל סְתִימִין. וְרוּחָא חֲדָא מֵעִנּוּגָא דְּהַהוּא עַתִּיקָא קַדִּישָׁא מִתְפַּשְׁטָא בְּכֻלְּהוּ עָלְמִין, וְסַלְקָא וְנַחְתָּא, וּמִתְפַּשְׁטָא לְכֻלְּהוּ בְּנֵי קַדִּישִׁין, לְכֻלְּהוּ נְטוּרֵי אוֹרַיְיתָא,

Venaichin benaicha shelim, mitneshei mikulehu, kol rugzin, kol dinin, vekhol pulchanin kashin. Hada hu dikhtiv, "beyom hiniach Adonai ... lakh meatzavekha umirogzekha umin ha avoda hakasha."

וְנַיְיחִין בְּנַיְיחָא שְׁלִים, מִתְנַשֵּׁי מִכֻּלְּהוּ, כָּל רוּגְזִין, כָּל דִּינִין, וְכָל פֻּלְחָנִין קָשִׁין. הֲדָא הוּא דִכְתִיב, (ישעיה יד) בְּיוֹם הָנִיחַ יְיָ לָךְ מֵעָצְבְּךָ וּמֵרָגְזֶךָ וּמִן הָעֲבוֹדָה הַקָּשָׁה:

Beginei kakh, shakil Shabta lakobel oraita, vekhol denatir Shabta, keilu natir oraita kula. Ukhtiv ashrei enosh yaase zot uben adam yachazik ba shomer Shabbat mechalelo veshomer yado me'asot kol ra. Ishtema, de man denatir Shabbat, keman denatir oraita kula.

בְּגִינֵי כַּךְ, שָׁקִיל שַׁבְּתָא לָקֳבֵל אוֹרַיְיתָא, וְכָל דְּנָטִיר שַׁבְּתָא, כְּאִילּוּ נָטִיר אוֹרַיְיתָא כֹּלָּא. וּכְתִיב (ישעיה נו) אַשְׁרֵי אֱנוֹשׁ יַעֲשֶׂה זֹאת וּבֶן אָדָם יַחֲזִיק בָּהּ שׁוֹמֵר שַׁבָּת מֵחַלְּלוֹ וְשׁוֹמֵר יָדוֹ מֵעֲשׂוֹת כָּל רָע. אִשְׁתְּמַע, דְּמַאן דְּנָטִיר שַׁבָּת, כְּמַאן דְּנָטִיר אוֹרַיְיתָא כֹּלָּא:

Come and see; throughout the six weekdays, at the time of Mincha, severe justice is dominant, and all the strict judgments are aroused. However, on the Shabbat day, when the time for Mincha arrives, the desire of desires is emitted, and *Atika Kadisha* reveals his *ratzon* (desire). All forms of judgment are then suspended; then, desire and joy flow down to all.

Moses, the prophet who was faithful and holy, left the world in such time of favor so that it would be known that his death was not an expression of strict justice. At that time, by the desire of *Atika Kadisha*, his soul left and hid in it [namely, in the *hekhal haratzon* (heavenly dimension of will of the world of *Beriyah*].

It is thus written, "no one knows his burial place;"[118] for, just like *Atika Kadisha* is the most concealed of all, and is not grasped neither Above nor below, so too, Moses's soul was concealed in this emanation of desire coming through to us at the time of Shabbat Mincha. Hence, as it is written, no one knows his burial place. His [soul] is more concealed than any other in the world, and strict justice has no power over him. Great is the portion merited by Moses.

We have learned that on this day the Torah is crowned in all its ways, that is, in all its commandments, in all its rabbinical decrees and executions of justice, in its seventy branches of light, radiating from all sides.

Who can gaze at the branches of light emerging from each of the branches? Its five main branches dwell in the Tree, to which are attached all the branches. Who saw the gates opening on Shabbat on each of the sides? These [lights] all radiate from the light flowing and flowing without ever ceasing.

---

118. Deut. 34:6.

A voice proclaims: Arouse yourselves, lofty, holy ones, and arouse yourselves, you holy chosen people, selected Above and below; arouse your joy before your Master, in order to be aroused with total joy.

Prepare for the three celebrations of joy of the three patriarchs, to accept the consciousness to receive a joy higher than any other joy. Fortunate are the People of Israel, holy in this world as in the other, for Shabbat is an inheritance for them only, among all idolatrous nations. It is thus written "between Me and the Children of Israel."

Said Rabbi Yehuda: It is surely [as above explained] and about this it is written: "Remember the Shabbat day to sanctify it."[119] It is also written, "Be holy…, [by means of the Shabbat holiness] for I am holy,"[120] and also, "Call the Shabbat a delight, and God's holy day honored."[121]

We have learned that on that day, all the souls of the righteous feel *oneg* by contact with *Atika Kadisha*, most concealed of all. And one spirit able to draw from the delight radiating from *Atika* which is extended downward to all the worlds, ascends and descends, infusing all the holy Children of Israel who are Torah observant.

These then attain a total harmony of inner peace, and forget about their causes for anger, and the strict judgment, and sadness or illness, and about all hard work [of the weekdays]. As the verse says, "On the Shabbat day Hashem relieves you from your pain and your anxiety, from the hard labor with which you worked."[122]

For this reason, Shabbat is equal to receiving the Torah, and when one observes Shabbat it is considered that s/he fulfills the entire Torah. As the verse says, "Praiseworthy is the man who does this and the person who grasps it tightly: who guards the Shabbat against desecrating

---

119. Ex. 20:8.
120. Lev. 19:2.
121. Namely: Sanctify yourselves with the Shabbat holiness because when you do, I – that is, *Zeir Anpin*, who is *Hashem* – am also sanctified, for the six lower sefirot are crowned with the three upper sefirot.
122. Is. 58:13. To paraphrase Isaiah 14:3: on Shabbat, by means of the additional Shabbat soul, Hashem gives you rest from the dinim (the pain that the outside forces cause us), from the anxiety caused by all sources of anger, and from the hard work we do during the week.

Key to the Locked Garden

it and guards his hand against doing any evil."[123] We derive that when one keeps the Shabbat it is as if s/he kept the entire Torah.[124]

UPON FINISHING THE THIRD SHABBAT MEAL ONE SHOULD SAY:

We have now completed the meals of perfect consciousness of the holy people Israel.

אַשְׁלִימוּ סְעוּדָתֵי דִּמְהֵימְנוּתָא שְׁלָמָתָא, דְּזַרְעָא קַדִּישָׁא דְיִשְׂרָאֵל

MELAVE MALKA: MEAL TO ESCORT THE QUEEN[125]
ZOHAR ON MELAVE MALKA

אַתְקִינוּ סְעוּדָתָא דִּמְהֵימְנוּתָא דָּא הִיא סְעוּדָתָא רְבִיעָאָה דְּדָוִד מַלְכָּא מְשִׁיחָא:

Prepare the meal of faith. This is the fourth meal, of David King Mashiach.

Patach Eliyahu veamar, Ribon Alma yehei raava dilakh deeima milin beorach mishor kideka yaut, culehu bamida bamishkal beshi'ur koma diShekhintakh. Patach veamar, "zot komatekh dameta letamar, veshadayikh leashkolot," mai letamar, ela lehahu deitmar beh "tzaddik catamar yifrach," kapot temarim, komatech vadai damia lelulav deleit kitzutz upirud, velav lemagana ukmuhu marei matnitin nifretzu alav pasul, lulav ihu domeh leshidra degufa, deihu vav, koma de khola, deihu shit bechushban, vechamesh

פָּתַח אֵלִיָּהוּ וְאָמַר, רִבּוֹן עָלְמָא יְהֵא רַעֲוָא דִילָךְ דְּאֵימָא מִלִּין בְּאֹרַח מִישׁוֹר כַּדְקָא יָאוּת, כֻּלְּהוּ בְּמִדָּה בְּמִשְׁקָל בְּשִׁעוּר קוֹמָה דִשְׁכִינְתָּךְ. פָּתַח וְאָמַר, (שיר זח) זֹאת קוֹמָתֵךְ דָּמְתָה לְתָמָר וְשָׁדַיִךְ לְאַשְׁכּוֹלוֹת, מַאי לְתָמָר, אֶלָּא לְהַהוּא דְאִתְּמַר בֵּיהּ (תהלים צב יד) צַדִּיק כַּתָּמָר יִפְרָח, כַּפּוֹת תְּמָרִים, קוֹמָתֵךְ וַדַּאי דָּמֵי לְלוּלָב דְּלֵית בֵּיהּ קִצּוּץ וּפֵרוּד, וְלָאו לְמַגָּנָא אוּקְמוּהוּ מָארֵי מַתְנִיתִין נִפְרְצוּ עָלָיו פָּסוּל, לוּלָב אִיהוּ דּוֹמֶה לְשִׁדְרָה דְגוּפָא, דְּאִיהוּ ו', קוֹמָה דְכֹלָּא, וְאִיהוּ שִׁית בְּחוּשְׁבָּן

---

123. Is. 56:2.
124. The verse is thus equating guarding oneself from desecrating any of the Shabbat laws with guarding oneself from doing any evil – namely, from desecrating any of the commandments in the Torah.
125. Tikunei Zohar 134a-b.

anfin mitpashtin mineh, veihu gufa de ilana be etmtzaita, ve chamesh anfin inun teren mehai sitra, utlat mehai sitra, vealaihu itmar "ve anaf etz arbot arbei nachal," anaf lismala, abot limina, etz beemtzaita, arbei nachal teren, abot tlat, vekhulehu chamesh veinun lakobel teren shokin ubrit, uteren dero'in, etrog lev beemtzaita, ikara deilana veanpoi, veihu iba deilana ubeh ihu etz peri ose peri lemino.	וְחָמֵשׁ עַנְפִין מִתְפַּשְׁטִין מִנֵּיהּ, וְאִיהוּ גּוּפָא דְאִילָנָא בְּאֶמְצָעִיתָא, וְחָמֵשׁ עַנְפִין אִינוּן תְּרֵין מֵהַאי סִטְרָא, וּתְלַת מֵהַאי סִטְרָא, וַעֲלַיְיהוּ אִתְּמַר (ויקרא כג מ) וַעֲנַף עֵץ עָבֹת וְעַרְבֵי נָחַל, עֲנַף לִשְׂמָאלָא, עָבוֹת לִימִינָא, עֵץ בְּאֶמְצָעִיתָא, עַרְבֵי נַחַל תְּרֵין, עָבוֹת תְּלַת, וְכֻלְּהוּ חָמֵשׁ, וְאִינוּן לָקֳבֵל תְּרֵין שׁוֹקִין וּבְרִית, וּתְרֵין דְּרוֹעִין, אֶתְרוֹג לֵב בְּאֶמְצָעִיתָא, עִקָּרָא דְאִילָנָא וְעַנְפוֹי, וְאִיהוּ אִיבָּא דְאִילָנָא, וּבֵיהּ אִיהוּ עֵץ פְּרִי עֹשֶׂה פְּרִי לְמִינוֹ:

Elijah the prophet said: Lord of the universe: May it be Your will that I merit to reveal Your heavenly mysteries as is proper, and explain the mysteries about the divine structure of Your *Shekhina*.

I have only translated the first line of this Zohar, due to its esoteric nature. According to the Kabbalists, reading the words of the Zohar aloud helps the *Shekhina* even if you do not understand them.

In the prayer book edited and published by Rabbi Mordechai Eliyahu, zt"l, it is written that in addition to the above Zohar, it is customary to read the first two sections of the prayer meditation *Petichat Eliyahu* (not to be confused with the above passage beginning *"Patach Eliyahu"*) during this meal in order to express our yearning for the prompt coming of the *Mashiach ben David*. The *Petichat Eliayahu* was translated by Abraham Sutton. The text and translation may be requested by writing to him: avraham.sutton@icloud.com

It is at the time that the Shabbat ends that it is important to alleviate the suffering of the *Shekhina* with our efforts from below by reading these holy words.

SONG OF KNESSET YISRAEL BELOW

We conclude this selection of mystical readings with a poem composed by another member of the Abuchatzira family, Rabbi Isaac Abuchatzira zt"l, known as *Ner Yitzhak* (the Light of Isaac). The acrostic of his name may be noticed at the beginning of every stanza. The subject of the song is an allegorical figure representing the female voice of Shir Hashirim. The inner dimension of the Torah distinguishes between *Knesset Yisrael Above* (our collective soul roots attached to Hashem on High,) and *Knesset Yisrael Below* – namely, our collective souls in the world below in a state of spiritual togetherness under our physical forms. *Knesset Yisrael Below* thus alludes to the collectivity of our souls even though each one of these seems to be an independent entity that gives life to our body. The feminine entity of this song is thus *Knesset Yisrael Below*.[126]

I will fly away and find a dwelling place![127] I would wander afar, and dwell in the desert;[128] maybe I would find my Beloved.	אָעוּפָה אֶשְׁכֹּנָה . וְאַרְחִיקָה נְדֹד. בַּמִדְבָּר אָלִינָה. וְאוּלַי אֶמְצָא דוֹד:
The weapon of His love burns within my heart. From the time that He distanced Himself from me, my soul is bitter.	נֶשֶׁק אַהֲבָתוֹ. בְּלִבִּי בֹּעֲרָה. מִיוֹם פְּרִדָתוֹ. נַפְשִׁי עָלַי מָרָה:
My beloved ran away from me; He abandoned me. Tell me which way He paved for me, and I will also go that way.	יְדִיד מֶנִי בָּרַח. הָלַךְ עֲזָבָנִי. אֵיזוֹ דֶרֶךְ אָרַח. וְאֵלְכָה גַם אָנִי:

---

126. In my desire to provide the reader with the exact meaning of this most beautiful and moving song, I have translated the words in an English that may sound awkward but it renders the thought behind the Hebrew words.
127. Paraphrasing Ps. 55:7 ("Then I said, 'If someone but would give me wings like the dove! I would fly and find rest!).")
128. Paraphrasing Ps. 55:8. ("Behold! I would wander afar, and dwell in the wilderness, selah").

I went out to ask for my Beloved among my friends. I was caught in a trap and the guards struck me.[129]	יָצָאתִי לְבַקֵּשׁ. דּוֹדִי בֵּין חֲבֵרִים. נִלְכַּדְתִּי בְּמוֹקֵשׁ. הִכּוּנִי הַשֹּׁמְרִים:
I waited for my Beloved; I wonder when He will come to me. He will then dress me in my ornaments and have mercy on me.[130]	צִפִּיתִי לְדוֹדִי. מָתַי יָבוֹא אֵלַי. יַלְבִּשֵׁנִי עֶדְיָי. וִירַחֵם עָלַי:
Expose your arm to gather those who are dispersed. Reveal the time of Your salvation and lift Your banner.	חֲשֹׂף זְרוֹעֶךָ. לְקַבֵּץ פְּזוּרִים. גַּלֵּה קֵץ יִשְׁעֶךָ. וְדִגְלְךָ הָרֵם:
Get up, My Unique One, and repent for your errors![131] My sister, My beloved, here, your Savior has come.	קוּמִי יְחִידָתִי וְשׁוּבִי בִּתְשׁוּבָה. אֲחוֹתִי רַעֲיָתִי. הִנֵּי גוֹאֲלֵךְ בָּא:
Sweet, precious one, distinguished by many qualities, chosen even over gold – please go out in a dance.	חֲמוּדָה יְקָרָה. רַבַּת הַמַּעֲלוֹת. גַּם מִפָּז נִבְחָרָה. צְאִי נָא בִּמְחוֹלוֹת:

---

129. Paraphrasing Shir Hashirim 5:7 ("The watchmen who patrol the city [the nations who destroyed the Temple in Jerusalem] struck me and wounded me").
130. Alluding to the spiritual ornaments that the People of Israel lost upon their involvement with the Golden Calf after the Giving of the Torah.
131. Hashem says (Shir Hashirim 7:1): "Return, Return O Shulamit; Return, return." Hakadosh Barukh Hu says the word shuvi (return) addressing Knesset Yisrael, calling upon them to return to Him.

I remember your kindness in the youth of the young.
I will establish your palace with stones of sapphire

זָכַרְתִּי לָךְ חֶסֶד. נְעוּרַיִךְ נְעוּרִים.
הֵיכָלֵךְ אֲיַסֵּד בְּאַבְנֵי סַפִּירִים:

The voice of My beloved has come, leaping over the mountains.[132]
Get up, My beloved,
for the end of your emptiness has arrived!

קוֹל דּוֹדִי הִנֵּה בָא. מְדַלֵּג עַל הֶהָרִים. קוּמִי לָךְ אֲהוּבָה. כִּי בָא קֵץ דְּרוֹרִים:

---

132. Paraphrasing Shir Hashirim, 2:8. ("Behold, the call of my Beloved! He is coming [to redeem me before the appointed time]. He is leaping over the mountains [in the merit of the patriarchs]. He is springing over the hills [in the merit of the matriarchs]).″

Bibliography

Abudarham, Rabbi David. *Pirush Haberachot Vehatefilot Aburdarham Hashalem.* Private publication. For information write to Ch. Gitler, R. Bilu 4, Tel Aviv.

Afjin, Avner (compiler). *Sefer Divrei Shalom.* Rosh Ayin: Yeshivat Emet veShalom, 5763). Copies may be obtained by calling 972-03-938 0410, fax 972-3-938-4999.

[Anonymous author]. Chemdat Yamim, Jerusalem: Yarid hasefarim, 2003.

[Anonymous author]. *Tevuot Shemesh.* Jerusalem: Makhon Yam *Chokhma*, Jerusalem, 5245.

Bar Urian, Rabbi Imanuel. *Matana Tova Yesh Li Beveit Genazai.* Jerusalem: private publication, 5763.

Ben Ish Chai. "Parashat Vayera." In *Chelek Hahalakhot.* Jerusalem: Merkaz Hasefer, 5754.

Benyosef, Simcha H. *Living the Kabbalah: A Guide to the Sabbath and Festivals in the Teachings of Rabbi Rafael Moshe Luria.* Jerusalem: Feldheim, 2006.

———. *The Beginning of Wisdom: Unabridged Translation of THE GATE OF LOVE from Rabbi Eliahu de Vidas' RESHIT CHOCHMAH.* New Jersey: Ktav Publishers, 2001.

Chok LeIsrael Hameforash: Lilmod Bechol Yom Keseder Parshiyot HaTorah, Mikraot min Torah, Neviim UKetuvim, Jerusalem: Bloom Sefarim, 5760.

Cordovero, Rabbi Moses. *Tomer Devorah.*

Drizin, Reb Rahmiel-Hayyim. *Shabbat Meal Meditations.* http://www.kabbalaonline-shop.com/Shabbat-Meal-Meditations-p/drizin-ebooks-shabbat.htm. Reb Rahmiel's translations and commentary on Zohar and other holy texts may be received daily upon request to zoharialev@aol.com.

Eisenbach, Rabbi Akiva Yosef (compiler). *Or HaShabbat: Yalkut Maamarim BeInyanei Shabbat Kodesh.* Jerusalem: private publication, (n.d.).

Frish, Daniel. *Zohar Matok Midevash.* Ramat Beit Shemesh, 2014.

Hillel, Rabbi Jacob. *Binyan Ariel: Kitzur Vetamtzit Sefer Etz Chayim.* Jerusalem: Machon Ahavat Shalom, 5766.

Kaplan, Rabbi Aryeh. *The Light Beyond: Adventures in Hassidic Thought.* New York: Moznaim Publishing Corp., 1981.

Kaplan, Rabbi Aryeh [trans.], *The Living Torah.* New York: Moznaim Publications, 1981.

Kassin, Rabbi Jacob S. *Till Eternity: With Explanations of the underlying reasons for the commandments and their esoteric significance.* Lakewood, N.J.: Orot Publications, 2006.

Luria, Rabbi Rafael Moses. *Sefer Beit Genazai al Parshiyot HaTorah, Kolel Biurim Uferushim Laparshiyot.* Jerusalem: R. M. Luria, 5761. [Cited as *"Sefer Beit Genazai al Parshiyot HaTorah."*]

_____. *Sefer Beit Genazai: Eretz Yisrael, Kolel Biurim Be'inyanei Kedushat Eretz Yisrael Umaaloteiha.* Jerusalem: private publication, 5771.

_____. *Sefer Beit Genazai:, Kolel Biurim Be'arba Mitzvot shel Simcha Shehaav Chayav Laben: Simcha shel Brit; Simcha shel Pidyon; Simcha shel Mitzvot; Simcha shel Nisuim.* Jerusalem: private publication, 5763.

_____. *Sefer Beit Genazai, Kolel Inyanei Teshuva Bechodesh Elul, Rosh Hashanah, Aseret Yemei Teshuva, Yom Hakippurim, Chag Hasukkot, Ushmini Atzeret Veavodat Yom Kippur Bamikdash Uviurim BaRambam Hilkhot Teshuva (Sefer Beit Genazai – Massekhet Teshuva – Hilkhot Teshuva).* Jerusalem: R.M. Luria, 5767. [Cited as *"Sefer Beit Genazai – Massekhet Teshuva – Hilkhot Teshuva."*]

_____. *Sefer Beit Genazai, Kolel Maamarim Uviurim al Derekh Haavoda Meyusadim al Divrei haAri z"l Luria, Be'inyanei Shabbat.* Jerusalem: Makhon Shaarei Ziv, 5753. [Cited as *"Sefer Beit Genazai: MaamareiShabbat,* 1st ed."].

_____. *Sefer Beit Genazai, Kolel Maamarim Uviurim al Derekh Haavoda Meyusadim al Divrei haAri z"l Luria, Be'inyanei Shabbat.* 2nd edition. Jerusalem: Jerusalem: private publication, 1963. [Cited as *"Sefer Beit Genazai: Maamarei Shabbat,* 2nd ed."]

_____. *Sefer Beit Genazai, Kolel Maamarim Uviurim Bemitzvot Tefilla... Uferushim Bedivrei HaArizal Beshaar Hakavanot (Sefer Pitchei Tefilla).* Jerusalem: R.M. Luria, 5762-5764. [Cited as *"Sefer Pitchei Tefilla."*]

_____. *Sefer Beit Genazai, Kolel Perush al Shir Hashirim Umaamarim Upeninim al Chodshei Nissan, Iyyar, Sivan, Shekolel Inyanei Chag HaPesach VeHagada shel*

Bibliography

Pesach, Yemei HaOmer VeChag haShavuot Matan Torah Jerusalem: private publication, 5762. [Cited as "*Sefer Beit Genazai: Shir Hashirim.*"]

———. *Sefer Geulat Mitzraim, Kolel Maamarim Uviurim al Derech Haavoda Meyusadim al Derech Ha Ari z"l Luria Be'Inyan Gezerat Brit bein Habetarim Veyetziat Mitzraim.* Jerusalem: private publication, 5749.

———. *Sefer Or Hamikdash, Kolel Maamarim Uviurim al Derekh Haavoda, Meyusadim al Divrei haArizal Luria, Be'inyanei Hamikdash…Vime Bein Hameitzarim.* Jerusalem: Makhon Shaarei Ziv, 5753.

———. *Sefer Ori Veyishi, Kolel Maamarim Uviurim al Derekh Haavoda, Meyusadim al Divrei haArizal Luria.* Jerusalem: Makhon Shaarei Ziv, 5753.

———. *Sefer Seder Leil Shimurim: Kolel Maamarim Uviurim al Derekh Haavodah: Meyusadim a"d HaArizal Luria Be'inyanei Seder Leil Pesach Vehaggada shel Pesach.* Jerusalem: private publication, 5750.

Luzzato, Rabbi Moses Chaim. *Siddur HaRamchal.* Jerusalem: Ramhal Institute, 2006.

Machzor Beit Yosef: The Complete ArtScroll Machzor. New York: ArtScroll Studios, 1987.

Machzor Kol Yaakov. Jerusalem: *Darkhei Horaa lerabanim*, (n.d.).

Mykoff, M.H., Gavriel Rubin and Moses Shapiro [trans.]. *The living Nach.* Jerusalem: Moznaim Publishing Corporation, 5758.

Or haShabbat: Siddur Rechovot haNahar. Jerusalem: Yeshivat Nahar Shalom, 5765.

Ramban (Nachmanides). *Commentary on the Torah.* Translated by Rabbi Dr. Charles B. Chavel. New York: Shilo Publishing House, 1976.

Scherman, Rabbi Nosson [ed.], *The Complete ArtScroll Siddur, Nusach Sefard.* New York: Mesora Publications, 1985.

Shemueli, Rabbi Benayahu Yissachar. *Parashat haKetoret; Seder haKorbanot.* Jerusalem: Yeshivat Nahar Shalom, (n.d.).

Siddur Kol Eliyahu Hashalem. Al pi Piskei Maran HaRishon LeTzion HaRav HaGaon Mordechai Eliyahu. Jerusalem: Hotzaa "Darkhei Horaa LeRabanim," 5762.

Siddur Rechovot Hanahar, Jerusalem: Yeshivat Nahar Shalom, 5765.

Sofer, Rabbi Jacob Chaim. *Shulchan Arukh: Orach Chaim, im Sefer Kaf HaChayim.* Jerusalem: private publication, 5775.

Sutton, Rabbi Avraham [trans.]. *Sefer Zemirot in Honor of Shabbos, from the Jerusalem Siddur.* New York: Targum Press, 1996.

Sutton, Rabbi Avraham. *Yearning for Redemption: The Psalms of King David,* (forthcoming).

Tanach: The Stone Edition. New York: Mesorah Publications, The ArtScroll Series, 1996.

Toldedano, Rabbi Eliezer [ed.], *The Orot Sephardic Yom Kippur Machzor*. Lakewood, New Jersey: Orot, Inc., 1962.

Vidal, Chaim ben Yosef. *Sefer Pri Etz Chayim*. Jerusalem: Rabbi Tzvi M. Vidavski, 5748.

———. *Shaar HaKavanot, Chelek Sheni*. Jerusalem: Rabbi Tzvi M. Vidavski, 5746.

———. *Shaar Maamarei Rashbi*. Saloniki: Saadi Ashkenazi, 5622.

Yosef, Rabbi Isaac. *Yalkut Yosef*. Jerusalem: Eliyahu Shitrit. Jerusalem, 5754.

Zlotowitz, Rabbi Meir [trans.]. *Shir Hashirm / Song of Songs: An Allegorical Translation based upon Rashi with a Commentary Anthologized from Talmudic, Midrashic, and Rabbinic Sources*. New York: ArtScroll/Mesorah, 2000.

Books on the Laws of Shabbat

Bitan, Rabbi Yisrael. *Yalkut Yosef - The Laws of Shabbat*, Jerusalem, Haketer Institute, (n.d.).

Chait, Rabbi Baruch. *The 39 Avoth Melacha of Shabbath*, Nanuet, NY, Feldheim Publishers, 1992.

Cohen, Rabbi Simcha Bunim. *The Laws of Shabbos* (7 volumes), Brooklyn, New York, ArtScroll Mesorah Publications, 2014.

Ribiat, Rabbi Dovid. *The 39 Melochos*, Nanuet, NY, Feldheim Publishers, 1999.

Glossary

A
achoti: my sister
ahava: love
ahava raba: passionate love
alot hashachar: dawn
Amida: the "standing prayer" said three times a day: morning, afternoon, and evening.
asiya: making
Aron: Ark
Arvit: Evening prayer
Ata kiddashta: You have sanctified
atkinu: prepare
avodat Hashem: divine service
Azara: Court

B
banim: children
baruch: blessed
bayit: home
Birkat HaMazon: grace after meals
bitachon: trust
bittul: nullification, surrender
boreh choshekh: Creator of darkness
brit mila: circumcision

C

chaya: a type of angel; one of the five soul levels
chemda: desire
Chochma: (divine) wisdom
chol: sand; weekdays
Chumash: Pentateuch

D

daat: intimate knowledge; consciousness
devekut: passionate attachment
dinim: Hashem's forces of severe strict justice
dira: dwelling place
dira batachtonim: dwelling place here below

E

Ein Sof: The Infinite Being
emunat Yisrael: the faith on which our *avodat Hashem* is based
Erev Shabbat: time prior to the actual beginning of Shabbat. Erev Shabbat begins at the fifth hour on Friday, counting from the point of *netz* (sunrise), and ends when we accept Shabbat upon ourselves.
eshet chayil: a woman of valor
etzem meatzamav: part of His essence.
eved: servant

G

geula: redemption

H

Halakha (plural: *halakhot*): law
Hallel: sequence psalms of praise recited on Rosh Hodesh and festivals
hasachat hadaat: diverting one's attention from the surroundings in order to zero in on one issue exclusively
hashpaa (plural: *hashpaot*): (divine) flow
Havaya: Being: a circumlocution for the Name spelled with four letters
Havdala: closing service

Glossary

I
ibur: gestation
ish: man
isha: woman, wife
ishto: his wife

K
Kabbalat Shabbat: prayers said to welcome Shabbat
kalla: bride
katnut: restricted consciousness
kavana (**plural:** *kavanot*): intention, intentions
kedusha: holiness
kelim: spiritual body parts, spiritual "vessels"
keruvim: cherubs
keter: crown
kiddush: prayer recited over wine to sanctify Shabbat and Yom Tov
kiddush Hashem: sanctification of Hashem's Name
kiddushin: first stage of the marriage ceremony
kishutim: ornaments
kli: vessel (container)
klippa (**plural:** *klippot*): evil husks
kodesh: holiness
Kodesh Kodashim: Holy of Holies
kohanim: priests
Kohen Gadol: High Priest

L
Lekha Dodi: Literally "Come O Beloved, a song composed by the Ari traditionally sung or recited each week to welcome Shabbat as part of the Kabbalat Shabbat prayers

M
Malkhut: Kingship
mashal: allegory, parable

Melacha (**plural:** *melachot*): creative activity (work) as defined by the Sages
Melave Malka: parting *seuda* to take leave of the Shabbat Queen
memshala: government
menora: candelabra
menucha: inner harmony
midbar: desert
mikve: ritual bath
Mincha: afternoon prayer
minyan: quorum of ten men
Mishkan: Portable Sanctuary
mitzva (**plural:** *mitzvot*): commandment
muktze: forbidden for use on Shabbat
Motzaei Shabbat: the end of Shabbat
Mussaf: additional *Amida*

N
nefesh: vital soul
neshama: higher soul
nesira: separation
ner: candle
netz: sunrise
nifradim: independent entities
nissuin: completion of the marital ceremony
noam: pleasantness

O
oneg: delight
ohel: tent
Olam Haba: The World to Come

P
parasha: weekly Torah section
pegam: spiritual flaw
peshat: plain meaning of the Torah

Glossary

R
rachamim: compassion
ratzon: will
reshut harabbim: public domain
reshut hayachid: private domain
Rishonim: Early Sages
Rosh Chodesh: the beginning of the month
ruach: spirit

S
sadeh: field
sefer keritut: bill of divorce
seuda (**plural:** *seudot*): meal, referring to the festive meals including bread and wine or grape juice had on Shabbat, Yom Tov, or special occasions.
shalhevet: (divine) flame
shalom zachar: a celebration held on the eve of Shabbat in honor of a newborn baby boy before his circumcision
shamor: observe
shefa: divine flow
shem: name
Shir Hashirim: Song of Songs
shira: song
shekia: sunset
shomer Shabbat: guarding the Shabbat laws
siddur: prayerbook
sukkat shalom: shelter of peace

T
taanug: delight
tahara: purification
tal: dew
talmid (**plural** *talmidim*): student
tefilla: prayer
teshuva: repentance
tikkun: spiritual repair

tosefet Shabbat: an additional ascending element granted from on High to those who take Shabbat upon themselves earlier than required.
tzaddik (**plural** *tzaddikim*)**:** righteous
tzedaka: charity for a Jewish cause

Y
Yesod: foundation
Yichud: unification, total togetherness only possible at the soul level
Yom Tov: festival

Z
zachor: remember

The fonts used in this book are from the Arno Koren family.

Menorah Books
Jewish Life & Spirituality in Practice
Koren Publishers Jerusalem Ltd.